The Art and Science of Virtual Content Creation

The Art and Science of Virtual Content Creation: Beyond the Screen is a wide-ranging guide that examines the dynamic fusion of creativity and technology in crafting immersive digital experiences. It explores how artistic vision and digital tools function as equal partners in the creation of compelling virtual media, moving beyond traditional boundaries to explore the vast creative potential of the digital realm. This book provides both theoretical foundations and practical strategies for conceptualizing, developing, and producing virtual content across multiple platforms and formats.

This book covers the complete life cycle of virtual content creation, guiding readers through every phase from initial concept development to postproduction. It explores the unique opportunities and challenges of virtual reality, augmented reality, and mixed reality, while introducing essential technical skills including 3D modeling, animation, spatial audio, and interactive design. Through real-world case studies and industry experiences, this book describes innovative storytelling methods and examines emerging technologies such as procedural generation, artificial intelligence, and blockchain as future drivers of virtual media. Equally important, it addresses the ethical and societal implications of virtual content, discussing critical issues of authenticity, representation, and privacy in increasingly lifelike digital experiences.

Beyond the Screen is designed for both newcomers seeking foundational knowledge and seasoned professionals looking to expand their expertise in virtual content creation. This book serves digital artists, game developers, filmmakers, UX designers, and media professionals who want to harness the power of immersive technologies. Academic researchers, students in digital media programs, and creative technologists will find valuable insights into the evolving landscape of virtual storytelling, while industry practitioners will benefit from actionable strategies and concrete methods for translating imaginative concepts into immersive digital realities.

The Art and Science of Virtual Content Creation
Beyond the Screen

Edited by
Raquel Victoria Benítez Rojas

CRC Press
Taylor & Francis Group
Boca Raton London New York

CRC Press is an imprint of the
Taylor & Francis Group, an **informa** business

Designed cover image: gettyimages-1417348387

First edition published 2026
by CRC Press
2385 NW Executive Center Drive, Suite 320, Boca Raton FL 33431

and by CRC Press
4 Park Square, Milton Park, Abingdon, Oxon, OX14 4RN

CRC Press is an imprint of Taylor & Francis Group, LLC

ISBN: 9781041138822 (hbk)
ISBN: 9781041142447 (pbk)
ISBN: 9781003673538 (ebk)

DOI: 10.1201/9781003673538

Typeset in Minion
by codeMantra

Contents

About the Editor

Raquel Victoria Benítez Rojas is an award-winning entertainment executive, academic leader, and researcher specializing in digital media, communication, and emerging technologies. As Associate Dean at the University of Niagara Falls, she has led global film and animation projects, published extensively on AI and the metaverse, and advised governments on media policy and innovation.

Contributors

Antonella Carpio Arias
Instituto Superior Tecnológico José
    Ortega y Gasset
Riobamba, Ecuador

Bassant Mohamed Attia
Arab Academy for Science,
    Technology, and Maritime
    Transport
College of Language and
    Communication
Alexandria, Egypt

Raquel Victoria Benítez Rojas
University of Niagara Falls
Niagara Falls, Ontorio, Canada

Wael Brahim
University of Niagara Falls
Niagara Falls, Ontorio, Canada

Elpidio del Campo-Cañizares
Universidad Miguel Hernandez
Alicante, Spain

Berna Çelikkaya
Istanbul Bilgi University
Istanbul, Turkey

Tamara Makana Chock
Syracuse University
Syracuse, NY

Rocío Cifuentes-Albeza
Universidad Miguel Hernandez
Alicante, Spain

Antonio Díaz-Lucena
Universidad Juan Carlos I
Madrid, Spain

David Gray
University of Niagara Falls
Niagara Falls, Ontario, Canada

Austin Hendy
Toronto Metropolitan University
Toronto, Ontario, Canada

Begoña Ivars Nicolás
Universidad Miguel Hernandez
Alicante, Spain

Francisco-Julián Martínez-Cano
Universidad Miguel Hernández
Alicante, Spain

Heba El Kamshoushy
University of Niagara Falls
Niagara Falls, Ontario, Canada

Cyndi McLeod
GUS North America

Victoria Mora de la Torre
Universidad Juan Carlos I
Madrid, Spain

André Plante
University of Niagara Falls
Niagara Falls, Ontario, Canada

Erkan Saka
Istanbul Bilgi University
Istanbul, Turkey

Foreword

IN TODAY'S RAPIDLY EVOLVING DIGITAL ERA, THE BOUNDARIES BETWEEN the real and the virtual are no longer clear lines. These boundaries are now dynamic intersections. This transformation, fueled by immersive technologies, artificial intelligence (AI), and the power of global connectivity, is reshaping the way we create, communicate, and experience the world. It is within this shifting landscape that unveiling *The Art and Science of Virtual Content Creation: Beyond the Screen* emerges as both a timely guide and an essential companion.

At once practical and visionary, this book invites readers to explore the multifaceted nature of virtual content creation, a field that demands both technical expertise and artistic imagination. It is a work that bridges theory and application, offering insights that are as valuable to students and educators as they are to industry professionals and innovators. From the foundations of immersive design to the complexities of AI and ethics, the following chapters capture the dynamic interplay between creativity and technology and explore the balance that defines our present and will continue to shape our future.

The author and editor of this volume, Dr. Raquel Victoria Benítez Rojas, brings a rare combination of scholarly rigor, artistic sensibility, and global leadership to the conversation. As Associate Dean of the Master of Arts in Digital Media and Global Communications at the University of Niagara Falls, Canada, she is guiding the next generation of creators, communicators, and critical thinkers. Her career has spanned continents and industries, including cinematography, broadcasting, animation, digital media, and AI, and equips her with a uniquely holistic perspective on the challenges and opportunities of virtual content.

She is not only a respected academic and award-winning professional but also a trailblazer in the discourse on AI ethics. In an age when technologies evolve faster than our ability to fully understand their implications, her voice reminds us of the responsibility that accompanies innovation. She has consistently advocated for a digital future where creativity thrives without compromising ethical values, where representation and inclusivity matter, and where the human spirit remains at the center of technological progress.

Beyond the Screen captures this ethos. Readers will find themselves immersed in explorations of how virtual content is conceived, built, and shared, detailing the movement from the artistry of storytelling to the science of simulation, from the tools of production to the platforms of distribution. This book addresses the ethical dimensions of digital creation with nuance and urgency, asking us to consider how representation, privacy, and authenticity can be safeguarded as immersive technologies become more pervasive. It also looks ahead, anticipating the trends that will define the next decade of virtual media: AI, blockchain, the metaverse, and beyond.

One of the most compelling aspects of this book is its accessibility. While deeply informed by research and experience, it never loses sight of the reader. It welcomes aspiring creators, seasoned professionals, and curious minds alike, encouraging each to step beyond the screen and into the expansive possibilities of digital creativity. The blend of case studies, theoretical insights, and practical guidance ensures that every reader will find both inspiration and utility in its pages.

For those of us working in higher education and industry alike, this book represents more than a contribution to scholarship. It is a call to action. It challenges us to nurture creativity responsibly, to lead with vision and empathy, and to recognize the transformative potential of virtual content as a force for cultural exchange, education, and human connection.

She exemplifies the kind of leader and thinker who can guide us through this journey. Her global academic and professional experience, her pioneering research in AI ethics, and her deep commitment to advancing knowledge make her an authority whose perspective is both authoritative and inspiring.

As you open this book, I encourage you to do so with curiosity and with a willingness to imagine what lies beyond the screen. In these pages, you will discover not only the art and science of virtual content creation but also the values and vision necessary to ensure that this rapidly expanding field enriches our lives and our societies.

It is with great admiration and respect that I recommend this important work to you.

—Dr. Cyndi McLeod
CEO, GUS North America

Introduction

WHEN THE TERM "TECHNOLOGICAL ADVANCES" IS MENTIONED, MY MIND always goes back to my great-grandmother. A lady who, through her life, witnessed the evolution from the horse and cart to mass-produced automobiles, a man landing on the moon, home computers, and the internet. At the time, as a young teenager, I had naively thought that there probably wouldn't be another era of such rapid technological advancement... how wrong I was.

We live in a digital age. Data and information are the new "gold", with companies expending vast amounts of money on strategies to capture, store, analyze, and use information to inform key business decisions. Each of us will have already engaged many times with AI during our day without even knowing it and yet there is a suspicion and fear about this digital world. It might be because these digital advances are not taking place out in the open but behind the scenes; 1's and 0's being used to drive our lives from the shadows, or, possibly, because these technological leaps are so sophisticated that, for most of us, they are difficult to comprehend.

Fear of the unknown is a human trait; it's built into our DNA as an evolutionary adaptation to maximize survival. It's far better to be cautious of something that you don't know or can't understand because, in our cave-dwelling days, it might just be dangerous and have eaten you. But in all seriousness, I am of an age where I can remember the reaction when the pocket calculator became easily accessible. It was going to make us all mindless zombies, unable to carry out basic arithmetic in our heads. Then came the digital watch...and the home computer? Well, that was going to be the end of life as we knew it.

We now know that none of these things came to pass; our fear of the unknown was not warranted. In fact, I think most of us would say that those advancements have benefitted humanity in significant ways, and yet here we are again, not learning from the past, but re-living it. AI is here and, let's be honest, many of us are scared of it. Is that fear warranted, or is it because we just don't understand it?

In history, whenever there has been a technological breakthrough, there have been two key groups that have been early adopters and implementers of that breakthrough—Agriculture and Artists. Agriculture and farmers were early users of the steam engine, automation, hydroponics, genetics, robots, drones—the list goes on. But if you really want to meet a group that truly pushes the boundaries of both driving and implementing technology, you need look no further than artists throughout our history.

I'm sure we have all seen pictures of the earliest cave paintings, created by prehistoric humans blowing ash on the outstretched hands to capture a picture on the cave wall that would last for thousands of years. Early carvings of pictures and words, the creation of massive structures like that of Stonehenge. The hieroglyphs found deep inside the pyramids of Giza—the adoption and use of different media such as inks, paints, oils, and brushes to capture moments in our history. Why would the digital space be any different?

In fact, digital and media artists really have embraced this as "their" space. They are comfortable in it as it truly removes creative barriers and allows their imaginations to thrive; and they've been quietly doing it for a while. We all visit our local cinema or movie house to watch Pixar or Disney animated movies, James Cameron's work with his Avatar movies? None of these would be possible without those 1's and 0's we are all so worried about. A lack of knowledge or understanding leads to fear and suspicion; the more you know and understand a thing, the better equipped you are to use it responsibly and to the betterment of yourself and humankind.

Universities have a key part to play in this and I'm a bit embarrassed to say it, but we haven't necessarily been doing a great job. Just like everyone else, when something new comes along, our first default setting is "suspicion". AI is a prime example. Instead of thinking "wow, this is an amazingly powerful tool, how can we prepare our students to better understand it, to use it in a responsible and ethical way?", many thought "students are going to use this to cheat and plagiarise…we need to focus our time on ensuring we put measures in place to stop it…in fact, let's stop them accessing AI". As someone who has worked in academia for over 25 years, all I can do is shake my head. Education is the key here; we must ensure that students, community members, and the public all have access to the knowledge they need to truly understand the recent technology breakthroughs, and be able to, impartially, see the benefits that they can bring.

I am proud to say that some Universities are taking this road less traveled. The University of Niagara Falls Canada (UNF) integrates AI and virtual/augmented reality into all of its programs and classes, ensuring that every one of our students will have the knowledge, skills, and competencies to be able to use these powerful tools in an ethical and responsible way. We have purposefully sought out and recruited experienced Professors in this academic space who truly understand this subject and have industry experience of its uses.

She is one of these inspirational individuals. An award-winning scholar in AI in media, she is currently the Associate Dean and academic lead of the Innovative and unique Master of Arts in Digital Media and Global Communications program at UNF. Having previously been the founder and Chief Executive Officer of Comet Entertainment Inc. Canada, one of Canada's largest digital animation studio, she brings decades of industry experience to the classroom. When not teaching, she is busy accepting invitations to present workshops and seminars on this important topic all over the world. Her passion and commitment to digital media and the ethical adoption of innovative technologies are mind-blowing and come across through every chapter of this book.

Through her global network of collaborators, she has managed to pull together a global "who's who" in the digital media space to collaborate on what is, in my opinion, a required read for anyone involved in, or surrounding, digital media.

Beyond the Screen emphasizes the symbiotic relationship between artistry and technology in the realm of virtual content creation. It explores how artists harness the power of digital tools to sculpt immersive environments, craft compelling narratives, and evoke emotional responses from audiences. From concept development to postproduction, each stage of the creative process is dissected, providing readers with practical strategies for realizing their creative visions in virtual space.

Beyond the Screen also acknowledges the ethical considerations and societal implications inherent in the creation and consumption of virtual content. As virtual experiences become increasingly indistinguishable from reality, questions of authenticity, representation, and privacy come to the forefront. By fostering a critical dialogue on these issues, this book encourages readers to approach virtual content creation with mindfulness and responsibility.

From the very first chapter, "An Introduction to Immersive Content Creation in Contemporary Media Ecosystems", she ensures that what could easily be a complex and difficult topic to engage with is accessible to all and, dare I say it, an enjoyable journey. With chapters covering topics such as "The Science behind Virtual Reality" to "Virtual Storytelling Techniques", from "The Art of Virtual Content Creation" to "Ethical Issues in the Use of VR in the Context of Artificial Intelligence", she and her team of collaborators ensure that every important aspect of this rapidly developing industry is covered in detail.

As an educator, an academic, and an artist, this book both excited me and inspired me to learn more about something that touches each one of us, every single day and, for the most part, we don't fully understand it, or even know it's happening. Let Dr. Benítez Rojas pull back the curtain and show you!

—**By David Gray**
President and Chair of the Board,
University of Niagara Falls, Canada

CHAPTER 1

Introduction to Virtual Content Creation in Contemporary Media Ecosystems

Raquel Victoria Benítez Rojas

1 INTRODUCTION

In the evolving landscape of digital media, content creation has undergone a profound transformation. What was once rooted in physical media and linear storytelling is now expanding into interactive, immersive, and often user-driven environments. This transformation is exemplified by the rise of virtual content creation, a practice that employs digital technologies to produce content that can be experienced across augmented reality (AR), virtual reality (VR), and mixed reality (MR) platforms. As media producers adapt to rapidly changing consumption habits and technological innovations, virtual content has emerged as a critical tool for engagement, education, commerce, and communication.

This chapter introduces the concept of virtual content creation, situates it within the broader context of modern media, and explores how it differs from traditional forms of content production. By analyzing its applications, affordances, and implications, this chapter aims to illuminate

DOI: 10.1201/9781003673538-1

the growing relevance of virtual content in shaping 21st-century media practices.

2 DEFINING VIRTUAL CONTENT

Virtual content refers to media outputs that are generated, displayed, or experienced within digitally constructed environments. Unlike traditional content—which may exist in physical formats such as print or analog film, or in digital but non-interactive formats like linear video—virtual content is typically designed to be immersive, interactive, and dynamic. It is often experienced through VR, AR, MR, or web-based 3D platforms and may be created using a suite of digital tools including game engines (e.g., Unity, Unreal Engine), 3D modeling software (e.g., Blender, Maya), and advanced rendering technologies.

The definition, as provided by Milgram et al. (1995), says that VR is a computer-generated simulation that utilizes three-dimensional near-eye displays and advanced pose-tracking technologies to create an immersive user experience within a digitally constructed environment. By engaging visual, auditory, and, in some cases, haptic senses, VR enables users to perceive and interact with virtual worlds as if they were physically present.

Likewise, Awati (2022) defines it as an artificial environment that offers immersive audio and visual experiences to users. These experiences are usually presented through specialized equipment. While the experience is realistic, the users' physical reality does not exhibit any change.

The applications of VR span a broad range of sectors. In entertainment, VR is particularly prominent in the video game industry, offering users fully immersive gameplay experiences. In education and professional training, VR is employed to simulate complex scenarios—such as medical procedures, safety drills, and military operations—allowing for risk-free experiential learning. In business contexts, VR facilitates virtual meetings, collaborative design, and remote presentations, enhancing productivity and engagement across distributed teams.

Positioned within the broader reality–virtuality continuum, VR represents one of the most immersive points along the spectrum of mediated experiences. It differs fundamentally from adjacent technologies such as AR and augmented virtuality (AV). While AR overlays digital content onto the physical world and AV integrates physical elements into predominantly virtual environments, VR fully replaces the user's sensory input with computer-generated stimuli, thereby creating a wholly immersive digital experience.

Virtual content encompasses a wide variety of applications, including but not limited to:

- Virtual learning environments and simulations.
- Interactive games and narratives.
- AR overlays in mobile apps.
- Digital replicas or "twins" of real-world spaces.
- Immersive advertising and marketing experiences.

What distinguishes virtual content is not only its form but also its user-centric orientation. Unlike passive media consumption, virtual content invites users to engage, manipulate, or co-create the experience, thereby altering traditional roles of authorship and audience.

The term virtual serves as a qualifier to world, and as such, it is essential to clarify what is meant by a "virtual world." Much like the term world, the notion of virtuality is multifaceted. It may be understood as a form of reality that is simultaneously ideal and real, or something experienced as if it were real. Deleuze (1990) provides a foundational conceptualization of the virtual by distinguishing it from the actual, yet not from the real. In this framing, the virtual is not unreal; rather, it possesses a real ontological status, even if it does not manifest in physical form. Our perception of the virtual, therefore, contributes to its reality.

This philosophical framing reveals a common pitfall in academic discourse: The tendency to describe virtual worlds as somehow "not real." Such assumptions are often grounded in a problematic dichotomy between the virtual and the actual. The term actual is frequently conflated with contemporary, physical existence, which further complicates the distinction. As Lehdonvirta (2010) argues, the persistence of binary thinking—such as real versus virtual identity—leads to flawed conceptual divisions in studies of online environments. These dichotomies obscure the complex, layered nature of identity and interaction in mediated spaces.

Rather than opposing the virtual to the real or actual, it is more productive to juxtapose the virtual with the physical, material, or natural world (Shields, 2003). This framing allows for a more nuanced understanding of how virtual experiences and identities are constructed and lived. It also acknowledges that individuals do not maintain a singular, unified "real" identity. Instead, identity is fluid and context-dependent, shaped by social relationships and spatial environments—whether virtual or physical.

VR technologies offer varying levels of immersion, each providing distinct experiences based on the degree to which users are engaged with and detached from their physical environment. Understanding these types of VR simulations is essential for recognizing their applications across fields such as gaming, education, training, and healthcare. The three primary categories—non-immersive, semi-immersive, and fully immersive VR—differ significantly in user interaction, sensory involvement, and technological requirements.

Max Burkhalter (2022) established five kinds of VR, these are:

1. Non-immersive VR

   Non-immersive VR refers to computer-generated environments that users interact with via standard input devices such as keyboards, mice, game controllers, or consoles, without becoming fully immersed in the virtual setting. The experience is mediated through a two-dimensional screen, and users remain acutely aware of their physical surroundings.

   Popular examples include strategy or role-playing video games such as World of Warcraft and Dota 2, where players control characters and actions within a virtual space but do not experience the sensation of being physically present in that space. This form of VR does not block the user's field of view or provide full sensory engagement, making it a cost-effective and widely accessible option for entertainment and basic simulation purposes.

2. Semi-immersive VR

   Semi-immersive VR offers a more engaging experience by partially immersing users in a virtual environment while maintaining their connection to the physical world. Typically facilitated through high-resolution monitors, projection systems, or head-mounted displays (HMDs) without full motion tracking or haptic feedback, this type of VR enhances the sense of spatial awareness and depth without complete physical isolation.

   A common application of semi-immersive VR is in professional and educational training environments. For instance, flight simulators used in pilot training replicate cockpit controls and instrumentation, enabling users to practice real-world procedures in a safe, controlled virtual setting. While these simulations deliver a convincing visual experience, they usually lack the tactile or full-body engagement characteristic of fully immersive systems.

3. Fully immersive VR

   Fully immersive VR provides the most advanced and realistic simulation by enveloping users in a computer-generated environment that engages multiple senses, including sight, sound, and, in some cases, touch. This experience requires specialized hardware such as VR headsets, motion sensors, haptic feedback devices (e.g., gloves or body suits), and spatial audio systems. These tools work in unison to track the user's movements and adjust the virtual environment accordingly, creating the illusion of true presence within the digital space.

   In this form of VR, users are not merely observing the virtual world—they are embedded within it. Applications in gaming, military training, surgical simulations, and therapeutic settings demonstrate the power of full immersion. In gaming, for example, players can navigate a room-scale environment, manipulate objects with their hands, and interact with the environment in real time. The perspective shifts from third person to first person, allowing users to perceive the virtual world as if it were their actual reality.

4. Augmented reality

   AR creates experiences where virtual entities or objects appear to exist in the real world, even though they are not physically present. Unlike VR, which immerses the user in a fully simulated environment, AR blends virtual content with the user's real surroundings. This integration enhances how we interact with digital information in everyday spaces.

   One of the most common applications of AR involves using the camera on a smartphone or tablet. When the user points their device at a space, a digital object—such as a character, item, or interface—can appear on the screen as though it exists in the physical environment. However, when the device is lowered or turned away, the virtual object disappears, highlighting its non-physical nature.

   This technology is already widely used across industries. In retail, for instance, home furnishing companies employ AR to assist customers in visualizing how products—like a couch, table, or lamp—might look in their own homes. Through AR-enabled apps, users can place virtual furniture in real spaces, adjust its position or size, and make more informed purchasing decisions without leaving home. These immersive features increase consumer confidence and bridge the gap between online and in-person shopping experiences.

5. Collaborative VR

It enables individuals from different locations to meet and interact within a shared simulated environment. In these virtual spaces, users are represented by 3D avatars or projected characters and can communicate in real-time using microphones and headsets. This immersive form of interaction adds a sense of presence and realism that traditional video conferencing often lacks.

One of the key applications of collaborative VR is in the corporate sector, where virtual meeting rooms are being used to conduct business meetings remotely. These digital environments offer the ability to present, brainstorm, and collaborate just as one would in a physical office space.

As our world becomes increasingly interconnected, VR is expanding the possibilities of human communication in unexpected ways. Following the global pandemic, the importance of maintaining strong interpersonal and professional connections has become more critical than ever. Collaborative VR helps address the challenges of remote work and social distancing, offering an innovative solution to bring teams together, no matter where they are in the world.

3 THE IMPORTANCE OF VIRTUAL CONTENT IN MODERN MEDIA

In the article by Talespin Team (2023), The Importance of Virtual Reality Technology, the prominence of virtual content in modern media is not merely a function of technological novelty; rather, it reflects a broader reconfiguration of how media is produced, circulated, and consumed in a networked society. The growing importance of virtual content can be understood through several interrelated dimensions:

3.1 Immersive Engagement

Virtual content offers unparalleled levels of immersion, transporting users into environments that simulate physical presence and spatial interaction. Whether exploring a historical reenactment in VR or navigating an interactive museum through AR, users become active participants rather than passive spectators. This depth of engagement fosters greater emotional investment and cognitive retention—qualities increasingly sought after in education, entertainment, and advertising.

3.2 Multisector Applications

The utility of virtual content extends far beyond the entertainment industry. In education, virtual laboratories and simulations provide risk-free environments for experimentation. In healthcare, AR assists with surgical planning and training. In architecture, digital walk-throughs allow clients to visualize unbuilt structures. These cross-sector applications underscore virtual content's capacity to enhance comprehension, reduce costs, and improve decision-making.

3.3 Alignment with Hybrid and Remote Models

In the wake of global disruptions such as the COVID-19 pandemic, there has been a shift toward remote learning, virtual events, and hybrid workplaces. Virtual content has been instrumental in enabling these transitions by offering alternatives to in-person interaction without sacrificing engagement or effectiveness. As digital infrastructure continues to expand, the demand for such content is poised to grow.

3.4 Creativity and Innovation

Virtual content creation fosters experimental and nonlinear modes of storytelling, allowing creators to design environments, characters, and narratives that defy the constraints of physical reality. Game designers, digital artists, and educators can leverage these platforms to imagine worlds and interactions previously impossible, thus expanding the boundaries of narrative form and pedagogical technique.

3.5 Personalization and Data Integration

Virtual environments offer real-time analytics that can inform personalized experiences. From adaptive learning modules to tailored product recommendations in AR commerce, virtual content integrates seamlessly with data-driven models, increasing efficiency and user satisfaction.

4 COMPARING VIRTUAL AND TRADITIONAL CONTENT CREATION

The term "virtual" has carried the meaning of "being something in essence or effect, though not in actual fact" since at least the mid-15th century

(Oxford English Dictionary, 2024). Its usage within the context of computing—specifically to denote something that does not physically exist but is simulated by software—emerged in 1959.

The conceptual roots of VR can be traced back to 1938, when French avant-garde playwright Antonin Artaud used the phrase *la réalité virtuelle* (virtual reality) in his influential collection of essays *Le Théâtre et son double*. In this work, Artaud reflected on the illusory and constructed nature of theatrical performance, where characters and objects are perceived as real, though they are not. The English translation of the book, published in 1958 as *The Theater and Its Double*, marks the earliest recorded use of the term "virtual reality" in print.

In the 1970s, the concept evolved further with the introduction of the term "artificial reality," coined by computer artist Myron Krueger to describe interactive environments that responded to human input in real time. Krueger's pioneering work laid the groundwork for future developments in human–computer interaction and immersive experience design.

The modern usage of "virtual reality" in a technological and cultural context was solidified in the 1980s. The term gained prominence through its use in science fiction, most notably in Damien Broderick's 1982 novel *The Judas Mandala*, where VR was depicted as a speculative future technology. Broader public recognition followed in the late 1980s, largely due to Jaron Lanier, a key figure in the development of VR hardware and software. Through his company VPL Research, Lanier introduced some of the first commercially available VR systems and popularized the term "virtual reality" in the media.

This popularization reached new heights with the release of the 1992 film The Lawnmower Man, which featured early representations of immersive digital environments and further cemented VR as a cultural and technological phenomenon (Faisal, 2017, 298–299).

While both virtual and traditional content share the goal of conveying meaning and engaging audiences, they differ significantly in terms of methodology, format, and user interaction. Table 1.1 outlines some key contrasts:

These differences are not merely technical—they represent a shift in media philosophy. Traditional content often presumes a fixed narrative and centralized authorship, whereas virtual content foregrounds interactivity, decentralization, and co-creation.

TABLE 1.1   Traditional vs Virtual Content Creation

Dimension	Traditional Content Creation	Virtual Content Creation
Format	Static or linear (e.g., print, video, photography)	Interactive and immersive (e.g., VR, AR, 3D simulations)
Tools and technologies	Cameras, printing presses, editing software	Game engines, 3D modeling tools, real-time rendering
Audience role	Passive consumption	Active participation and manipulation
Workflow	Linear production (pre-production to distribution)	Iterative, modular, often nonlinear
Distribution	Physical and digital (books, broadcasts)	Digital-only; scalable and cloud-based
Updateability	Static once published	Dynamic and updatable post-launch
Accessibility	High; minimal hardware requirements	Variable; often requires specific devices or applications

Created by the author.

5 CHALLENGES AND CONSIDERATIONS

While virtual content creation offers tremendous opportunities for innovation, interaction, and creative expression, it also presents a complex set of challenges that demand critical reflection. These challenges span technical, economic, social, ethical, and regulatory domains. Understanding these limitations is essential not only for developers and content creators but also for educators, policymakers, and scholars who seek to implement or study virtual content in diverse contexts.

5.1 Technical and Financial Barriers

The creation of high-quality virtual content often requires advanced technical infrastructure and specialized skill sets. Unlike traditional media production, which may rely on relatively accessible tools such as video cameras or word processors, virtual content development frequently involves:

- Real-time rendering engines (e.g., Unreal Engine, Unity).

- 3D modeling and animation software (e.g., Maya, Blender).

- High-performance computing systems with powerful graphics processing units.

- Cross-platform optimization for web, mobile, VR, and AR devices.

The steep learning curve associated with these tools can limit participation to those with formal training in computer graphics, game development, or immersive design. Additionally, producing content for virtual environments is both time-intensive and resource-heavy, often involving teams of programmers, designers, sound engineers, and testers.

Small organizations, independent creators, and institutions in lower-income regions may find it difficult to enter or compete in this space, creating a digital stratification in terms of who can create and distribute immersive content. The cost of licensing software, purchasing hardware (e.g., VR headsets, light detection and ranging scanners), and hiring qualified personnel can be prohibitively high, especially when ongoing updates and maintenance are required.

5.2 Access, Equity, and the Digital Divide

While virtual content promises enhanced user engagement, it also risks deepening existing inequities in digital access. Immersive experiences often require devices such as VR headsets, smartphones with AR capabilities, or high-bandwidth internet connections—resources not universally available. This disparity affects not only individuals but also institutions such as schools, libraries, and small businesses.

The digital divide—shaped by geography, socioeconomic status, infrastructure, and education—limits the ability of certain populations to access, interact with, or benefit from virtual content. In educational contexts, for instance, students in rural or underfunded school systems may be excluded from the benefits of virtual learning tools, thereby exacerbating structural inequalities.

Addressing these challenges will require investment in public infrastructure, the development of low-bandwidth or offline-capable virtual solutions, and the promotion of inclusive design principles that accommodate diverse levels of ability and access.

5.3 Ethical and Psychological Implications

Virtual content creation raises a host of ethical questions that demand serious scrutiny. Immersive environments have the capacity to simulate lifelike experiences, which can have profound effects on user perception, cognition, and emotional response. This power introduces risks such as:

- Manipulation: Sophisticated environments may be used to subtly influence user decisions, especially in advertising, political messaging, or behavioral nudging.

- Addiction and escapism: Highly immersive virtual worlds can be habit-forming, leading some users—particularly adolescents or individuals with mental health vulnerabilities—to spend excessive time in digital environments to the detriment of real-world relationships or responsibilities.

- Content appropriateness: The realism of virtual content also raises concerns about exposure to graphic violence, explicit material, or culturally insensitive representations, particularly when age restrictions and moderation systems are inadequate.

From a design perspective, creators must grapple with the implications of realism, consent, and emotional safety. For example, should simulations of traumatic historical events be rendered in photorealistic VR and how can users be ethically prepared for such experiences?

Furthermore, the psychological impact of embodied presence in virtual environments remains an area of ongoing research. Concepts such as "virtual trauma," "simulation sickness," and "identity disorientation" highlight the need for careful consideration of user well-being during both the design and deployment stages.

5.4 Data Privacy and Surveillance

Virtual content platforms often rely on data-intensive technologies to deliver personalized and interactive experiences. These may include:

- Motion tracking and eye-tracking.

- Biometric data (e.g., heart rate, gaze direction).

- Behavioral analytics and spatial movement within VR/AR environments.

While these capabilities can enhance user immersion and adapt content to individual preferences, they also raise significant concerns around surveillance, consent, and data ownership. In immersive environments, the boundary between public and private information becomes blurred, and users may be unaware of the extent to which their actions are being monitored or recorded.

This has led to calls for stricter regulation of immersive data collection, particularly regarding minors, medical simulations, and workplace-based virtual training. Questions also arise about the ownership and portability of data generated in virtual spaces, especially when content is hosted on third-party platforms or cloud-based systems.

5.5 Interoperability and Standards

As virtual content creation becomes more widespread, there is a growing need for interoperable standards that ensure compatibility across platforms, devices, and ecosystems. Currently, many immersive applications are siloed within proprietary environments (e.g., Meta's Horizon Worlds, Apple's Vision Pro, or Microsoft's HoloLens), each with its own development protocols and user access rules.

This fragmentation hinders scalability, collaboration, and sustainability, particularly for educational and public service applications that may not have the resources to develop for multiple ecosystems. It also limits users' ability to move content, avatars, or identities between platforms—a critical consideration as the concept of the "metaverse" evolves.

Efforts such as the Metaverse Standards Forum and WebXR are working to address these challenges, but widespread adoption remains uneven. Until robust standards are implemented, creators may face redundancies and inefficiencies in their workflow, and users may experience frustration in accessing or navigating content.

5.6 Environmental Sustainability

The production and delivery of virtual content, particularly in high-fidelity formats such as VR and real-time 3D rendering, demand considerable energy and computational resources. Data centers that host and stream this content can have significant carbon footprints, especially as immersive applications scale to global audiences.

From an environmental perspective, the lifecycle of virtual content—encompassing device manufacturing, server operation, software maintenance, and data transmission—must be carefully evaluated. Some sustainability considerations include:

- The energy consumption of rendering and simulation engines.
- E-waste generated by obsolete VR/AR hardware.
- Cooling demands for cloud infrastructure and edge computing systems.

Creators and organizations will increasingly need to balance the benefits of virtual immersion with the imperative to design for energy efficiency and circular resource use. This may include optimizing code, using cloud platforms powered by renewable energy, and encouraging device longevity.

5.7 Health Concerns

April Miller (2022) talks about a recently emerging term in the VR community is VR sickness, which refers to the physical discomfort some users experience while immersed in virtual environments. Symptoms commonly include eye strain, nausea, dizziness, disorientation, and general motion sickness.

Because VR sickness is still a relatively new concept, there is no universal solution for addressing it. However, as developers gain a better understanding of how and why it occurs, they can begin to design VR experiences that minimize its effects. Reducing rapid movements, improving frame rates, and refining user interface design are just some of the strategies being explored.

Ongoing research is essential to uncover the underlying causes of VR sickness and to guide the development of more user-friendly experiences. As the technology continues to evolve, developers have a crucial role in ensuring that VR becomes not only more immersive but also more comfortable and accessible for all users. Other authors such as Ben Lawson (2014), Paola Araiza-Alba et al. (2022), and Kaylee Fagan (2018) speak about this issue.

The most common being:

- Motion sickness: A common issue where users experience nausea and dizziness due to a mismatch between visual and physical sensations.

- Eye strain and fatigue: Prolonged use can lead to eye strain, headaches, and blurred vision.

- Ergonomics: Headsets can be heavy and poorly balanced, causing neck strain and discomfort.

- Heat dissipation: Poor heat management can lead to discomfort and even skin burns.

6 TYPES OF VIRTUAL CONTENT

6.1 Introduction

In the digital era, content creation has expanded far beyond static text or images to embrace a rich and multifaceted spectrum of virtual media. As users, creators, and institutions engage more deeply with immersive technologies, understanding the taxonomy of virtual content becomes essential. Virtual content comprises a wide range of digital assets and experiences produced or delivered through computational means and often mediated by interactive interfaces or spatial computing environments.

From fully immersive VR to two-dimensional graphic design, the diversity of virtual content reflects the converging pathways of art, design, computing, and storytelling. The six primary categories explored here are VR, AR, MR, 3D Modeling and Animation, Digital Art and Graphic Design, and Gaming and Interactive Media. Each represents not just a technological approach, but a cultural and communicative mode with specific affordances and implications.

6.2 Virtual Reality

6.2.1 Definition and Characteristics

VR refers to a fully immersive digital environment that simulates physical presence and spatial interaction. It typically requires the use of an HMD and, in more advanced settings, haptic controllers or full-body tracking systems. VR content is three-dimensional, computer-generated, and experienced from a first-person perspective, enabling users to look, move, and interact within an artificial world.

6.2.2 Applications

VR has expanded beyond its initial niche in gaming to become a powerful tool in education, healthcare, architecture, and the arts. For instance:

Education: Simulations of historical events or complex scientific phenomena allow learners to engage actively with curriculum material.

- Healthcare: VR is used for pain management, phobia treatment, surgical training, and rehabilitation.

- Design and architecture: Professionals use VR to prototype spaces and test usability before construction.

- Art and culture: VR installations are redefining museum exhibits and performance art.

6.2.3 Affordances and Limitations

The primary strength of VR lies in its capacity for deep immersion and embodied experience. However, limitations such as hardware cost, user motion sickness, and the need for specialized development tools remain significant barriers to mass adoption.

6.3 Augmented Reality

6.3.1 Definition and Characteristics

AR superimposes digital content onto the physical world, typically viewed through smartphones, tablets, or wearable devices like AR glasses. Unlike VR, which replaces reality, AR enhances it by adding context-aware information or visuals in real time.

6.3.2 Applications

AR has rapidly gained traction due to its accessibility and versatility. Key application areas include:

- Retail: Virtual try-ons for clothing, makeup, or furniture placement.

- Tourism and navigation: AR guides offering location-based data and historical context.

- Education: Interactive textbooks and lab simulations that overlay digital elements onto physical materials.

- Maintenance and manufacturing: Overlaid instructions and diagnostics for complex machinery.

- Entertainment: Games like Pokémon Go popularized AR as a mainstream interactive experience.

6.3.3 Affordances and Limitations

AR's real-world integration enhances usability and relevance, particularly in mobile contexts. Its ability to deliver contextual content at the point of need increases its functional value. However, challenges include a limited field of view, latency, and the need for precise environmental mapping to achieve seamless integration.

6.4 Mixed Reality

MR represents the convergence of physical and digital environments, allowing real and virtual elements to interact in real time. MR is often misunderstood as a subset of either VR or AR, but it is better understood as an evolutionary midpoint between the two. While AR simply overlays data, MR enables anchored, persistent, and spatially aware digital objects to respond to physical space and user behavior dynamically.

6.4.1 Definition and Characteristics

MR integrates physical and virtual environments into a single, unified interface. Users can interact with digital elements as if they were part of the physical world—manipulating, rotating, or walking around them. MR systems often involve sophisticated spatial mapping, environmental tracking, and gesture recognition, and are typically accessed through advanced wearable devices such as Microsoft HoloLens, Magic Leap, or Qualcomm Snapdragon XR headsets.

6.4.2 Applications

Industrial design: MR is used to visualize and manipulate complex product prototypes in physical space, enhancing rapid prototyping.

Collaborative work: Remote teams can meet in shared MR spaces with holographic avatars and shared documents.

Medical training: MR facilitates advanced surgical planning and procedural simulation with layered anatomical data.

Cultural heritage: Museums use MR to animate artifacts and reconstruct historical settings on-site.

6.4.3 Affordances and Limitations

MR's strength lies in its contextual intelligence—the ability to detect and adapt to physical surroundings. Unlike AR, MR allows for two-way interaction between real and virtual elements. However, MR devices remain costly, and the development ecosystem is still maturing. Designing for MR requires careful calibration of spatial fidelity, interaction design, and user safety (Table 1.2).

6.5 3D Modeling and Animation

6.5.1 Definition and Characteristics

3D modeling and animation involve creating three-dimensional digital representations of objects, characters, environments, or abstract forms. While 3D models are static structures, animation involves giving these models motion and lifelike behavior through keyframes, simulations, or procedural techniques.

These assets serve as foundational components in VR and AR experiences, digital twins, architectural visualizations, simulations, and gaming.

TABLE 1.2 Comparison Chart between VR, AR, and MR

Aspect	VR	AR	MR
Definition	Fully immersive digital environment that replaces the real world	Digital overlays that enhance the real world	Integration of digital and real-world elements with dynamic interaction
User experience	Isolated from the physical environment; complete immersion	Views the physical world with added digital content	Engages with both real and virtual objects that respond to each other
Hardware required	VR headset (e.g., Oculus Rift, HTC Vive), motion controllers	Smartphone, tablet, or AR glasses (e.g., Magic Leap Lite)	Advanced headsets with spatial mapping (e.g., HoloLens, Magic Leap)
Spatial awareness	Virtual space only	Partial awareness of real-world space	High-level spatial awareness and environmental understanding
Interaction type	Interaction within virtual environments only	Limited interaction with overlaid content	Bi-directional interaction between real and digital objects
Level of immersion	High	Low to moderate	Moderate to high
Mobility	Typically tethered or confined to VR-safe spaces	Highly mobile with smartphones or lightweight devices	Semi-mobile; depends on advanced tracking and mapping
Use cases	Gaming, simulation, virtual training, therapy, virtual tourism	Retail, education, navigation, live events	Industrial prototyping, remote collaboration, advanced medical training
Design complexity	High: Requires fully virtual world creation	Moderate: Digital elements overlaid on real environment	Very high: Real-time interaction and spatial coherence required
Cost and accessibility	Moderate to high hardware costs	Low: Accessible via consumer devices	High cost, limited commercial accessibility
Examples	Beat Saber, Google Earth VR	IKEA Place app, Pokémon Go	Microsoft Dynamics 365 Guides, HoloAnatomy

Created by the author.

Software such as Blender, Autodesk Maya, Cinema 4D, and ZBrush enables high-fidelity modeling and animation workflows.

6.5.2 Applications

Entertainment: Used extensively in film, television, and video games to produce visual effects and character animation.

Product design: Companies use 3D prototypes to test aesthetics and function before manufacturing.

Medical visualization: Anatomical models assist with surgical planning and patient education.

Virtual production: Real-time rendering pipelines integrate 3D animation with live-action footage.

6.5.3 Affordances and Limitations

3D content allows for realistic visualization, reusability, and interactivity, particularly when paired with game engines. However, production can be labor-intensive, and high-quality models often demand significant computing power and artistic expertise.

6.6 Digital Art and Graphic Design

6.6.1 Definition and Characteristics

Digital art and graphic design refer to two-dimensional visual content created using digital tools such as Adobe Creative Suite (Photoshop, Illustrator), CorelDRAW, Procreate, and other specialized software. This content may be static (e.g., logos, posters) or dynamic (e.g., motion graphics, UI design), and it plays a central role in shaping digital aesthetics across platforms.

6.6.2 Applications

- Digital design is a pillar of virtual content creation in various domains:

- Branding and marketing: Logos, advertising campaigns, and visual identities.

- Web and interface design: UX/UI for websites, apps, and software platforms.

- Publishing: E-books, infographics, and interactive PDFs.

- Motion graphics: Animated titles, explainer videos, and digital signage.

- NFT art: Digital artworks tokenized and traded on blockchain platforms.

6.6.3 Affordances and Limitations

Graphic design is accessible and widely practiced, offering a rich visual language for conveying complex messages in minimal space. It is highly portable, platform-agnostic, and central to visual communication. However, its impact depends on aesthetic coherence, audience literacy, and platform constraints such as screen size or resolution.

6.7 Gaming and Interactive Media

6.7.1 Definition and Characteristics

Gaming and interactive media are forms of virtual content where the user is not just a viewer but an active participant. These experiences are governed by game mechanics, narrative structures, and input-feedback loops that allow users to affect outcomes in real time. This category includes video games, serious games, simulations, and interactive storytelling applications.

6.7.2 Applications

- Entertainment: AAA games, indie games, mobile games, and VR-based game experiences.

- Education: Game-based learning platforms like Kahoot! or immersive history simulations.

- Training and simulation: Flight simulators, emergency response training, or business simulations.

- Narrative innovation: Interactive films and transmedia storytelling across platforms.

6.7.3 Affordances and Limitations

Interactive media offers high levels of engagement, agency, and replayability. Gamification elements—such as scoring, leveling, or achievements—can boost motivation and user retention. However, development is complex, often requiring interdisciplinary collaboration between designers, writers, developers, and testers. Furthermore, balancing interactivity with narrative cohesion remains a significant design challenge.

6.8 Intersections and Hybrid Forms

In practice, the boundaries between these types of virtual content are increasingly blurred. For instance:

- A VR experience may incorporate 3D models, animation, and interactive game mechanics.

- AR applications often rely on graphic design elements for intuitive interfaces.

- A digital art installation may include both real-time 3D environments and audio interactivity.

The rise of extended reality (XR) and metaverse platforms further encourages hybridization, where users move fluidly between modalities, devices, and experiences. These intersections highlight the need for cross-disciplinary literacy in virtual content creation and the importance of integrated workflows that accommodate multiple content types.

7 TOOLS AND SOFTWARE FOR VIRTUAL CONTENT CREATION

7.1 Introduction

As virtual content becomes increasingly embedded in digital culture, media production, and immersive technologies, the tools and software used to create such content have grown in sophistication and diversity. From 3D modeling environments and animation suites to immersive development platforms for virtual and AR, the landscape of digital creation is rapidly expanding. Mastery of these tools is crucial for professionals working in media design, game development, education, entertainment, and other sectors reliant on interactive and immersive experiences. These tools are not only technical assets but also enablers of new forms of creative expression and audience engagement.

7.2 3D Design Software

3D design is foundational to the creation of immersive and interactive content. Whether for use in games, simulations, architecture, or product visualization, 3D design software provides creators with the ability to model, sculpt, texture, and render digital environments and objects.

- Blender is an open-source 3D creation suite that has become a go-to tool for both independent creators and professional studios. It supports the entire 3D pipeline: Modeling, rigging, animation, simulation, rendering, compositing, and motion tracking. Its flexibility and robust community make it a powerful tool for real-time and pre-rendered content creation.

- Autodesk Maya is a professional-grade 3D software used widely in the film, television, and game industries. Known for its advanced animation capabilities and robust modeling toolkit, it is favored for high-end visual effects and character animation.

- Cinema 4D, developed by Maxon, is prized for its intuitive interface and motion graphics capabilities. It is frequently used in advertising, broadcasting, and digital art, especially in conjunction with Adobe After Effects.

7.3 VR Platforms and Tools

VR platforms and tools enable the development of immersive 3D environments where users can navigate and interact in real time. These tools encompass game engines, SDKs (software development kits), and hardware integration modules.

- Unity is one of the most popular game engines for VR development due to its flexibility, scalability, and cross-platform capabilities. Its component-based architecture and strong asset store make it accessible for both indie developers and large studios.

- Unreal Engine, developed by Epic Games, is a high-fidelity game engine used for VR experiences that demand top-tier graphics. Its blueprints visual scripting system allows for rapid prototyping without deep programming knowledge.

- SteamVR and OpenXR are frameworks that allow developers to build VR applications that work across multiple hardware platforms. OpenXR, managed by the Khronos Group, is particularly valuable for creating standardized, future-proof applications.

7.4 AR Development Tools

AR development requires tools that can track real-world environments and overlay digital content in a seamless, interactive manner. These tools often include SDKs, AR-specific engines, and computer-vision libraries.

- ARKit is Apple's framework for creating AR experiences on iOS devices. It combines device motion tracking, camera scene capture, and advanced processing to allow digital objects to interact with the real world.

- ARCore is Google's platform for building AR applications on Android devices. It provides similar capabilities to ARKit, enabling environmental understanding and motion tracking.

- Vuforia is a widely adopted AR SDK that supports both marker-based and markerless AR experiences. It is compatible with multiple development environments and devices.

- Spark AR Studio, developed by Meta (formerly Facebook), is used to create AR effects for Instagram and Facebook. It emphasizes ease of use and accessibility for creators with a limited technical background.

8 ANIMATION SOFTWARE

Animation is a central element in virtual content, giving life and motion to static objects. Animation tools range from traditional keyframing systems to procedural and motion-capture-based platforms.

- Adobe After Effects is the industry standard for 2D animation, compositing, and visual effects. It is widely used for motion graphics, video post-production, and integrating animated content into larger media projects.

- Toon Boom Harmony is a professional 2D animation tool used extensively in television and film production. It supports both traditional frame-by-frame animation and rig-based animation.

- MotionBuilder specializes in real-time 3D character animation and motion capture processing. It is used in virtual production, game development, and cinematic animation.

- Spine is a lightweight 2D skeletal animation tool often used in mobile games and interactive content. It allows for fluid animations with minimal file size (Table 1.3).

TABLE 1.3   Tools and Software for Virtual Content Creation: Key Features

Category	Software	Key Features
3D creation suites	Blender	• Non-destructive modeling workflow • Physics and particle simulations • Cycles and Eevee renderers • Python scripting support
	Autodesk Maya	• Advanced rigging and animation tools • Arnold renderer • MASH motion graphics support • Game engine integration (Unity, Unreal)
	Cinema 4D	• MoGraph for procedural animation • Adobe Creative Cloud integration • Fast viewport/rendering • User-friendly interface
VR platforms and tools	Unity	• Real-time rendering and physics • VR support (Oculus, Vive, etc.) • C# scripting • Extensive plugin marketplace
	Unreal Engine	• Lumen and Nanite photoreal rendering • Blueprint visual scripting • VR motion controller support • Open-source customization
	SteamVR and OpenXR	• Hardware-agnostic VR development • Open input/rendering standards • Game engine compatibility • Promotes device interoperability
AR development tools	ARKit (Apple)	• High-res environment mapping • Face/body tracking • Reality composer/SceneKit support • Exclusive to iOS
	ARCore (Google)	• Plane detection and light estimation • Simultaneous localization and mapping-based motion tracking • Android Studio and unity integration • Cloud Anchors support
	Vuforia	• Marker/markerless tracking • Unity/native SDK integration • Model targets for industry • Broad hardware compatibility
	Spark AR Studio	• Drag-and-drop interface • Face/gesture tracking • Mobile device previews • Built-in asset library
Animation software	Adobe After Effects	• Layer-based animation • Plugin-rich ecosystem • Adobe Suite integration • Expression-based scripting support

(Continued)

TABLE 1.3   (Continued)

Category	Software	Key Features
	Toon Boom Harmony	• Vector/bitmap drawing tools • Advanced deformers/rigging • Storyboard Pro integration • Cross-platform rendering
	Autodesk MotionBuilder	• Real-time 3D animation preview • Multi-system motion capture • Maya and 3Ds Max interoperability • Python scripting
	Spine	• Bone-based animation system • Efficient export to Unity and other engines • Mesh deformation and skinning • Timeline-based editing

Created by the author.

9 NAVIGATING THE LANDSCAPE: CHALLENGES AND FUTURE TRENDS IN VIRTUAL CONTENT CREATION

In an era increasingly defined by immersive experiences and digitally mediated storytelling, virtual content creation has emerged as a critical frontier across industries—from entertainment and education to marketing, design, and beyond. This field, driven by rapid technological advances, continues to evolve in complexity and possibility. However, as creative professionals, technologists, and educators strive to harness its potential, they encounter a variety of formidable challenges. At the same time, a new wave of innovation—anchored in artificial intelligence (AI), machine learning, and the metaverse—is reshaping the possibilities for virtual content, offering fresh opportunities for creative expression and audience engagement.

9.1 Challenges in Virtual Content Creation

9.1.1 Technical Limitations

Despite considerable progress in rendering software, real-time engines, and XR platforms, technical limitations remain a persistent barrier to virtual content creation. One of the most significant challenges lies in the accessibility and interoperability of tools. Many professional-grade platforms, such as Unreal Engine or Blender, require steep learning curves and substantial computing power. Rendering high-quality 3D environments, volumetric video, or photorealistic avatars demands not only high-performance hardware but also deep technical expertise.

Furthermore, compatibility across devices and platforms continues to be a stumbling block. Content designed for one VR headset or operating system may not function properly on another. Network infrastructure, especially in regions with limited broadband connectivity, also restricts access to cloud-based rendering or real-time streaming of interactive content, reducing the scalability of virtual productions.

9.1.2 Creative Hurdles

The creative process in virtual environments is both liberating and demanding. The nonlinear, interactive nature of virtual content requires creators to think beyond traditional storytelling. Crafting meaningful user experiences in immersive spaces calls for interdisciplinary collaboration among artists, coders, designers, and writers. This convergence of roles often leads to creative tensions, misaligned visions, or breakdowns in communication.

Additionally, maintaining narrative coherence in dynamic environments—where users can explore freely, make choices, and affect outcomes—poses unique narrative design challenges. Creators must strike a balance between agency and structure, ensuring that interactive elements enhance rather than detract from the story's emotional and thematic impact.

9.1.3 Resource and Time Constraints

Producing high-quality virtual content can be resource-intensive. From previsualization and asset design to programming and quality assurance, each phase of development demands time, specialized labor, and financial investment. Smaller studios or independent creators often lack the funding or personnel to compete with larger organizations capable of deploying expansive virtual experiences. The iterative nature of designing interactive or immersive environments—frequently requiring testing across devices and user scenarios—further extends production timelines. Agile workflows and real-time feedback loops can help mitigate delays, but only if sufficient resources are allocated for ongoing revisions and optimization.

9.2 Future Trends in Virtual Content Creation

9.2.1 Emerging Technologies: AI and Machine Learning

AI and machine learning are rapidly transforming the virtual content landscape. Tools like generative AI models, procedural content generators, and intelligent animation systems are streamlining workflows and expanding creative possibilities. Text-to-image platforms, for instance, allow concept artists to generate visual ideas in seconds, while AI-assisted voice synthesis and motion capture reduce the need for costly studio sessions.

Machine learning algorithms are also being used to enhance realism in avatars, simulate complex environmental interactions, and personalize content in real time based on user behavior. These innovations not only speed up production but also democratize access, allowing smaller teams to produce sophisticated virtual experiences previously out of reach.

However, the use of AI also introduces new ethical and creative concerns, including questions around authorship, originality, and algorithmic bias. As these tools become more integrated into content pipelines, creators will need to engage critically with both their benefits and limitations.

9.2.2 The Rise of the Metaverse

The concept of the metaverse—persistent, shared digital environments where users interact through avatars—represents a paradigm shift in virtual content consumption and production. In this emerging ecosystem, content is not merely viewed or played but inhabited. As such, creators are being called upon to design not just linear experiences, but entire worlds.

This shift demands new forms of storytelling, architecture, and social interaction design. The metaverse also raises practical considerations: Interoperability of assets, moderation of user-generated content, and the economics of virtual goods and spaces. For content creators, this presents not only a frontier rich with opportunity, but also uncertainty. Understanding the evolving expectations of metaverse participants will be key to crafting engaging and sustainable virtual environments.

9.2.3 The Role of Virtual Content in Digital Storytelling

As audiences grow more comfortable with immersive technologies, virtual content is poised to become a central mode of storytelling. From virtual museums and branded experiences to educational simulations and live performances in XR, virtual content is reshaping how narratives are crafted and consumed.

Storytelling in virtual environments allows for multisensory engagement, emotional depth, and personal agency. These features enable creators to move beyond passive media consumption, inviting audiences to co-create meaning and memory within the narrative space. Whether in documentaries enhanced with AR layers or virtual theater productions staged in 3D worlds, the future of digital storytelling lies in its capacity to be experiential, interactive, and deeply immersive.

10 CONCLUSION

Virtual content creation stands at the intersection of technological innovation, cultural transformation, and media evolution. As this chapter has shown, the shift from traditional to virtual content represents more than a change in tools or formats—it reflects a fundamental reimagining of how stories are told, how knowledge is transmitted, and how users participate in mediated experiences. From non-immersive gaming environments to fully embodied simulations in VR, the spectrum of virtual content is broad and continually expanding. This expansion enables increasingly rich, personalized, and multisensory engagements across sectors, including education, healthcare, entertainment, design, and commerce.

The philosophical exploration of virtuality reveals that virtual experiences are not "unreal" but occupy a legitimate place within human perception and cultural practice. The ontological status of the virtual, as framed by Deleuze (1990) and others, underscores its role in shaping identity, interaction, and meaning in ways that are no less authentic than those grounded in physical environments. By moving beyond binary distinctions between real and virtual, scholars and creators alike can engage more critically with the layered realities that users now navigate.

At the same time, the development of virtual content is marked by significant challenges. Technical complexity, high production costs, and limited accessibility remain barriers to entry. Ethical concerns, including data privacy, user consent, and psychological impacts, demand careful attention from designers, developers, and regulators. The risk of exacerbating digital divides—both in terms of access and participation—poses serious questions about equity and inclusion in future digital ecosystems.

Looking ahead, emerging trends such as generative AI, machine learning, and the rise of the metaverse are reshaping the landscape of content creation. These technologies promise to reduce barriers, enhance personalization, and support new forms of interactivity. Yet, they also call for critical scrutiny regarding authorship, control, and the socio-cultural implications of automated content generation.

Ultimately, virtual content creation is not just a technical endeavor but a cultural and ethical project. As the tools grow more powerful and the experiences more immersive, creators, educators, and institutions must continually reflect on the purposes, audiences, and values that drive their work. In doing so, they can help shape a digital future that is not only innovative but also inclusive, responsible, and deeply meaningful.

REFERENCES

Araiza-Alba, Paola; Keane, Therese; Kaufman, Jordy (August 8, 2022). "Are we ready for virtual reality in K-12 classrooms?" *Technology, Pedagogy and Education*. 31 (4): 471–491.

Artaud, Antonin (1958). *The theatre and its double*. Trans. Mary Caroline Richards. New York: Grove Weidenfeld.

Awati, Rahul (January 10, 2022). *Virtual*. https://www.techtarget.com/searchitoperations/definition/virtual

Burkhalter, Max (May 19, 2022). *The five kinds of virtual reality*. https://www.perle.com/articles/the-five-kinds-of-virtual-reality-40194293.shtml

Deleuze, Gilles (1990). *Bergonism*. Trans. H. Tomlinson; B. Habberjam. New York: Zone Books (1988).

Fagan, Kaylee (March 4, 2018). *Here's what happens to your body when you've been in virtual reality for too long*. New York City: Business Insider.

Faisal, Aldo (2017). "Computer science: Visionary of virtual reality". *Nature*. 551 (7680): 298–299.

Lawson, Ben D. (2014). "Motion sickness symptomatology and origins". In Hale, Kelly S.; Stanney, Kay M. (eds.). H*andbook of Virtual Environments*. pp. 531–599. Boca Raton, FL: CRC Press (an imprint of Taylor & Francis).

Lehdonvirta, V. (2010). "Virtual worlds don't exist: Questioning the dichotomous approach in MMO studies". *The International Journal of Computer Game Research*, 10(1).

Milgram, Paul; Takemura, Haruo; Utsumi, Akira; Kishino, Fumio (1995). "Augmented reality: A class of displays on the reality-virtuality continuum". In Das, Hari (ed.). *Telemanipulator and Telepresence Technologies*. Vol. 2351. pp. 282–292. Bellingham: Society of Photo-Optical Instrumentation Engineers (SPIE) (also referred to as SPIE – The International Society for Optical Engineering).

Miller, April (June 1, 2022). *7 challenges in VR product development*. https://arinsider.co/2022/06/01/7-challenges-in-vr-product-development/

Oxford English Dictionary (2024). https://www.oed.com/search/dictionary/?scope=Entries&q=virtual

Shields, Rob (2003). *The virtual*. New York: Routledge.

Talespin Team (July 10, 2023). *The importance of virtual reality technology*. https://www.talespin.com/reading/the-importance-of-virtual-reality-technology

CHAPTER 2

Understanding Virtual Environments

Francisco-Julián Martínez-Cano
and Tamara Makana Chock

1 INTRODUCTION

One of the most important technological advancements of the 21st century is virtual environments (VEs). Users can interact with digital information in ways that confuse virtual and physical realities in these computer-generated environments that mimic real or imagined worlds. From the first text-based adventures like Zork (Anderson et al., 1977) to the photorealistic virtual reality (VR) simulations of today, the development of VR has been propelled by the rapid expansion of computing power, artificial intelligence (AI), and research on human–computer interaction (HCI).

VEs are complex socio-technical systems that combine computer science, communication, cognitive psychology, and HCI. They may be classified depending on the type of device that's been used for their creation and consumption. Let's say that a console video game can be considered a VE, regardless of whether it is 2D or 3D; a virtual social network for on-screen consumption such as Second Life (Linden Lab, 2003); a VR film to be consumed with a head-mounted display (HMD) such as *Queerskins: A Love Story* (Szilak and Tsiboulski, 2018); or a social network for immersive

DOI: 10.1201/9781003673538-2

consumption such as AltspaceVR (Altspace Inc., 2015) or VRChat (VRChat Inc., 2014) can be considered VEs, whose difference based on the consumption device for their creation and design is the degree of immersion they offer.

A VE may be displayed on a head-mounted device, a computer monitor, or a large projection screen. Head and hand tracking systems are used to enable users to observe, navigate, and interact with the VE (Mandal, 2013). In this chapter, we will put the focus on immersive virtual environments (IVEs). For their definition, there has been a debate since the 1990s, where the major features of these media were considered to be telepresence, simulation, and full-body immersion (Heim, 1998). Coates' definition (2003) sets VR as electronic simulations of environments experienced via head-mounted goggles and wired clothing, enabling the audience to interact in realistic three-dimensional settings. Greenbaum included movement in the definition of VR and described it as an alternate world filled with computer-generated images that respond to human movements. Pimental (1995) defines VR as an interactive, immersive experience generated by a computer, moving forward from a device-driven to an experience-content-oriented definition.

As Martínez-Cano et al. (2023) established, at the end of the 20th century and the beginning of the 21st, an agreement seemed reached to define the "three common features of VR: immersion, presence, and interaction" (Cruz-Neira, 1993), as noted by Biocca (1997), Biocca et al. (2001a, 2001b), Bailenson et al. (2006), Slater (2009), Mandal (2013), Lopreiato et al. (2016), and Cipresso et al. (2018). Blascovich et al. (2002) highlight a definition of VR that is based on its goal: to trick the senses into believing that a synthetic representation of reality exists. Bown et al. (2017, p. 255) explained VR as a simulation that is regarded as real, mediated by "presence as the effect caused by perceiving an essential copy," after physical transcendence. On the contrary, Yoh (2001) noted that the term is imprecise because its meaning varies depending on the situation.

VR tries

> to alter one's perception of reality by tricking the senses, by providing artificial computer-generated stimuli. The ultimate goal of VR is to create a perfect illusion, an artificial experience so realistic that it is practically indistinguishable from the real thing.
>
> *(Stanković, 2015, p. 4)*

Martínez-Cano et al., in their 2023 systematic review, introduce VR definition as "the use of advanced hardware and software capabilities to create user-centered high fidelity emotional experiences that go beyond the two-dimensional screen." Therefore, through VR technologies, high-level IVEs are generated, where human senses are substituted by computer-generated signals, and the user's movements are tracked and mirrored. Carefully designing VR experiences will enhance immersion and, consequently, increase the audience's sense of presence.

2 THEORETICAL FOUNDATIONS OF VES

2.1 Immersion and Presence

Lombard and Ditton (1997) establish that "the ultimate goal of virtual environments is to create a sense of presence—making users feel as though they are truly 'inside' the digital world." As a result, a fundamental idea in VE research and development is presence. According to Biocca (1992), it is the feeling of being in a VE as opposed to a real one, which leads to psychological phenomena that encourage user involvement and is reinforced by sensory reality and response interaction. Whether VR is utilized for social interaction, teaching, gaming, or treatment, its usefulness is largely dependent on this psychological phenomenon called presence. Immersion technologies like VR, augmented reality, and mixed reality are becoming more widely available, which has increased their use in a variety of sectors, including healthcare, remote and cooperative work, education, and entertainment.

As stated by Slater and Wilbur (1997), the idea of presence is the user's psychological reaction to immersion, whereas the concept of immersion is an objective feature of the technology (such as field of vision or display quality). As Steuer (1992) explains, immersion is a function of the system's capacity to deliver an inclusive, extensive, surrounding, and vivid illusion of reality, highlighting users' movement tracking:

> Various nonimmersive "three-dimensional" visual systems, including the ViewMaster, "three-dimensional" films, and holograms, attempt to accurately portray a sense of depth across part of the visual field, while immersive visual displays such as stereoscopic head-mounted displays create a sense of presence by presenting a visual environment that moves with the viewer.

> *(Steuer, 1992, p. 14)*

These ideas are intertwined, and the distinction between virtual and real-world experiences is blurred as they evolve with the use of 3D graphics, spatial audio, and haptic feedback to achieve a high degree of immersion. In this manner, these technical characteristics enhance immersion, which in turn fosters the sense of presence, or the perception of being present in the VE (Sanchez-Vives & Slater, 2005).

McGowin and Fiore (2024) clarified this distinction. They contend that technical immersion, including multimodal concurrency and HMDs with a high field of view (technological features), needs to be separated from interaction realism or narrative involvement (subjective dimensions of the experience). In other words, immersion is determined by the setting of the scene, while presence depends on how well the stage conforms to our sensory expectations. When sensory contingencies in VEs match real-world patterns, the presence is improved even in situations where story elements are deemed lacking.

Immersion and presence in VEs are conceptualized using a tiered framework. Hardware fidelity, sensory modalities, and tracker accuracy are all included in the technology layer. Motion, gesture, feedback, and proprioception alignment are all inside the sensorimotor layer. Emotional involvement, flow, presence, and psychological absorption are all part of the cognitive-affective layer.

Recent studies have expanded this framework by investigating the impact of AI-driven interactions on presence. Adaptive virtual agents that respond to user behavior in real time have been shown to significantly increase perceived presence and engagement. These findings indicate that AI can dynamically adjust VEs to sustain immersion, a concept referred to as dynamic fidelity. Dynamic fidelity is defined as the degree to which simulations replicate real-world systems (Harris et al., 2020) and can be categorized into four key dimensions: physical, functional, psychological, and social fidelity. The representation of the virtual body and embodiment strategies are critical components within these dimensions.

2.2 Embodiment and the Virtual Body

The embodiment phenomenon is directly connected with presence. Slater et al. define embodiment as "the illusion of transfer of body ownership," (2010, p. 1) or the "temporary subjective illusion of ownership of the virtual body [...]" (2010, p. 2). To clarify, the sensation of body ownership in a virtual environment facilitates better user interaction and learning outcomes. The following crucial components are listed by Kilteni et al. (2015):

synchronized multimodal feedback, congruent motion control, alignment of virtual and real posture, and a realistic body shape. These ideas have significant implications, as people's perceptions of space, threat sensitivity, pain management, and social connection all change when they feel embodied.

The feeling of control over a virtual body, or embodiment, is another important psychological component of VEs. Kilteni et al. (2012) demonstrated that when users see a virtual limb moving in sync with their own actions, they experience a strong sense of embodiment, which can alter their perceptions and behaviors. This phenomenon has significant ramifications for applications such as virtual rehabilitation, in which patients engage with virtual limbs to restore motor abilities (Riva et al., 2019; Matamala-Gómez et al., 2022).

Your senses must all agree for something to truly feel like a part of you. It should be consistent with what you see, hear, and feel. This isn't something that happens automatically. Porssut et al. (2023) found that if these senses clash, people might feel disconnected from the experience, which can make it less immersive and even cause discomfort.

Nevertheless, embodiment is not simple. Highly lifelike avatars have been shown to actually reduce internal body awareness. According to a CHI 2023 study by Döllinger et al. (2023), internal body awareness can be reduced by extremely lifelike avatars, indicating that embodiment may divert attention from interoceptive cues that are important in mental health settings.

Forster et al. (2022) introduce the Implied Body Framework (IBF), a theoretical paradigm that integrates presence and embodiment. According to the IBF, presence and embodiment become stronger the more a virtual body indicates suitable sensorimotor contingencies—a conceptual synergy that is frequently disregarded in conventional designs.

2.3 Interactive Meaning and Embodied Cognitive Processes

Embodied cognition, which maintains that bodily observation and action are the foundation of cognitive functioning, also yields theoretical insight. Wilson (2002) makes the case that cognition developed to facilitate adaptive action in contextual situations, which is directly relevant to VE design, especially in applications related to education or the arts. The space design or scenography also plays an important role. Bachelard states that the spatial layout of an environment is not only a vessel for action but also a stage for memory and imagination (1994).

In VR, for example, users can navigate and alter spaces using gestures in virtual art and design instruction because VR combines mental images with physical action. According to Mills et al. (2022), this type of VR setup encourages people to think more imaginatively about their bodies, despite the fact that experiencing things like missing a body could ruin their VR experience. This suggests that a true corporeality may require the integration of sensory feedback in a harmonious manner.

Emotions are not confined to the mind but emerge from the sensory and spatial interactions of the body with its surroundings. These ideas emphasize that cognition occurs in action rather than only in the brain and are applicable to social simulation, education, and rehabilitation. The ability to move, gesture, and engage with the body in VR environments extends cognition beyond the head into situated, sensorimotor space. Following these ideas, we move from VEs to IVEs.

2.4 Affordances, Design of Interaction, and AI Adaptation

In IVEs, it's a major feature to consider the way users get to know and identify potential actions. Therefore, affordance theory (Norman, 1999; Gibson, 2014) has been adapted. From exploring areas to grabbing virtual tools, VEs must make it obvious when there are interactive options. Following Norman's affordance theory, an intuitive way and easy engagement and interaction with a well-designed virtual object should be evident (for example, a virtual button should look pressable). When consumers find it difficult to navigate or control the environment, poor affordance design causes frustration (LaViola, 2000).

Current IVEs are evolving into dynamic and adaptive by using AI. Many traditional elements from VEs are getting a major update; amid them are Non-Playable Characters (NPCs) that are becoming more natural and realistic through natural language models, props, and landscapes content that is generated automatically as the user navigates and moves forward in the virtual space (procedural content generation), and behaviors that are dynamic (real-time behavior shaping). Adaptive Virtual Neuroarchitecture is actually a notion put up by Jain et al. (2023): IVEs that dynamically react to the user's physiological, cognitive, and emotional state—modifying lighting, space, or interactivity to improve well-being in real time, "[...] buildings can be an important focal point for promoting wellbeing by optimizing the occupant's experience of the indoors space. We believe bodily perceptual processes can similarly form the basis of built environment design in virtual reality (VR)" (Jain et al., 2023, p. 2).

AI-enhanced VR is also connected to recent research on haptic feed-back. Puttur Venkatraj et al. (2024) found that participants' sense of agency and copresence were significantly impacted by the distribution of vibrotactile feedback and control when they shared agency of a single avatar. Similarly, Seinfeld et al. (2022) found that when using haptics, users experienced greater emotive touch than when using visual-only stimuli. This suggests that visuotactile input enhances emotional embodiment.

2.5 Social Presence in IVEs

Seldom does virtual interaction occur in a vacuum. Interpersonal and social presence are crucial in collaborative IVEs. The Transformed Social Interaction (TSI) idea developed by Bailenson et al. (2004) emphasizes how virtual systems can change the way people connect with one another—for instance, enabling a presenter's avatar to make eye contact with several users at once (Bailenson, 2005).

In the research and design of IVEs, the idea of social presence has taken on a greater significance. Often called "being with others" in mediated places, social presence is different from similar ideas like spatial presence (the feeling of "being there") and self-presence (the link to one's virtual self). The emergence of immersive settings such as VR headsets and online immersive platforms with multiple users has brought social presence back into the spotlight as a factor in psychological well-being, communication quality, learning outcomes, and the efficacy of cooperation. Even though it is mediated electronically and digitally, this phenomenon is impor-tant because it can reduce the psychological distance between people who are spread out, creating an experience that is similar to face-to-face conversations.

There are a few aspects that affect how social presence develops in IVEs. According to research on volumetric capture avatars, technological accuracy is crucial because realistic motion and appearance boost users' experience of copresence and trust, especially in dynamic tasks where three-dimensional cues are crucial (Cho et al., 2020).

Social influence is captured by TSI together with imitation and empa-thy. An avatar can be more persuasive, less discriminatory, and more cohesive when its embodiment is in line with the demographics of its users. Matching users' ethnicity and gender with their avatar significantly enhanced embodiment, including self-location and ownership beliefs, according to Do et al. (2024).

The level of social connection is influenced by contextual factors, such as how shared tasks and spaces are designed. For instance, it has been demonstrated that cooperative problem-solving in educational simulations improves social presence through interaction and reciprocal attention (Bulu, 2012). Lastly, the degree to which people sense social presence is modulated by individual characteristics, such as self-perception, cultural background, or immersion tendencies. Some users need richer connections or better fidelity to obtain the same psychological participation, while others easily transfer social cues into mediated areas.

A key component of social presence is the design of avatars and interaction methods. One field with a lot of potential is haptic technologies. Haptic cues in VR have the potential to enhance social presence in a variety of settings, including online collaboration, long-distance communication, and treatment.

Social presence is the cornerstone of meaningful engagement in IVEs. From remote teams and collaborative classrooms to senior citizen well-being programs, the sense of "being with others" affects learning, emotional outcomes, and enjoyment. It is a product of both social and technological production and is contingent upon the caliber of interaction and communication as well as the accuracy of representation.

3 AI-DRIVEN IVES TOWARD REALITY SIMULATIONS

The field of IVEs is changing due to AI, which is influencing educational simulators, immersive VR spaces, and the developing Metaverse. AI-powered IVEs evolve, react, and enhance user engagement in a way that goes well beyond static, pre-scripted experiences. VEs offer immersive locations for learning, working, collaborating, and socializing. These range from social media platforms and instructional simulations to expansive VR ecosystems. AI transforms IEVs from static into responsive, adaptive, and personalized simulations. Realism and immersion, together with presence, interaction, and collaboration, are boosted by the implementation of AI in IVEs.

The development of presence, or the feeling of "being there" and "being with others," is a primary goal in IVEs. This is made possible in large part by AI technologies, such as intelligent avatar systems, procedural modeling, and real-time environment generation. Another reason for the recent surge in interest in generative artificial intelligence (GenAI) is the continuous progress being made in the field of human-AI interaction. Natural language processing, for example, allows conversational bots and NPCs to react in real time, mimicking the impromptu nature of human communication. Meanwhile, machine learning techniques are improving motion capture and gesture recognition which turns into avatars with more realistic facial emotions and body language. By lowering the perception distance between the virtual and physical worlds, these AI-powered features improve social and spatial presence.

Large language models and diffusion models have pushed further the GenAI trend. Relevant and customized conversations can be had with conversational avatars, and virtual landscapes can be procedurally improved to offer more contextual complexity and diversity through AI models that analyze the links between items and spaces in a particular setting: spatial reasoning (Kobenova et al., 2024, pp. 3–4). All of these developments contribute to more socially engaging, realistic, and responsive settings and empower their applications in augmented and VR experiences, robotics, and gaming.

3.1 Personalization in IVEs

Personalization is essential to the efficacy of training simulations and immersive virtual learning environments. Real-time feedback, adaptive content difficulty, and performance-based scaffolding are all capabilities of intelligent tutoring systems integrated into VR platforms. The system can dynamically modify the learning pace or instructional style by employing AI to process eye-tracking data, physiological signals, and behavioral logs to estimate degrees of attention, motivation, or cognitive load. AI-powered adaptive scenarios, for instance, can pose increasingly difficult problems to learners in medical or engineering simulations, simulating real-world decision-making under duress.

The development of intelligent, self-governing, and user-controlled avatars is one of the most significant developments in IVEs. In order to serve as instructors, allies, or enemies, artificially intelligent avatars can imitate complex behavioral patterns. These avatars assist in bridging the gaps in remote teams operating in collaborative environments by serving as flexible mediators or simulation aids in training scenarios.

3.2 AI Generative Models for IVEs

GenAI is causing rapid changes in the creation, populating, and experiencing of virtual worlds. While in traditional VEs, content was handcrafted as 3D models with manually placed textures and hand-coded scripts, in generative IVEs, trained priors are used to generate geometry, appearance, and behavior from textual, visual, and/or sparse sensor input. Diffusion models of 3D tasks designed for generative modeling, neural implicit scene representations, especially Neural Radiance Fields (NeRFs), and 3D scene reconstruction are the three most significant families of techniques related to IVEs that hybrid pipelines utilize 2D scene generative models. Geometry and rendering generative work have been boosted by NeRFs. Through these models, IVEs can support realistic view synthesis, which results in consistent-appearance multi-view VR scenes where the users can move as they please during their navigation through virtual space (Gao et al., 2025).

On the other hand, models created for high-quality 2D image synthesis such as Diffusion are currently applied and adapted to 3D graphics generation as they are combined with NeRFs or other differentiable renderers. For instance, before optimizing a 3D representation triggered by text prompts, "DreamFusion framework uses a pretrained text-to-image diffusion model to generate realistic 3D models from text prompts" (Poole et al., 2022, p. 2), avoiding the need for a large 3D dataset in this domain. There are also other Single-Stage Diffusion NeRF (SSDNeRF) models "which models the generative prior of scene latent codes with a 3D latent diffusion model (LDM)" (Chen et al., 2023, p. 2). In this realm, "the Magic3D framework revolutionizes high-quality 3D content synthesis using text prompts, surpassing the design limitations of DreamFusion" (Fang, 2024, p. 8). This SSDNeRF can enhance resolution and cross-view coherency while cutting down on production time. It is therefore demonstrated the potential of these early-stage models for the generation of high-resolution meshes suitable for downstream use in IVEs (Lin et al., 2023).

Practical avatar pipelines have used generative components to speed up capture and rigging in tandem with NeRF/diffusion advancements. By transforming "in-the-wild" monocular video into photorealistic portrait avatars using techniques like Gaussian splatting and neural volumetric avatars, the difficulty of producing credible participants in IVEs is significantly reduced. Recent work gives game engine-compatible editing tools and recreates photorealistic avatars using Gaussian splatting, an essential step in production integration (Zhang et al., 2025; Nehvi et al., 2024). Within the benefits of GenAI models for IVEs, we found the most important ones: content scalability (props and asset creation on demand from text prompts), customization (user-personalized avatars from pictures or videos), and dynamic world procedural generation, creating scenes that adapt to users' behavior and interaction).

But what's next from a research point of view? It is certain that IVE's development is in need of deeper research that goes from physical simulation and affordance-ready asset generation that allows user interaction, continuing the hybrid model pipelines explorations to keep improving and shortening generative computing processes, AI-generated NPCs and agents that are able to express coherent and natural nonverbal communication, and the development of governance frameworks that include user consent, provenance, and on-device privacy protections. These dimensions are highlighted in recent surveys and research articles, which urge interdisciplinary study integrating ethics, HCI, and graphics.

4 CONCLUSIONS

The conceptual and technological development of VEs has been mapped out, from simple simulations to the complex, AI-powered ecosystems of today. In summary, key concepts of IVEs were shared: affordance, or how to make interaction more natural and affordable for the user; presence or the "feeling of being there"; immersion, or how to create deep engaging experiences where the users forget they are not in a real-world environment; and embodiment, which is related to creating the strong experience of having a virtual body. These ideas are not only theoretical; they form the foundation for developing IVEs that are interesting, meaningful, useful, engaging, and available in a variety of fields.

These pillars are intricately linked, as the theoretical debate demonstrated. The scene is set via technological immersion, which is accomplished by precise tracking, spatial audio, and high-fidelity graphics. Nonetheless, the alignment of sensory dependencies—in which a virtual body precisely mimics a user's movements—is what causes the feeling of embodiment. This embodiment works as a mediator and as a moderator that enhances immersion and therefore presence, changing completely users from passive viewers to active participants in IVEs. It's worth becomes clear in areas like motor skill recovery, where patients reconnect with virtual body parts, and in social VEs, where avatars help grow communication and trust, connecting individuals from distant or non-usually related communities, "not only by embodying one's own role, but by embodying another (otherness theory)" (Martínez-Cano et al., 2023).

AI is changing the digital world we live in during the first quarter of the 21st century. Virtual worlds that are immersive are not an exception. Consider living in an IVE that can adjust to you and your interests in real time. It can detect your heart rate, temperature, and brain activity, use all of this information to react to your individual physical and mental state, which is connected to your mood and physiological state, and then provide you with the exact experience you require at that specific time. As the new conductor of these experiences, this review highlights the significance of AI. Combining basic components with AI transforms virtual worlds from static landscapes into simulations that respond and change. Through adaptive tutoring systems that adjust learning based on physiological feedback, AI enhances cognitive and affective engagement.

By building intricate and contextually aware worlds from basic text instructions, generative models such as diffusion pipelines and NeRFs enable AI to address content scalability concerns in IVEs. On the other hand, AI-powered avatars and NPCs allow IEVs to enhance social presence through enabling natural language in communication processes, which contribute to the improvement of social presence by implementing natural dialogue and accurate nonverbal cues, which boost the authenticity of shared narratives and teamwork.

Ethical considerations from the combination of immersion, embodiment, and AI result in a necessity for future research in these fields. As discussed above, high-fidelity avatars might diminish the sense of owning a virtual body, which results in questions about psychological effects and the impact of embodiment during long lapses of time. Future development must be guided by the tremendous issues and ethical implications that come with this potent convergence. Strong governance frameworks that give user consent, data provenance, and on-device privacy protections top priority are required since AI can create hyper-realistic content and adaptable environments. Incorporating these principles into generative pipelines is mentioned in this chapter as an urgent necessity for responsible innovation, not as a utopian ideal. The trend of IVEs suggests that experiences will become more ubiquitous and customized in the future. Smart IVEs are not science fiction anymore. By providing individualized experiences that empower, support healing and treatment, IVEs have the potential to become more than just a simulation of reality.

Finally, understanding VEs is a task that requires a multidisciplinary effort, one that combines perspectives and insights from different areas of knowledge. EVs have shifted from sensory trick experiences to an AI-driven "ultimate display." (Sutherland, 1965) shows a field that evolves nonstop in its pursuit of achieving higher immersion experiences and more meaningful interactions. At this intersection of human intelligence and cutting-edge technology, the problem and the potential are in effectively utilizing these potent instruments. We shall move closer to a future of higher human potential and tighter ties if IVEs are designed to be not only technologically advanced but also moral and human-centered.

REFERENCES

AltspaceVR, Inc. (2015). *AltspaceVR* [Social VR Platform].

Anderson, T., Blank, M., Daniels, B., & Lebling, D. (1977). *Zork* [Video game]. MIT Lab for Computer Science.

Bachelard, G. (1994). *The poetics of space* (Boston, MA: Beacon Press).

Bailenson, J. N. (2005). Transformed social interaction in virtual environments. *NSF Award Number 0527377. Directorate for Computer and Information Science and Engineering, 5*(527377), 27377.

Bailenson, J. N., Beall, A. C., Loomis, J., Blascovich, J., & Turk, M. (2004). Transformed social interaction: Decoupling representation from behavior and form in collaborative virtual environments. *Presence: Teleoperators & Virtual Environments, 13*(4), 428–441.

Bailenson, J. N., Yee, N., Merget, D., & Schroeder, R. (2006). The effect of behavioral realism and form realism of real-time avatar faces on verbal disclosure, nonverbal disclosure, emotion recognition, and copresence in dyadic interaction. *Presence: Teleoperators and Virtual Environments, 15*(4), 359–372.

Biocca, F. (1992). Communication within virtual reality: Creating a space for research. *Journal of Communication, 42*, 5.

Biocca, F. (1997). The cyborg's dilemma: Progressive embodiment in virtual environments. *Journal of Computer-Mediated Communication, 3*, JCMC324. doi: 10.1111/j.1083-6101.1997.tb00070.x

Biocca, F., Burgoon, J., Harms, C., & Stoner, M. (2001a). Criteria and scope conditions for a theory and measure of social presence. *Presence, 10*, 2001. doi: 10.1162/105474601753132722

Biocca, F., Harms, C., & Gregg, J. (2001b). The networked minds measure of social presence: pilot test of the factor structure and concurrent validity. In *4th annual international workshop on presence*, Philadelphia, PA, pp. 1–9.

Blascovich, J., Loomis, J., Beall, A. C., Swinth, K. R., Hoyt, C. L., Bailenson, J. N. (2002). Immersive virtual environment technology as a methodological tool for social psychology. *Psychological Inquiry, 13*, 103–124. doi: 10.1207/ S15327965PLI1302_01

Bown, J., White, E., & Boopalan, A. (2017). Looking for the ultimate display: A brief history of virtual reality. In *Boundaries of self and reality online*, eds J. Gackenbach, and J. Bown (Cambridge, MA: Academic Press), 239–259. doi: 10.1016/B978-0-12-804157-4.00012-8

Bulu, S. T. (2012). Place presence, social presence, co-presence, and satisfaction in virtual worlds. *Computers & Education, 58*(1), 154–161. doi: 10.1016/j. compedu.2011.08.024

Chen, H., Gu, J., Chen, A., Tian, W., Tu, Z., Liu, L., & Su, H. (2023). Single-stage diffusion NeRF: A unified approach to 3D generation and reconstruction. In *Proceedings of the IEEE/CVF international conference on computer vision* (Paris: IEEE), 2416–2425. doi: 10.48550/arXiv.2304.06714

Cho, S., Kim, S. W., Lee, J., Ahn, J., & Han, J. (2020, March). Effects of volumetric capture avatars on social presence in immersive virtual environments. In *2020 IEEE conference on virtual reality and 3D user interfaces (VR)* (Atlanta, GA: IEEE), 26–34.

Cipresso, P., Giglioli, I. A. C., Raya, M. A., & Riva, G. (2018). The past, present, and future of virtual and augmented reality research: A network and cluster analysis of the literature. *Frontiers in Psychology, 9*, 2086. doi: 10.3389/fpsyg.2018.02086

Coates, N. (2003). 13.4: Head mounted display for simulation and visualisation. In *SID symposium digest of technical papers*, Volume 34, No. 1 (Oxford: Blackwell Publishing Ltd), 184–187. doi: 10.1889/1.1832234

Cruz-Neira, C. (1993). Virtual reality overview. In *SIGGRAPH 93 course notes 21st International conference on computer graphics and interactive techniques* (Orlando, FL: Orange County Convention Center).

Do, T. D., Protko, C. I., & McMahan, R. P. (2024). Stepping into the right shoes: The effects of user-matched avatar ethnicity and gender on sense of embodiment in virtual reality. *IEEE Transactions on Visualization and Computer Graphics, 30*(5), 2434–2443.

Döllinger, N., Wolf, E., Botsch, M., Latoschik, M. E., & Wienrich, C. (2023, April). Are embodied avatars harmful to our self-experience? The impact of virtual embodiment on body awareness. In *Proceedings of the 2023 CHI conference on human factors in computing systems* (New York: Association for Computing Machinery), 1–14.

Fang, S. (2024). Exploring the capabilities of NeRF in generating 3D models. *EAI Endorsed Trans AI Robotics, 3*. doi: 10.4108/airo.5360

Forster, P. P., Karimpur, H., & Fiehler, K. (2022). Why we should rethink our approach to embodiment and presence. *Frontiers in Virtual Reality, 3*, 838369.

Gao, R., Gao, Q., & Wang, X. (2025, May). Enhancing 3D scene reconstruction with a modified NeRF approach. In *2025 5th international conference on computer, control and robotics (ICCCR)* (Hangzhou: IEEE), 578–583.

Gibson, J. J. (2014). The theory of affordances (1979). In J. J. Gieseking, W. Mangold, C. Katz, S. Low, & S. Saegert (Eds.), *The people, place, and space reader* (Routledge), 56–60. doi:10.4324/9781315816852

Greenbaum, P. (1992). The lawnmower man. *Film Video, 9*, 58–62. doi: 10.1353/jfv.2010.0011

Harris, D. J., Bird, J. M., Smart, P. A., Wilson, M. R., & Vine, S. J. (2020). A framework for the testing and validation of simulated environments in experimentation and training. *Frontiers in Psychology, 11*, 605. doi: 10.3389/fpsyg.2020.00605

Heim, M. (1998). *Virtual realism*. Oxford, New York. doi: 10.1093/oso/9780195104 264.003.0007

Jain, A., Maes, P., & Sra, M. (2023). Adaptive virtual neuroarchitecture. In A. Simeone, B. Weyers, S. Bialkova, R. W. Lindeman (Eds.), *Everyday virtual and augmented reality*. Human–Computer Interaction Series. Springer, Cham, 227–249. doi: 10.1007/978-3-031-05804-2_9

Kilteni, K., Groten, R., & Slater, M. (2012). The sense of embodiment in virtual reality. *Presence 21*, 373–387. doi: 10.1162/PRES_a_00124

Kilteni, K., Maselli, A., Kording, K. P., & Slater, M. (2015). Over my fake body: Body ownership illusions for studying the multisensory basis of own-body perception. *Frontiers in Human Neuroscience, 9*, 141.

Kobenova, A., DeVeaux, C., Parajuli, S., Banburski-Fahey, A., Fernandez, J. A., & Lanier, J. (2024). Social conjuring: Multi-user runtime collaboration with AI. In *Building Virtual 3D Worlds*. arXiv preprint arXiv:2410.00274.

LaViola Jr, J. J. (2000). A discussion of cybersickness in virtual environments. *ACM Sigchi Bulletin, 32*(1), 47–56.

Lin, C. H., Gao, J., Tang, L., Takikawa, T., Zeng, X., Huang, X., Kreis, K., Fidler, S., Liu, M. Y., & Lin, T. Y. (2023). Magic3D: High-resolution text-to-3D content creation. In *Proceedings of the IEEE/CVF conference on computer vision and pattern recognition* (Vancouver, BC: IEEE), 300–309.

Linden Lab. (2003). *Second Life* [Virtual world]. https://secondlife.com/

Lombard, M., & Ditton, T. (1997). At the heart of it all: The concept of presence. *Journal of Computer-Mediated Communication, 3*, JCMC321. doi: 10.1111/j.1083-6101.1997.tb00072.x

Lopreiato, J. O., Downing, D., Gammon, W., Lioce, L., Sittner, B., Slot, V., Spain, A. E., The Terminology & Concepts Working Group (2016). *Healthcare simulation dictionary*. Available online at: https://www.ssih.org/dictionary (accessed September 25, 2022).

Matamala-Gomez, M., Slater, M., & Sanchez-Vives, M. V. (2022). Impact of virtual embodiment and exercises on functional ability and range of motion in orthopedic rehabilitation. *Scientific Reports, 12*(1), 5046.

Mandal, S. (2013). Brief introduction of virtual reality and its challenges. *International Journal of Scientific & Engineering Research, 4*, 304–309. Available online at: https://api.semanticscholar.org/CorpusID:8070706

Martínez-Cano, F. J., Lachman, R., & Canet, F. (2023). VR content and its prosocial impact: predictors, moderators, and mediators of media effects. A systematic literature review. *Frontiers in Communication, 8*, 1203242.

McGowin, G., & Fiore, S. M. (2024, September). Mind the gap! Advancing immersion in virtual reality—Factors, measurement, and research opportunities. In *Proceedings of the human factors and ergonomics society annual meeting* (Sage, CA; Los Angeles, CA: Sage Publications), Vol. 68, No. 1, 1648–1654.

Mills, K. A., Scholes, L., & Brown, A. (2022). Virtual reality and embodiment in multimodal meaning making. *Written Communication, 39*(3), 335–369.

Nehvi, J., Kabadayi, B., Valentin, J., & Thies, J. (2024, September). Volumetric portrait avatar. In *DAGM German conference on pattern recognition* (Cham: Springer Nature Switzerland), 3–19.

Norman, D. A. (1999). Affordance, conventions, and design. *Interactions, 6*(3), 38–43.

Pimental, K. (1995). *Virtual reality. Through the new looking glass* (New York: McGraw-Hill).

Poole, B., Jain, A., Barron, J. T., & Mildenhall, B. (2022). Dreamfusion: Text-to-3D using 2D diffusion. arXiv preprint arXiv:2209.14988

Porssut, T., Iwane, F., Chavarriaga, R., Blanke, O., Millán, J. D. R., Boulic, R., & Herbelin, B. (2023). EEG signature of breaks in embodiment in VR. *PLoS One, 18*(5), e0282967.

Riva, G., Wiederhold, B. K., & Mantovani, F. (2019). Neuroscience of virtual reality: From virtual exposure to embodied medicine. *Cyberpsychology, Behavior, and Social Networking, 22*, 82–96. doi: 10.1089/cyber.2017.29099.gri

Sanchez-Vives, M. V., & Slater, M. (2005). From presence to consciousness through virtual reality. *Nature Reviews Neuroscience, 6*(4), 332–339.

Szilak, I., & Tsiboulski, C. (Creators). (2018). *Queerskins: A love story* [Virtual reality experience]. Cloudred.

Slater, M. (2009). Place illusion and plausibility can lead to realistic behaviour in immersive virtual environments. *Philosophical Transactions of the Royal Society of London. Series B, Biological Sciences, 364*, 3549–3557. doi: 10.1098/rstb.2009.0138

Slater, M., Spanlang, B., Sanchez-Vives, M. V., & Blanke, O. (2010). First person experience of body transfer in virtual reality. *PLoS One, 5*(5), e10564.

Slater, M., & Wilbur, S. (1997). A framework for immersive virtual environments (FIVE): speculations on the role of presence in virtual environments. *Presence 6*, 603–616. doi: 10.1162/pres.1997.6.6.603

Stanković, S. (2015). Virtual reality and virtual environments in 10 lectures. *Synthesis Lectures Image Video Multimedia Process, 18*, 1–197. doi: 10.1007/978-3-031-02254-8

Steuer, J. (1992). Defining virtual reality: Dimensions determining telepresence. *Journal of Communication, 42*, 73–93. doi: 10.1111/j.1460-2466.1992.tb00812.x

Sutherland, I. (1965). The ultimate display. In *Proceedings of the IFIPS congress* 65 (New York: IFIP), 506–508. Available online at: https://papers.cumincad.org/data/works/att/c58e.content.pdf (accessed August 8, 2025).

VRChat Inc. (2014). *VRChat* [Social VR platform].

Venkatraj, K. P., Meijer, W., Perusquía-Hernández, M., Huisman, G., & El Ali, A. (2024). *ShareYourReality: Investigating haptic feedback and agency in virtual avatar co-embodiment*. In F. F. Mueller, P. Kyburz, J. R. Williamson, C. Sas, M. L. Wilson, P. Toups Dugas, & I. Shklovski (Eds.), *Proceedings of the CHI Conference on Human Factors in Computing Systems* (Article 100). Association for Computing Machinery. https://doi.org/10.1145/3613904.3642425

Wilson, M. (2002). Six views of embodied cognition. *Psychonomic Bulletin & Review, 9*(4), 625–636.

Yoh, M. S. (2001). The reality of virtual reality. In *Proceedings seventh international conference on virtual systems and multimedia* (Berkeley, CA: IEEE), 666–674.

Zhang, R., Watkins, A., & Sarkar, N. (2025). GSAC: Leveraging Gaussian Splatting for Photorealistic Avatar Creation with Unity Integration. arXiv preprint arXiv:2504.12999

CHAPTER 3

The Historical Evolution of Virtual Reality Technologies

Raquel Victoria Benítez Rojas

1 INTRODUCTION

Virtual reality (VR), often associated with contemporary digital environments and immersive simulations, has a historical lineage that extends far beyond the computer age. The development of VR reflects a long-standing human aspiration to transcend physical limitations and construct alternate realities, a pursuit that has shaped diverse innovations across art, science, and technology. This exploration traces the conceptual and technical evolution of immersive media, beginning with pre-digital visual devices and culminating in the sophisticated, interactive systems of the present day.

The earliest forms of VR-like experiences – such as 19th-century panoramic paintings and stereoscopic viewers – demonstrated an emerging understanding of human visual perception, particularly depth and spatial immersion. Innovations by figures like Sir Charles Wheatstone and Sir David Brewster in stereopsis and lens-based viewing laid foundational principles for later developments. As technology progressed, these principles were extended into electromechanical systems like the Link Trainer and digital defense projects such as SAGE, marking the convergence of simulation, computation, and human–computer interaction.

DOI: 10.1201/9781003673538-3

Mid- to late-20th-century advancements brought significant momentum to the field. Pioneering inventions, including Morton Heilig's Sensorama and Ivan Sutherland's head-mounted displays (HMDs), introduced multisensory and interactive dimensions to virtual environments. These innovations gradually evolved into practical applications across military, medical, and entertainment contexts, culminating in the emergence of commercially available VR systems in the 1990s and 2000s.

By examining these historical milestones, the analysis reveals how VR technologies emerged through iterative innovation and interdisciplinary collaboration. The resulting narrative situates VR not as a sudden technological leap, but as the product of cumulative advances driven by a persistent desire to enhance and extend human experience through immersive simulation.

2 HISTORICAL EVOLUTION

2.1 XIX–XX Century – Panoramic Paintings

VR, often associated with advanced digital technology, has roots that stretch far into the past. If we define VR as the creation of an illusion that places the viewer in a different location, then the 360-degree panoramic paintings of the 19th century represent one of its earliest forms. These massive murals were designed to occupy the viewer's entire field of vision, immersing them in scenes of battles, landscapes, or important historical events. By eliminating the edges of the image and surrounding the viewer completely, these works aimed to transport spectators into another place and time. Though lacking digital interactivity, the intention behind these panoramic paintings parallels that of modern VR: to simulate presence in a space beyond one's immediate physical surroundings. Viewers would often stand on specially constructed platforms in circular rooms, surrounded by imagery, enhancing the sense of immersion. These early attempts reflect humanity's longstanding desire to escape physical limits and explore distant or imagined worlds, a goal that continues to drive VR development today.

A clear example of this technique is the picture Battle of Moscow, 7th September 1812, by Louis-François Lejeune, 1822. The picture is also known as the Battle of Borodino or Battle of the Generals (Shishov, 2012), is 2.64 meters long and 2.10 meters high, and is in the Castle Museum in Versailles, France (Buckler & Hazzard, 2016).

2.2 1838 – Sir Charles Wheatstone's Stereopsis

Dom Barnard (2024) describes how, in 1838, Sir Charles Wheatstone made a groundbreaking contribution to the understanding of human vision by being the first to describe stereopsis – the perception of depth from the slightly different views seen by each eye. This discovery revealed how the brain merges two images, each seen from a slightly different angle, to create a single, three-dimensional perception of the world. For this pioneering work, Wheatstone was awarded the Royal Medal of the Royal Society in 1840.

Wheatstone's research led him to invent the first stereoscope, a device that demonstrated how binocular vision could be used to create the illusion of depth. His original stereoscope design used two mirrors positioned at 45-degree angles to the viewer's eyes. These mirrors reflected two separate images located off to the sides, simulating how each eye naturally views the world from a slightly different perspective. When viewed through the device, the brain combined the images into a single 3D scene, producing a sense of depth and immersion.

This contribution laid the foundation for modern 3D imaging and VR technologies. His work not only advanced scientific understanding but also introduced a new way for people to experience visual media, foreshadowing future developments in immersive visual experiences.

2.3 1849 – The Lenticular Stereoscope by Sir David Brewster

The Lenticular Stereoscope, invented by Sir David Brewster in 1849, was a significant advancement in the field of 3D image viewing. This portable device used prismatic lenses to merge two slightly different photographs taken from different angles, creating a convincing three-dimensional effect. By combining the images into a single visual experience, the stereoscope gave viewers the illusion of depth, making flat images appear lifelike and immersive.

Compared to Sir Charles Wheatstone's earlier reflecting stereoscope, Brewster's design was far more compact, easier to handle, and portable. These practical improvements helped the Lenticular Stereoscope gain widespread popularity, bringing stereoscopic viewing into the homes of everyday users.

Brewster, already renowned for his work in optics and the discovery of Brewster's angle, contributed significantly to the development of visual technology through this invention. The Lenticular Stereoscope not only advanced scientific understanding of human vision but also laid the groundwork for the popular enjoyment of 3D images. It marked a major step in the evolution of immersive media and helped pave the way for future innovations in photography, entertainment, and virtual visual experiences (International Stereoscopic Union, 2006).

2.4 1929 – Link Trainer, the First Flight Simulator

In 1929, Edward Link invented the "Link Trainer," considered the first commercial flight simulator. Patented in 1931, the Link Trainer was an entirely electromechanical device designed to provide a safe and realistic environment for pilots to learn instrument flying. Using his background in pumps, valves, and bellows from working at his father's Link Piano and Organ Company, Ed Link engineered a simulator that accurately mimicked real flight controls. Motors connected to the rudder and steering column simulated changes in pitch and roll, while a motor-driven mechanism reproduced turbulence and in-flight disturbances.

The need for safer pilot training methods was urgent, and the U.S. military recognized the potential of Link's invention. They purchased six of the trainers for $3,500. The original trainer became essential during World War II, where more than 10,000 "blue box" Link Trainers were used to train over 500,000 pilots. These devices helped pilots gain crucial skills in instrument flying, reducing the risk of accidents during training.

The Link Trainer marked a pivotal moment in aviation history, laying the foundation for modern flight simulation. It demonstrated how mechanical ingenuity and innovation could transform pilot education and significantly enhance flight safety (De Angelo, 2000).

2.5 1935 – Stanley G. Weinbaum's Pygmalion's Spectacles

American science fiction writer Stanley G. Weinbaum introduced a visionary concept of VR in his 1935 short story Pygmalion's Spectacles. In this story, the protagonist encounters a professor who has developed an extraordinary pair of goggles. These goggles allow the wearer to fully immerse themselves in a fictional world – not just through sight and sound but also through taste, smell, and touch. The story describes an experience where the user becomes part of the narrative: "You are in the story, you speak to the shadows (characters) and they reply [...] the story is all about you, and you are in it" (Weinbaum, 1935).

Weinbaum's fictional invention closely mirrors the ambitions of today's VR technology. Though created long before the digital era, his concept includes many of the elements that define VR today: total sensory immersion, interactivity, and user-centered narratives. His story predated even the earliest physical VR prototypes by decades, making Weinbaum a remarkable early visionary in the field.

In hindsight, Pygmalion's Spectacles can be seen as one of the first conceptual blueprints for immersive virtual experiences. Weinbaum's imagination anticipated not only the technological developments of the future but also the emotional and narrative power that modern VR strives to achieve today.

2.6 1939 – The View-Master

The View-Master is a trademarked line of stereoscopes that became widely popular for its innovative use of stereoscopic 3D imagery. Each View-Master reel is a thin cardboard disk containing seven pairs of small, transparent color photographs on film. When viewed through the device, these image pairs combine to create a vivid three-dimensional scene, offering an immersive visual experience. Originally manufactured and sold by Sawyer's, the View-Master was introduced to the public in 1939, just four years after the invention of Kodachrome color film. This film made it possible to produce sharp, colorful images in a compact format, which suited the View-Master's design perfectly.

In its early years, the View-Master focused on reels showcasing tourist attractions and travel destinations, allowing users to explore famous landmarks from around the world. These reels appealed to both children and adults, serving as both entertainment and educational tools. Over time, however, the content shifted more toward children's themes, with reels featuring popular cartoon characters, stories, and educational topics. Despite changing trends and advances in digital technology, the View-Master remains an iconic piece of visual history, symbolizing the lasting appeal of stereoscopic imagery and early virtual experiences (Sell et al., 2000).

2.7 1939 – Cinerama Wide-screen Film Format
by Fred Waller and Ralph Walker

In the words of Mark R. Baldock (1995), Cinerama was the brainchild of Fred Waller, a prolific inventor and special effects engineer whose wide-ranging innovations included water skis, a 360-degree panoramic camera, and the Waller Gunnery Trainer – a device that could be seen as a precursor to both arcade games and flight simulators. Among his most ambitious projects was the development of Cinerama, a wide-screen film process that aimed to revolutionize cinematic experiences by mimicking the way humans perceive reality.

Attempts at wide-screen formats had been made as early as the 1890s and again in the 1920s, but they failed due to resistance from film studios and theater owners. Studios feared these new formats would devalue their existing film libraries, while exhibitors were reluctant to invest in new, non-standard equipment. Despite this resistance, Waller pursued his vision, rooted in his understanding of human depth perception. He believed that, at longer distances, the brain relied more on peripheral vision and visual cues like perspective and parallax, rather than stereoscopic depth.

While working with architect Ralph Walker on a visual exhibit for the 1939 New York World's Fair, Waller had a breakthrough. Realizing that normal human vision is arc-shaped, he concluded that replicating reality on screen required a curved display. Together, they patented a system called Vitarama, using 11 interlocked 16-millimeter cameras and projectors to create an immersive experience. Although they secured funding from Lawrence Rockefeller and Time Magazine, the fair organizers declined to use the system, and the film industry initially ignored the invention. Still, Vitarama laid the foundation for Cinerama and influenced the future of immersive visual technologies.

2.8 1940s – Project Whirlwind and SAGE (Semi-Automated Ground Environment)

Project Whirlwind and the SAGE system not only revolutionized military air defense but also laid key foundations for the development of VR. Whirlwind, originally designed as a flight simulator, used digital computers to create real-time simulations of aircraft, linking them to cockpit mock-ups. This early form of interactive simulation marked one of the first instances of humans engaging with a digital environment in a lifelike, immersive manner – a core principle of VR.

SAGE extended these ideas by integrating data from multiple radar sources into a unified, interactive display. Human operators used light pens to interact with the system, an early form of graphical user interface that mirrors VR's emphasis on real-time user input and spatial interaction. The massive computing infrastructure behind SAGE demonstrated the potential for computers to manage and render complex, real-time environments.

The concepts developed in Whirlwind and SAGE – simulation, real-time feedback, human–computer interaction, and immersive environments – directly influenced the trajectory of VR. Today's VR systems use many of the same principles to create interactive 3D environments for training, gaming, and design. Thus, these Cold War-era defense projects helped shape not only military technology but also the immersive digital experiences that define VR today.

As a summary, it can be said that SAGE was a system of large computers and associated networking equipment that coordinated data from many radar sites and processed it to produce a single unified image of the airspace over a wide area (Wragg,1973).

2.9 1956 – Morton Heilig's Sensorama

In the mid-1950s, cinematographer Morton Heilig envisioned a revolutionary concept he called "Experience Theater," which sought to fully immerse audiences by stimulating all the senses – not just sight and sound. This vision culminated in the creation of the Sensorama; a groundbreaking arcade-style theater cabinet patented in 1962. This invention is now recognized as one of the earliest examples of VR and multimodal technology (Regrebsubla, 2015, p. 5).

The Sensorama featured a stereoscopic 3D display, stereo speakers, fans, odor emitters, and a vibrating chair, creating a rich, multi-sensory environment. It was designed to transport the viewer into the action, allowing them to "feel" the film as much as see and hear it. Heilig produced six short films for the device – Motorcycle, Belly Dancer, Dune Buggy, Helicopter, A Date with Sabina, and I'm a Coca-Cola Bottle! –all of which he wrote, directed, and edited himself. One of the most notable experiences involved simulating a motorcycle ride through New York City, where the viewer would feel the wind, hear the traffic, and even smell city aromas like pizza or bus exhaust, thanks to precise chemical releases (Craig et al., 2009, p. 4; Grau, 2003, p. 1786).

Though the Sensorama offered a deeply immersive experience, it lacked interactivity. Users could not influence the film's outcome or respond to it dynamically, a feature that would become central to future VR technologies. Nonetheless, it paved the way for later advancements by demonstrating how sensory stimulation could enhance realism.

Heilig's concept was ahead of its time. Despite his innovations, he failed to secure the financial support needed to develop the Sensorama commercially. Still, his work left a lasting impression. Writer Howard Rheingold praised the device in his 1991 book Virtual Reality, recalling a 1950s Sensorama film that offered an unforgettable, fully immersive experience even decades later (Srivastava et al., 2014).

Though limited by the technology of its time, the Sensorama laid the groundwork for the immersive, interactive experiences that define VR today.

2.10 1960 – Morton Heilig's Telesphere Mask: The First HMD

In 1960, Morton Heilig patented the Telesphere Mask, widely considered the first HMD. Building on his vision of "Experience Theater," Heilig designed the Telesphere Mask to deliver a more immersive cinematic experience by engaging multiple senses. Though it lacked modern motion tracking, it featured stereoscopic 3D visuals, a wide field of view, and stereo sound, offering a significant step toward VR as we know it today.

Unlike interactive VR headsets, the Telesphere Mask was created for non-interactive film experiences. It aimed to deepen immersion by simulating environmental effects – TechRadar notes it included features such as scents and air breezes, enhancing the illusion of presence within the on-screen world. Heilig's device was not intended for user input or real-time interaction but instead focused on enveloping the viewer in a rich, multi-sensory environment.

Although it did not achieve commercial success or widespread adoption, the Telesphere Mask marked a crucial milestone in VR history. It introduced many concepts – such as head-worn immersive displays and sensory enhancement – that remain central to modern VR. Heilig's pioneering work laid essential groundwork for the development of future interactive and immersive technologies (USC HMH Foundation Moving Image Archive, 2025).

2.11 1961 – Headsight: The First Motion-Tracking HMD

Engineers Comeau and Bryan in 1961 from the Philco Corporation developed the Headsight, a pioneering device that marked a major milestone in the evolution of HMD technology. This was the first HMD to incorporate motion tracking, using a magnetic tracking system linked to a closed-circuit camera. Each eye had its own video screen, and the user's head movements would control a remote camera, allowing them to look around a remote environment in real time.

Although Headsight is a direct ancestor of modern VR systems, it was not created for entertainment or simulation. Instead, it was developed for military applications, providing personnel with the ability to observe hazardous situations remotely, such as handling dangerous materials or navigating combat zones. By mimicking the user's head movements with a remote camera, the device allowed for natural and immersive observation of environments that would otherwise be too dangerous to approach directly.

While Headsight lacked the computer-generated imagery and interactive environments we now associate with VR, it introduced key technological concepts that are central to today's systems – head tracking, stereoscopic visuals, and immersive perspective. Though not designed as a VR headset,

Headsight's innovative approach laid the groundwork for future developments in VR and remote sensing.

2.12 1965 – Ivan Sutherland's "Ultimate Display" and the Vision of True VR

In 1965, computer scientist Ivan Sutherland introduced the concept of the "Ultimate Display," a visionary idea that laid the intellectual foundation for modern VR. Sutherland imagined a system so immersive and convincing that users would be unable to distinguish it from physical reality. His concept marked a major turning point in the evolution of VR, pushing beyond passive visual experiences to propose a fully interactive, multi-sensory virtual environment.

Sutherland's Ultimate Display envisioned a virtual world viewed through a HMD, enhanced with 3D sound and tactile feedback. He proposed that this environment would be generated and maintained in real time by computer hardware capable of simulating a dynamic, responsive world. Most importantly, users would be able to interact realistically with virtual objects, blurring the line between digital and physical existence.

In his own words, "A chair displayed in such a room would be good enough to sit in... a bullet displayed in such a room would be fatal" (Sutherland, 1965, pp. 506–508). This bold idea foreshadowed not only the immersive nature of VR but also the potential seriousness of its applications.

Though purely theoretical at the time, Sutherland's paper became a blueprint for VR development, inspiring generations of researchers and developers. His vision of complete sensory immersion and interaction remains central to the goals of contemporary VR technologies. The "Ultimate Display" continues to influence the design of virtual environments, reminding us that the future of VR lies in its power to replicate – and perhaps surpass – reality itself.

2.13 1966 – Thomas Furness and the Birth of Modern Flight Simulation and VR

Thomas Furness, a military engineer, began developing in 1966 the first advanced flight simulators for the U.S. Air Force – marking a key moment in the evolution of VR. Known as the "grandfather of VR," Furness spent over 50 years pioneering virtual and augmented reality (AR), starting with efforts to help fighter pilots cope with the increasing complexity of jet cockpits.

Furness's early work focused on helmet-mounted displays and visually coupled systems that allowed pilots to view and control aircraft data more naturally. His most notable project, the Visually Coupled Airborne Systems Simulator (VCASS), demonstrated in 1982, enabled pilots to immerse themselves in a symbolic data environment. Using head tracking and CRT displays, VCASS revolutionized how pilots interacted with information mid-flight.

This led to the Super Cockpit program in the late 1980s, which integrated 3D maps, radar imagery, voice commands, and gesture-based controls into a fully immersive flight experience. The technology reduced cockpit complexity while enhancing decision-making under pressure.

After leaving the military, Furness founded the Human Interface Technology Lab at the University of Washington and helped develop virtual retinal display technology. He later launched the Virtual World Society, promoting VR for education and global problem-solving. His lifelong mission: using VR to change how we learn, communicate, and experience the world (Kentbye, 2015).

2.14 1967 – Ivan Sutherland's Bell Helicopter

In 1967, computer graphics pioneer Ivan Sutherland partnered with Bell Helicopter to develop an HMD system, a project that evolved into the groundbreaking "Sword of Damocles." Funded in part by the CIA, the device was originally intended for helicopter pilot training and simulation. Due to its heavy construction, the headset was suspended from the ceiling – hence the name.

This early VR prototype used simple wireframe graphics but was revolutionary in its ability to immerse users in a digital environment. A key test demonstrated the sense of presence when a subject instinctively ducked as a ball was thrown toward the camera (Computer History Museum).

Bell Helicopter's involvement provided both funding and practical application goals, highlighting early interest in HMDs for aviation training. Sutherland's work laid essential foundations for immersive VR and also built on his earlier innovation, Sketchpad, the first interactive computer graphics system.

2.15 1968 – The Sword of Damocles: The First Computer-Connected HMD

In 1968, computer scientist Ivan Sutherland, along with his student Bob Sproull, created the first HMD connected to a computer rather than a

camera. Known informally as the "Sword of Damocles" due to its imposing, ceiling-suspended design, this prototype marked a major milestone
in the development of both VR and AR (Sutherland, 1965, pp. 506–508).

The device earned its nickname from its heavy, intimidating frame
that required users to be strapped into a chair beneath it. Its actual
name was simply the "HMD," and Sutherland preferred the term
"Stereoscopic-Television Apparatus for Individual Use." The system displayed primitive wireframe graphics – simple 3D rooms and shapes – that
changed perspective in response to the user's head movements, thanks to
an integrated tracking system. While visually basic, this interaction demonstrated an essential concept of immersive environments: responsive,
real-time visual feedback based on the user's orientation (Werner, 2024).

Though it remained a lab project due to its size and complexity, the
Sword of Damocles is considered the first functional AR system, as it featured optical transparency, allowing users to see both virtual and real elements simultaneously. It was also one of the earliest devices to use the
now-standard term HMD.

Sutherland's work at MIT's Lincoln Laboratory, with contributions from
Bob Sproull, Quintin Foster, and Danny Cohen, established key foundations for interactive computer graphics. Coming after Morton Heilig's
Telesphere Mask (1960), the Sword of Damocles shifted the field from passive viewing to interactive, computer-generated environments, embodying Sutherland's vision of the "Ultimate Display" – a system capable of
simulating any experience or environment.

2.16 1969 – Myron Krueger and the Birth of Artificial Reality

Computer artist Myron Krueger pioneered the concept of "artificial
reality" – a form of interactive computer-generated environment that
responded to the presence and actions of users. Unlike traditional VR
systems that required headsets or equipment, Krueger's work focused on
unencumbered interaction, allowing users to engage with digital environments using only their bodies and natural movements. His early projects,
GLOWFLOW, METAPLAY, and PSYCHIC SPACE, were progressive
experiments in combining computer graphics, video, and sound to create
responsive and immersive digital spaces.

These projects culminated in the development of VIDEOPLACE, one
of the most innovative interactive systems of its time. VIDEOPLACE
allowed multiple users, located miles apart, to interact in a shared
computer-generated environment through video recognition. It tracked

users' silhouettes and movements in real time and displayed them in a dynamic digital space filled with colorful graphics and sound. This groundbreaking system laid the foundation for modern concepts in both VR and AR.

Krueger's ideas were formally explored in his influential book Artificial Reality, published in 1983, and later expanded in Artificial Reality II (1991). These works examined how technology could allow users to enter immersive worlds without physical gear, relying on visual and auditory cues to shape their experience. Krueger emphasized that visualization is central to creating meaningful artificial realities – by tapping into human sensory systems, users could naturally understand and interact with digital environments.

For over 16 years, Krueger refined his systems to better connect human gestures with computer responses. His visionary work not only helped define early immersive technology but also significantly influenced the evolution of human–computer interaction, making him a foundational figure in the history of VR. 1972 – General Electric Builds a Digital Flight Sim (Krueger, 1983).

2.17 1975 – VIDEOPLACE: The First Interactive VR System

Developed by Myron Krueger, VIDEOPLACE is widely regarded as the first interactive VR system. Unlike modern VR, it did not require headsets or gloves. Instead, it used a combination of computer graphics, light projection, video cameras, and large screens to create an immersive experience. Users entered dark rooms where their movements were captured and translated into visuals projected around them. First showcased at the Milwaukee Art Center, VIDEOPLACE allowed people to interact with a virtual environment using only their bodies, making it a groundbreaking achievement in early augmented and VR technology.

2.18 1977 – The Aspen Movie Map: A Precursor to Virtual Tourism

The MIT Media Lab developed the Aspen Movie Map, an early VR project that allowed users to explore Aspen, Colorado, from a first-person perspective. Using footage captured by a car driving through the city, the system enabled users to "move" through the streets by interacting with a computer interface. It featured three modes – summer, winter, and a polygon-based version – to showcase the city's environment under different conditions. Although it didn't use HMDs, the Aspen Movie Map demonstrated how technology could simulate travel and hinted at VR's potential to transport users to distant places.

2.19 1979 – The McDonnell Douglas VITAL Helmet

The VITAL helmet, developed by McDonnell Douglas, was one of the first practical VR HMDs used outside the lab. Designed for military pilots, it featured a head tracker that followed eye movements, allowing users to view computer-generated imagery aligned with their gaze – marking a major step in applied VR technology.

2.20 1980 – StereoGraphics Stereo Vision Glasses

In 1980, StereoGraphics developed stereo vision glasses, enabling users to experience 3D visuals by delivering separate images to each eye. This innovation played a key role in advancing stereoscopic displays and laid important groundwork for modern virtual and AR systems.

2.21 1982 – Sandin and DeFanti's Sayre Gloves

In the early 1980s, Daniel Sandin and Thomas DeFanti invented the Sayre gloves, the first finger-tracking VR gloves. Using optical sensors, they converted finger movements into electrical signals, laying the foundation for gesture recognition and future data gloves in VR systems.

2.22 1985 – VPL Research Inc. is Founded

In the 1980s, Jaron Lanier and Thomas Zimmerman founded VPL Research, the first company to sell VR headsets and gloves, including the pioneering DataGlove and EyePhone HMD, shaping commercial VR.

2.23 1986 – Furness Invents the Super Cockpit

Between 1986 and 1989, Tom Furness developed the Super Cockpit, an advanced Air Force flight simulator. It used real-time CG graphics, gesture, speech, and eye-tracking to train pilots in immersive virtual environments.

2.24 1987 – VR

In 1987, Jaron Lanier, founder of VPL Research, coined (or popularized) the term "virtual reality," giving a name to a rapidly evolving field. Through VPL, Lanier and Tom Zimmerman developed pioneering VR equipment, including the DataGlove and EyePhone HMD. VPL became the first company to commercially sell VR goggles and gloves, with the EyePhone HRX priced at $49,000 and the DataGlove at $9,000. These innovations marked a major step in VR haptics. Around the same time, British Aerospace created a Virtual Cockpit with speech recognition, inspired by Furness's Super Cockpit. Dimension International also contributed by developing PC software for building 3D virtual worlds.

2.25 1989 – NASA's Project VIEW

In the late 1980s, NASA, with Crystal River Engineering, developed Project VIEW, a VR simulator for astronaut training. It featured gloves for touch interaction and 3D binaural audio, directly inspiring the Nintendo Power Glove. VIEW marked a major step toward modern, immersive VR experiences.

2.26 1990 – Jonathan Waldern Exhibited Virtuality, a VR Arcade Machine

In 1990, Jonathan Waldern showcased Virtuality, a VR arcade machine, at the Computer Graphics 90 exhibition in London, offering a glimpse into the future of immersive gaming.

2.27 1991 – Virtuality Group Arcade Machines

In 1991, the Virtuality Group introduced the first publicly accessible VR arcade machines, marking a major step in consumer VR. These systems featured VR goggles, immersive stereoscopic 3D visuals, and real-time response with latency under 50 milliseconds. Some units were even networked for multiplayer gaming, bringing early virtual worlds to arcades before home VR was feasible.

2.28 1991 – Medina's VR Mars Rover

In 1991, NASA engineer Antonio Medina developed a VR system called "Computer Simulated Teleoperation" that allowed operators to control Mars rovers in real time, despite the signal delay between Earth and Mars. This pioneering technology helped overcome the challenges of remote rover navigation.

2.29 1992 – The Lawnmower Man Movie

The 1992 film The Lawnmower Man brought VR to the mainstream. Loosely inspired by Jaron Lanier's early work in VR, the movie featured Pierce Brosnan as a scientist using VR therapy. Real VR equipment from

Lanier's company, VPL Research, was used in the film, with director Brett Leonard acknowledging VPL's influence on the project.

2.30 1993 – SEGA Announces New VR Glasses

In 1993, SEGA announced the Sega VR headset for Genesis with head tracking and LCD screens. Priced at $200, it never launched due to technical issues. SEGA later released the VR-1 arcade machine, while VictorMaxx released CyberMaxx.

2.31 1993 – The First Telesurgery Equipment Was Developed at SRI International

In 1993, Stanford Research Institute developed the first telesurgery prototype, the Green Telepresence System, funded by the Department of Defense. A key component, the AESOP robotic camera arm, gained FDA approval in December 1993, marking a milestone in surgical technology. The first robotic surgery took place in 1998 (Moro et al., 2017).

2.32 1995 – Nintendo Virtual Boy

In 1995, Nintendo launched the Virtual Boy, the first portable console to display true 3D graphics. Despite its innovation, it was a commercial failure due to red-black visuals, limited software support, and uncomfortable design. Discontinued in 1996, it coincided with the release of other VR headsets like I-Glasses and VFX1.

2.33 1997 – Landmark VR PTSD Treatment

In 1997, Georgia Tech and Emory University developed Virtual Vietnam, a VR-based PTSD treatment for war veterans. By simulating combat scenarios, therapists could safely expose patients to traumatic triggers. This groundbreaking use of VR remains vital in PTSD therapy and research today.

2.34 1999 – The Wachowski Siblings' Film The Matrix

In 1999, The Matrix premiered, portraying a fully simulated world where most humans are unaware of reality. Unlike earlier films like Tron, its cultural impact was immense, pushing VR and simulated worlds into mainstream discussion and popular imagination.

2.35 2001 – SAS Cube, the First PC-based Cubic Room

SAS3, the first PC-based cubic VR room, was developed by Z-A Production, Barco, and Clarté in Laval, France. It later inspired the Virtools VR Pack add-on.

2.36 2007 – Google Street View

In 2007, Google launched Street View with 360-degree images by Immersive Media. By 2010, Street View gained a 3D mode. Meanwhile, Palmer Luckey prototyped the Oculus Rift, a DIY VR headset, leading to a breakthrough after connecting with gaming legend John Carmack.

2.37 2010 – Microsoft Kinect

Microsoft's Kinect was a motion-sensing device using cameras and infrared to enable real-time gesture and skeletal tracking, plus voice control. It supported speech recognition and advanced depth mapping but was eventually discontinued despite its innovative features.

2.38 2011 – iPhone Virtual Reality Viewer

The iPhone Virtual Reality Viewer is a pair of 3D goggles that deliver an immersive, three-dimensional experience. Featuring 360-degree movement, the goggles work with existing mobile devices to enhance VR viewing.

2.39 2012 – The Oculus Kickstarter Campaign

Palmer Luckey's Kickstarter for the Oculus Rift raised nearly $2.5 million, marking a pivotal moment that separated past VR failures from the beginning of the modern VR revolution.

2.40 2013 – Tactical Haptics VR Motion Controller

The Tactical Haptics VR Motion Controller is a responsive gaming joystick that simulates pushing, pulling, and twisting forces through its grip. Launched on Kickstarter in 2013, the campaign fell short of its $175,000 goal.

2.41 2014 – Google Cardboard, PSVR, Facebook Buys Oculus, and Sony Announced Their VR Project

In 2014, Facebook acquired Oculus, propelling Palmer Luckey to wealth. That year also saw the launch of Google Cardboard, PSVR, and Samsung Gear VR, igniting widespread VR interest. Additionally, Sony announced a VR add-on for PS4, sparking curiosity about its performance on less powerful hardware.

2.42 2015 – Increased VR Accessibility

Increased VR accessibility brought unique experiences to the public, such as:
The Wall Street Journal's VR roller coaster simulating the Nasdaq's fluctuations.

The BBC's 360-degree video of a Syrian migrant camp.

The Washington Post's VR tour of the Oval Office during the White House Correspondents' Dinner.

RYOT's Confinement, a VR film on solitary confinement in U.S. prisons.

Additionally, Gloveone successfully funded its Kickstarter campaign, creating gloves that allowed users to feel and interact with virtual objects.

2.43 2016 – Microsoft HoloLens

Microsoft HoloLens is an AR and mixed reality (MR) headset powered by the Windows Mixed Reality platform on Windows 10. Its positional tracking technology traces its origins to the Microsoft Kinect, an accessory introduced in 2010 for Xbox 360 and Xbox One consoles.

2.44 2016–2017 – The Evolution of VR Technology and the Rise of Sensor-Based Tracking

By 2016, numerous companies were developing VR products, with most headsets featuring dynamic binaural audio. Haptic interfaces, like Gloveone gloves, were still in early stages, meaning handsets mostly relied on buttons. HTC released the HTC Vive SteamVR headset, the first to offer sensor-based tracking for free movement.

In 2017, companies such as HTC, Google, Apple, Amazon, Microsoft, Sony, and Samsung continued to develop VR headsets. Sony was reportedly working on location-tracking technology similar to HTC Vive for the PlayStation 4.

2.45 2018 – The Half-Dome HMD

Oculus introduced a groundbreaking prototype HMD called the "Half-Dome," marking a major leap forward in VR technology. This prototype featured several innovative enhancements designed to improve the user experience and immersion in VR environments.

One of the standout features of the Oculus Half-Dome was its impressive 140-degree field of view, significantly wider than the 90–100 degrees commonly found in most VR headsets. This expanded view contributed to a more natural and immersive experience, allowing users to feel more enveloped in the virtual world.

Another key advancement in the Half-Dome prototype was its use of varifocal lenses. These motorized lenses could adjust their focus in real time, responding to eye tracking to mimic how the human eye naturally focuses on objects at varying distances. This feature enhanced visual clarity and comfort, particularly when switching between objects at different focal lengths.

Additionally, the Half-Dome prototype incorporated moving screens that adjusted based on eye tracking. These screens physically shifted to maintain sharp focus, even when users looked at objects up closely. This innovation helped eliminate blurriness or discomfort when viewing near-field content in virtual environments.

Overall, the Oculus Half-Dome aimed to improve both comfort and immersion by combining a wide field of view, advanced varifocal lenses, and dynamic screen adjustments. These features together promised to take VR experiences to the next level, offering sharper visuals and a more comfortable, lifelike interaction with virtual worlds.

2.46 2019 – Nintendo Labo: VR kit

Released in 2018, Nintendo Labo includes individual kits with cardboard cut-outs and materials to build "Toy-Con" creations, along with a Switch game card for assembly instructions and interactive software. The Toy-Con interacts with the Switch or Joy-Con controllers in unique ways. Players can customize the cardboard parts, and more advanced users can invent new ways to play. The Variety and Robot Kits launched in April 2018, with additional accessories and replacement parts available for purchase.

2.47 2020–2026 – New and Upgraded Headsets Enter the Market

In 2020, Meta unveiled the Oculus Quest 2, a highly successful VR headset, receiving positive reviews and selling millions globally. In 2021, Pico launched the Pico Neo 3 as a competitor, later acquired by ByteDance. Meta committed $10 billion to its metaverse division, Facebook Reality Labs. In 2023, Apple entered the VR market with the Apple Vision Pro, priced at $3,499, while Meta released the Meta Quest 3 with major improvements in display and tracking, priced at $499. By 2024, VR and AR headsets were becoming more advanced, offering immersive experiences. Apple Vision Pro debuted in the U.S. in February, generating mixed reactions. Meta launched the Quest 3S with enhanced features in September 2024, while Pico introduced the Pico 4 Ultra, a powerful competitor priced at $469, further expanding the VR market. In 2025, VR advancements focus on AI integration, lighter, more comfortable headsets, and higher resolution micro-OLED displays. Wireless connectivity, extended battery life, and improved depth tracking enhance immersion. Devices like the Apple Vision Pro and Samsung's "Project Moohan" showcase these innovations, with the latter expected to be a premium headset on Android XR.

3 CONCLUSION

The evolution of VR is not merely a narrative of technological progress, but a reflection of humanity's enduring impulse to simulate, explore, and inhabit alternative realities. From the immersive illusions of 19th-century panoramic art to the interactive, sensor-driven systems of the 21st century, VR has consistently developed at the intersection of science, engineering, art, and human perception. Each milestone – whether rooted in optics, electromechanics, computer graphics, or interface design – represents a cumulative effort to overcome the constraints of physical experience and extend the boundaries of sensory engagement.

What began with attempts to replicate depth and spatial awareness through stereoscopy evolved into complex systems capable of real-time interaction, multi-sensory stimulation, and spatial computing. Key innovations, including the Link Trainer, Sensorama, HMDs, and later commercial and medical applications, underscore the interdisciplinary nature of VR's development. Moreover, the influence of defense, entertainment, and healthcare sectors highlights how diverse motivations have shaped both the form and function of immersive technologies.

This historical perspective demonstrates that VR is not a recent phenomenon, but the culmination of a long and varied technological heritage. Understanding this lineage is essential for contextualizing current VR applications and anticipating future directions. As the field continues to mature – with advancements in AI, haptics, and MR – the foundational ideas and innovations of the past remain deeply embedded in its ongoing evolution.

REFERENCES

Baldock, Mark R. (1995). *Cinerama Format.* https://sunnycv.com/steve/filmnotes/cinerama2.html

Barnard, Dom (October 17, 2024). *History of VR – Timeline of Events and Tech Development.* VirtualSpeech. https://virtualspeech.com/blog/history-of-vr

Buckler, Julie; Hazzard, Samuel. (2016). *Humanities 54: The Urban Imagination.* https://hum54-15.omeka.fas.harvard.edu/exhibits/show/1812commemoration/museum-panorama-the-battle-of-

Computer History Museum. (1996). *Virtual Reality before It Had that Name.* https://www.computerhistory.org/collections/catalog/102639877

Craig, Alan; Sherman, William; Will, Jeffrey (2009). *Developing Virtual Reality Applications: Foundations of Effective Design.* Morgan Kaufmann Publishers. ISBN 9780080959085.

De Angelo, Joseph (June 10, 2000). *The Link Flight Trainer* (PDF). ASME. https://www.asme.org/wwwasmeorg/media/resourcefiles/aboutasme/who%20we%20are/engineering%20history/landmarks/210-link-c-3-flight-trainer.pdf

Grau, Oliver (2003). *Virtual Art: From Illusion to Immersion*. MIT Press. ISBN 0262572230.

International Stereoscopic Union (2006) "Stereoscopy", Numbers 65–72, p. 18. "In 1849 Scottish scientist Sir David Brewster invents the lenticular stereoscope, the first practical, portable, 3D viewing device. This stereoscope used refractive lenses and began the protocol of having the stereo pairs mounted side by side."

Kentbye (November 17, 2015). *50 years of VR with Tom Furness: The Super Cockpit, Virtual Retinal Display, HIT Lab, & Virtual World Society. #245.* https://voicesofvr. com/245-50-years-of-vr-with-tom-furness-the-super-cockpit-virtual-retinal-display-hit-lab-virtual-world-society/

Krueger, Myron (1983). *Artificial Reality*. Addison-Wesley. ISBN 0-201-04765-9

Moro, Christian; Štromberga, Zane; Raikos, Athanasios; Stirling, Allan (November 2017). *The Effectiveness of Virtual and Augmented Reality in Health Sciences and Medical Anatomy* (PDF). Anatomical Sciences Education. https://anatomypubs. onlinelibrary.wiley.com/doi/abs/10.1002/ase.1696

Regrebsubla, Namron (2015). *Determinants of Diffusion of Virtual Reality*. GRIN Publishing. ISBN 9783668228214.

Sell, Mary Ann; Sell, Wolfgang; Van Pelt, Charley (2000). *View-Master Memories*. M. A. and W. Sell, ISBN B0006S314I, Self-Published.

Shishov, Alexei (2012). *Кутузов. Фельдмаршал победы [Kutuzov: Fieldmarshal of victory]. Великие исторические персоны (Great historical persons)* (in Russian). Вече. ISBN 978-5-4444-0596-3.

Srivastava, Kalpana; Chaudhury, S.; Das, R. C. (July 2014, 01). "Virtual reality applications in mental health: Challenges and perspectives". *Industrial Psychiatry Journal*. 23 (2): 83–85. https://doi.org.10.4103/0972-6748.151666. PMC 4361984. PMID 25788795.

Sutherland, Ivan Edward (1965). "The Ultimate Display". Proceedings of IFIP 65, vol 2.

USC HMH Foundation Moving Image Archive (2025). *Morton Heilig: Inventor Vr.* https://hmharchive.com/morton-heilig-inventor-vr/

Weinbaum, Stanley Grauman (1935) *Pygmalion's Spectacles*. https://www.gutenberg. org/files/22893/22893-h/22893-h.htm

Werner, John (February 2024, 23). "Catchup with Ivan Sutherland – Inventor of the First AR Headset". *Forbes*. Retrieved 19 July 2025. https://www.forbes. com/sites/johnwerner/2024/02/23/catchup-with-ivan-sutherlandinventor-of-the-first-ar-headset

Wragg, David W. (1973). *A Dictionary of Aviation* (first ed.). Osprey. p. 232. ISBN 9780850451634.

CHAPTER 4

The Art of Virtual Content Creation

Heba El Kamshoushy and Bassant Mohamed Attia

1 INTRODUCTION

Without creative art, the world would lack depth and meaning. Art transforms everything, giving it a soul – it turns objects from plain to lively and from cold to warm and emotional. VR has been a transformative advancement in technology, turning reality into imaginary scenes. It has created a sense of illusion and blurred the boundaries between reality and fantasy. However, it is interesting to question why some VR experiences are more engaging and feel more realistic than others. The answer lies in the art of the virtual content creation – not only in how it appears to the viewer but also in how it feels. The sense of immersion in a virtual world, rather than simply observing it, is what creates an emotional and psychological connection with the viewer – one that resonates deeply and stays long after the experience.

This chapter will explore several dimensions in the art and creativity behind the virtual environments, helping in understanding the role of creative expressions in shaping the virtual space. It begins with discussing the factors that shape the aesthetic experience in VR, such as arousal, fascination, and creative interpretation. After that, it explores the role of colour, and the psychological reactions, identifying how they affect cognition and immersion, putting into consideration the challenging aspects of colour choices in VR, addressing insights into colour constancy. Also, the successful use of avatars is addressed, exploring the connection between

DOI: 10.1201/9781003673538-4

presence and avatar realism, embodiment, empathy, and social connected-ness, while understanding the diverse psychological and behavioural con-sequences of immersive VR technology.

2 THE AESTHETIC EXPERIENCE IN VIRTUAL REALITY

The aesthetic experience is a complex process, it is not merely perceiving the beauty within a visual content, but it involves how we respond to exter-nal aesthetic inputs that stimulate our emotional and cognitive responses, Fu et al. (2023) defined the *aesthetic experience* as "the experience that differs from everyday life, in which psychological focuses are completely on the subject at hand" (p. 177). While in *virtual reality*, it might have a different perspective, as it involves the individual's engagement with all the different sensory inputs and how they are transformed into feelings of wonder and fascination, which results in a heightened state of awareness.

The aesthetic experience process begins with arousal, where the user's attention is captured and all their senses are engaged at the same time. Next comes the deeper level of cognitive engagement, where interpretation of the aesthetic content occurs; however, those experiences within the vir-tual reality are not passive but involve active participation that enhances the overall experience and contributes to the *qualitative immersion* in VR.

Fu et al. (2023) explain that virtual environments introduce a new form of aesthetic engagement, with three different dimensions; aesthetic fasci-nation, *which they defined as the complete sensory and phycological pillar that captures the user's attention, second is the aesthetic interpretation or appraisal, which involves all the cognitive and the interpretive process dur-ing the experience, where the users analyse the narrative structure, symbols, and metaphors, and this process is also closely connected to the role of* aes-thetic creativity, where users engage in the artistic co-creation of the vir-tual environment. Their model provides a good analysis for understanding the cognitive and interactive aesthetic experiences that users have in VR.

2.1 Aesthetic Fascination: The Foundation of Immersion

Aesthetic fascination acts as a main pillar of the immersive experience within the VR. It is the immediate attention, focus, and direct emotional engagement towards a specific subject within a *simulated presence*. This immediate attention – where the user lacks self-awareness and becomes disconnected from the physical environment – resembles a psychologi-cal state like mental flow – (Fu et al., 2023) where users can transcend from consciousness and experience a form of time distortion, where min-utes feel like seconds. Within VR, this state is extensive because of the medium's immersive nature, which engages multiple senses at once and promotes deep focus. That fascination in VR is not the direct reaction to visual stimuli but a complex multidimensional sensory and cognitive process that works together to create a sense of wonder, creating a state of heightened attention and arousal, where users become deeply absorbed in the virtual experience and become a part of the virtual scenario. To analyse this phenomenon, we can break down the metrics for analysing fascination in VR into *immersion* and presence, and each can be explored by examining the sensory and psychological dimensions.

2.1.1 The Sensory and Psychological Dimensions in VR

Immersion is the extent to which a virtual environment captures all the user's sensory focus and simulates an alternate reality combined with *tactile displays* and *haptic feedback*. It is a fully engaging and holistic experience that requires the complete focus and thought processes of the user (Fu et al., 2023). As Buttazzoni et al. (2022) state:

> We seek the same feeling from a psychologically immersive experience that we do from a plunge in the ocean or swimming pool: the sensation of being surrounded by a completely other reality … that takes over all of our attention, our whole perceptual apparatus … in a participatory medium, immersion implies learning to swim, to do the things that the new environment makes possible.
>
> (p. 2)

This description illustrates the nature of VR's immersive and psychological capabilities, where users are enveloped in a *simulated environment* to such a degree that the separation between the actual and virtual world ceases to exist. The metaphor of learning to swim is very expressive because it underlines the active dimension of *immersion*, which involves *interaction*, not simply watching a virtual space. This strengthens the case that the focus of VR designers should not only be on the *photorealistic* details of the environment, but also on creating conditions that encourage active exploration and qualitative involvement.

But reaching a strong level of qualitative involvement and interaction requires the use of advanced methods that integrate multiple sensory channels, including sight, sound, touch, and *extended sensory feedback* that can integrate smell, and other physical sensations like wind, temperature, and vibrations to create a richly textured environment that helps in the separation of the user and the medium and integrate them more deeply, increasing the user's sense of presence and engagement (Fu et al., 2023).

Finkler et al. (2025) conducted a study to examine whether 360° virtual-reality nature films might function as e-health interventions to improve emotional resilience and well-being. Their study included 63 adults, where presence, mood change, interaction quality, and nature connectedness were analysed before and after the VR experiences. The research showed that almost all participants reported a strong presence, and during follow-up, they described emotions such as cognitive withdrawal and renewed affinity with those natural environments. The study therefore provides a good discussion that VR environments can mirror the psychological effect obtained in physical nature. As the authors concluded that head-mounted nature experiences have shown a positive impact on well-being and reducing stress, especially for people with limited access to natural physical environments, taking into consideration the technological and sensory limitations that might affect the results, e.g. resolution and supplementary multisensory cues.

2.2 The Aesthetic Interpretation: Cognitive Dimensions

The aesthetic experience in virtual reality expands beyond intellectual engagement and content analysis. It extends to considering virtual reality frameworks and their design in ways that result in placing the viewer beyond the interface. The user must undertake some form of artistic linguistic exploration to grasp the structural and symbolic components.

When exploring the VR interactive designs today, they demand content and systems to narrate, compose, and construct virtual worlds. Elements such as gaze, physical movement in the scene, and selective attention may determine the chronological events that one undergoes in stages within the experience. This control can enhance emotional engagement but may also result in *story gaps* (Fu et al., 2023). The reason is that the VR experience provides the user freedom to control his or her gaze in all directions, and to preserve story coherence, designers must control gaze direction using *binaural audio, environmental sensing,* and *strong spatial audio cues,* unlike traditional media, where the user is a passive viewer.

From this perspective, we can describe creativity in VR as something that frequently arises to "surface" almost simultaneously. Participants – as they are actively co-creating the virtual space – are doing what we can refer to as interpretive creativity. This is when the metaphors applied in interaction design show their greatest strength, as it aims to improve the user's psychosensory participation by means of symbolic actions that evoke emotions. As Djokic et al. (2021) explained, *metaphorical thinking acts as a bridge between embodiment and abstraction and helps to flexibly organize human knowledge and behavior* (p. 1). Such metaphorical frameworks are, in turn, augmented in virtual reality by the sensory richness of the medium, which heightens users' focus and allows users to naturally "be a butterfly" for example, and as a result, cause users to fly upwards and vertically towards blooming, as the virtual world does not have to be constrained to a literal, rigid, one-to-one gesture mapping because it can be more analogical and qualitative (Djokic et al., 2021).

2.2.1 The Role of Colour in VR

It is known that colour is a main design component in experience design, but in immersive VR, colour can do a lot more than being just a part of the aesthetic virtual composition; it is an important aspect supporting the multiple sensory dimensions. Every colour is described through three primary attributes: hue, chroma, and brightness (as cited in Xia et al., 2023). Hue is how we perceive a colour, as red, blue, or green. Chroma describes the colour's intensity or the pureness and vividness of the hue, while brightness describes the level of lightness or darkness of the colour. Research on colour in VR shows that the users' feeling of presence and cognitive performance can be enhanced by the correct use of chroma and brightness levels, as conducted by Xia et al. (2023).

Colour psychology provides a good framework for understanding how colour can evoke different emotions and physiological responses. Where high saturated warm colours are known to help increase the feeling of excitement, cooler hues can help in relaxation and calmness. Those emotional reactions to different colours can be explored in three different levels: unconscious, semi-conscious, and conscious (as cited in Xia et al., 2023). Unconscious reactions to colour result from biological responses, which can be used for reducing stress, or in managing mood. Semi-conscious reactions result from the cultural background and experiences of the participants, while the conscious level is connected to the personal preferences of colours. This three-level classification of the emotional reactions to colour is illustrated in Figure 4.1. putting into consideration that our perception of colour depends on many other interconnecting factors such as the viewing distance, our viewing angle, the ambient lighting, and the surrounding colours (as cited in Elliot, 2015).

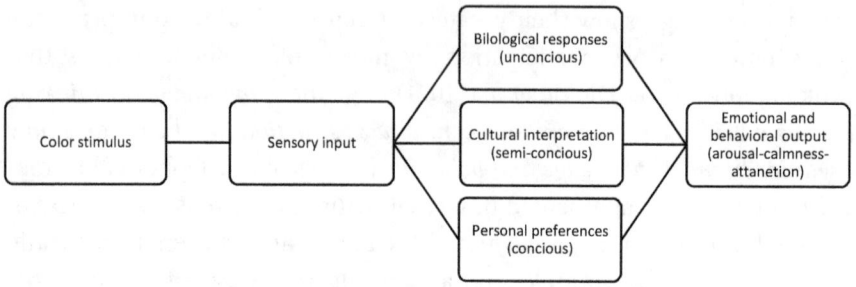

FIGURE 4.1   Emotional Responses to Colour Stimuli in Virtual Reality.

Source: Xia et al. (2023).

Note: Author-generated diagram adapted from information in Kauppinen-Räisänen (2014, as cited in Xia et al., 2023).

As the emotional reactions to colour may affect arousal in the VR experiences, it's important to understand the relation between arousal and cognitive performance, which can be reasoned through the Yerkes-Dodson law – the psychological principle introduced by Robert Yerkes and John Dillingham Dodson in 1908 discussing the use of colour in design. The theory proposes a good explanation for the connection between arousal and cognitive performance, mentioning that a moderate level of arousal is helpful to better cognitive performance, while higher levels of arousal can somehow lower attention and overall performance (Pietrangelo, 2020). For example, a moderate level of stress before an exam may enhance focus and help retain information, while excessive anxiety can make focus difficult, and the user is unable to recall the correct information. The same rule applies in VR settings; the use of intense colours that increase arousal within VR environments will cause more user impulsivity (Xia et al., 2021). Consequently, highly saturated and overly bright colours in VR might be a reason for lowering the overall performance due to increased arousal.

2.2.2 Colour Constancy in VR Environments

Our visual system identifies colours by analysing the light waves reflected from the objects. But what's interesting is that we can easily identify and perceive the same object colour even when seen under different illuminations and surrounding conditions, such a phenomenon is called colour constancy, which has three main strategies the human visual system seems to use for maintaining it. The first, local surround, which is how colour shifts at the edges between the object and its background: as lighting changes, the colour edges still signal to the brain that the object's colour hasn't changed. The second, maximum flux, happens when the brain works to analyse the brightest part of the image as reference white. The third, spatial mean, suggests that the visual system works to adapt to the average colour of the scene (as cited in Gil Rodríguez et al., 2024).

When then compared to the immersive VR context, the HMDs and the rendering in high resolution sustain a spatial stability replicating the natural environment. In comparison to the real world, achieving colour constancy in virtual reality relies on the same human cognitive and interpretive capabilities. In VR, the lighting is simulated to resemble the natural environment, relying on rendering engines and high-resolution HMDs, which then must be strongly manipulated and enhanced through the spatial cues, background colour, and overall scene illumination. But what we must consider is that our brains do not define colours on a pixel-based structure, but interpret the colour based on the context. We recognize the objects in a scene, and our cognitive abilities automatically adjust for the light waves emitted from the objects and reflected to our retina, which makes the VR colour feel the same in different situations while relying on interpreting the scene as a whole and not as separate objects (Gil Rodríguez et al., 2024).

2.3 Character Design and Presence in AR/VR

Even though the visual aesthetic aspect of virtual content creation is central to *the immersive experience* of users, the visual and behavioural style of avatars plays an essential role in how users respond to them when navigating the space. Some individuals may view *avatars* as just tools whose primary function is to act as a catalyst pushing the narrative forward; nevertheless, they are the fundamental component for an *immersive experience*. Without *avatars*, no emotions will be evoked, nor will a high *user's immersion level* be achieved. Avatars are now known for their contribution to constructing a sense of identification with the people involved in such an experience.

When focusing on achieving a deeper level of immersion, avatar design is a key element to be explored. The way avatars appear alongside their personalities is extremely associated with the user's degree of affinity. They improve the perception of presence, hence allowing the avatars to be seen as more appealing, compelling, and realistic in VR immersive environments (Zibrek et al., 2018). It is significant to mention that recent studies emphasized that facial resemblance and entire body synchronization make the psychological line between *lifelike avatars* and users less distinct

(Suk & Laine, 2023). The more realistically detailed these avatars are, the deeper the level of immersion is converted into a high-quality perception, synthesizing the virtual world and the real world, heightening the cognitive/intellectual immersion during *multimodal interactions* (Figure 4.2).

Visual realism is essential in creating avatars that boost *stimulated presence*. The illusion of physical tangibility could be attained through simple yet influential elements like uneven bone structure, dermal flaws, Eye wetness, and live-rendering shadows. It is worth noting that also, the illusion of place (Pi), which highly contributes to the level of realism in any Immersive environment, could be easily triggered by producing lifelike avatars that accurately resemble human movement, bodily dimensions,

Cycle of Avatar Realism

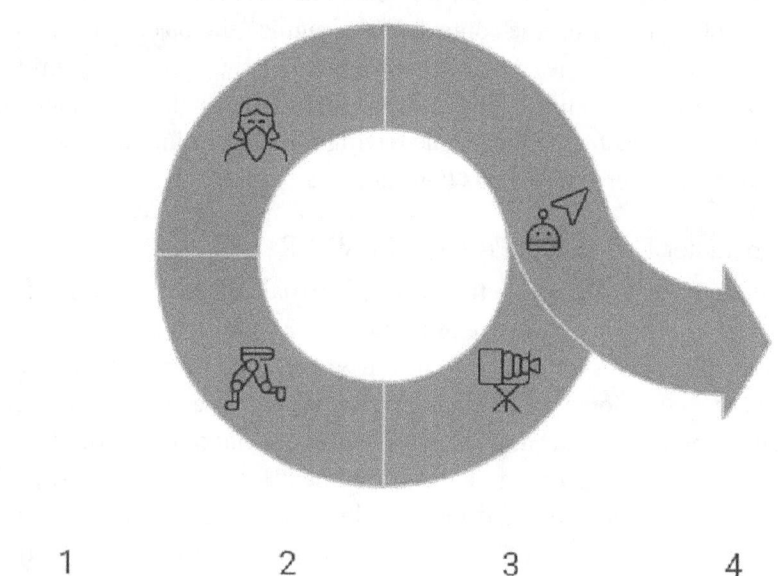

1	2	3	4
Capture Motion	Simulate Kinetics	Enhance Realism	Achieve Behavioral Realism
Use advanced tracking systems to record real-world movements.	Apply kinetic simulations to make avatar movements fluid.	Improve avatar appearance and behavior for lifelike quality.	Ensure avatars act autonomously and believably.

FIGURE 4.2   Avatar Realism Cycle.

Note: Diagram created by the author.

topography, and facial anatomy. Hence, Plausibility illusion (Psi) is evoked by Pi. By doing so, an actable avatar that is so believable in the virtual realm is accomplished.

3 AVATARS IN MOTION: A POWERFUL STEP TO ACHIEVE A HIGH IMMERSION LEVEL

It is extremely vigorous to let avatars depict real-life motion. The actions undertaken by avatars in a virtual atmosphere should be recognized as the same as those of individuals in real life. This defines the core aspect of the *gesture recognition* concept. For an avatar to act and move in a naturalistic way, cutting-edge tracking systems, whole body dynamics, natural blinking reflex, and subtle facial cues should be taken into consideration. Stressing that *Kinetic simulation* and motion tracking systems increase the accuracy of gestures made by the avatars, uplifting their realistic response, which forms the underlying mechanism of Behavioural realism (avatar acts in a lifelike manner).

With the intention of achieving a greater user gratification level and connectedness in VR experience, it has been proven that having lifelike avatars that display realistic behaviour is far more influential than having avatars that provide *unrealistic feedback. Eye gaze tracking, body tracking,* and synchronized lip movements are nuanced techniques that boost user engagement and trust. And any *interface lag* related to these minutes' techniques could effortlessly demolish the perception of realistic interaction.

3.1 First-Person Embodiment: User Engagement and Empathy in Virtual Reality/Augmented Reality

Beyond the visual and behavioural realism, First-person embodiment sets a key factor for strong user engagement and amplified emotional response. When users assume a first-person view of *gaze-based control*, it is not an experience of witnessing an avatar; it becomes them. The virtuality of the above alignment is immersive and creates a psychological effect where a person starts having a virtual body. The user does not take control of a character at the safe distance of a video game but internalizes the actions and responses of the character as part of themselves. This uplifting experience has been called body transfer or embodied presence, which makes such experiences more genuine and increases emotional connectedness to the *virtual identity.*

Furthermore, the engrossment of neuroscientific evidence proves that such embodiment awakens the major brain networks related to self-perception and threat detection. For instance, members taking part in a simulation of domestic violence in a first-person perspective displayed greater synchrony in the front-parietal network and the amygdala reaction areas associated with the body self and emotional processing (de Borst et al., 2020).

Moreover, the use of virtual reality in a pilot study allowed students to take on the role of a patient in a virtual sense, one that covered their typical daily routine, the symptoms that they experience, and the response to care providers. Being able to go through the Embodied Labs modules allowed first-year medical students to have a first-hand experience concerning either having a terminal illness or being informed that there are no more treatments available and later seeing the reaction of the loved ones. The number of statistics attained because of surveys and reflections revealed that place illusion, plausibility, and user embodiment were at a high level. Such a high immersion led to creating more comfort in discussing end-of-life issues, creating a larger insight into what patients and their families go through (Elzie & Shaia, 2021).

Collectively, this perceptual fusion, made possible by first-person perspective, gaze-based control, bespoke avatar match, low interface lag, and high degrees of tracking fidelity, causes participants to not only see through the eyes of the *empathetic virtual avatars*, but to incrementally feel like the avatar. The subjective reports of empathy production, along with brain synchronization objectively measured, show that *qualitative immersion* and long-term engagement are high in users, and in many cases, the engagement extends into the world past the VR experience itself. As a result, the user interaction becomes at very high levels of empathy. Since users identify themselves in the virtual environment both mentally and emotionally, they experience the virtual scenarios using the emotional accounts. So, placing the avatars outside a meaningful context or lacking instructional simulation may hinder this evocation of empathy; such a disconnection between the user and the Virtual world weakens the desired emotional reaction of the users.

4 IMPACT OF THE AR/VR IMMERSIVE EXPERIENCE ON USERS

The impact of having a realistic avatar goes far beyond evoking empathy. This part of this chapter will delve deeper into the various effects of being immersed in a Virtual environment as a user. When users encounter the virtual versions of their own, they become more aware of how their behaviour and actions could come off in realistic scenarios. The higher and more accurate level of imitation and human reactions the avatar maintains, the more precise the users will be when it comes to decision-making. This genuine simulation, hence, enriches the ability of mental predictability and adaptability of users to diverse situations.

4.1 Immersive Experience: Enhancing Predictability

Such a simulation enables them to have more of a comparative analysis of what could happen in both the virtual and the physical worlds and how they would react in much clearer aspects. Moreover, users are given secure settings to show off their behaviour through cognitive rehearsals while undergoing different scenarios without encountering the jeopardy of human responses that might not always be as predictable and safe as they might seem. Henceforth, enforcing realism plays as a crucial anticipatory mechanism that enhances practical intelligence (Griffith et al., 2020).

4.2 Immersive Experience: A New Approach for Developing Problem-Solving Skills

Furthermore, Virtual reality proposes an accommodating approach for problem-solving. This is, in fact, a complementary force that supports users' decision-making in a later stage, as it offers an engaging environment that highly reflects hazardous challenges that need to be tested and analysed thoroughly. Nonetheless, it offers various solutions and scenarios to deal with such challenges. In that light, virtual reality encompasses both the brain and bones to comprehensively enable users to acquire imperative life skills, such as critical thinking (Fitkin, 2015). It is worth mentioning

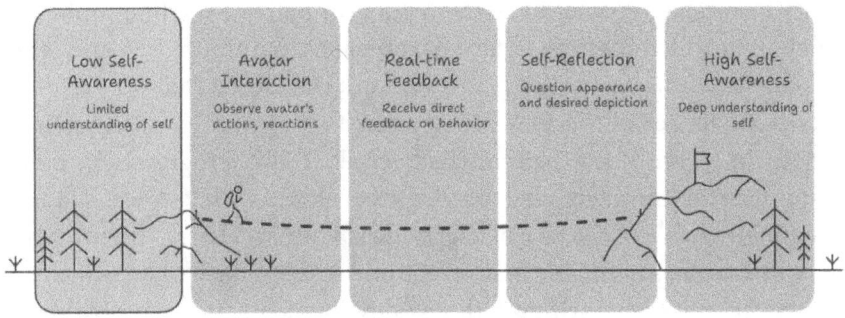

FIGURE 4.3   Impact of Lifelike Avatars on the Self-Awareness Process.

Note: Diagram created by the author.

that breaking down non-verbal annotations, reading micro-expressions, and engaging in negotiations in simulated immersive environments are significant for users to adequately comprehend human interactions.

The realism makes the users too sensitive to nuance and the non-immediate meaning of behaviour. It makes them understand that solutions do not necessarily have to be linear or in isolation, but are because of consciousness of tone, context, and timing. This, in turn, strengthens their disposition to solve interpersonal and professional problems (Figure 4.3).

4.3 Lifelike Avatars: A New Method for Self-Awareness

Furthermore, a lifelike avatar also increased self-awareness. Through observing an avatar in action, reaction, and body movements in a virtual world that is highly resembling of real-life settings, users obtain direct feedback regarding themselves in real-time. The user starts to think about the following question: how do I appear to other people? Do I move, talk, and make decisions that reflect how I desire to be depicted? These questions begin to surface when dealing with the human-like avatar, which primarily reflects the traits of the user. In return, such analytical thinking immensely elevates self-adjustments and realignment with people's values and beliefs. As these corrective actions are the core of cognitive behaviour, they not only reflect the user's physical appearance but also the way their mind functions. This virtual interaction further proliferates self-awareness and longs for personal growth.

4.4 Virtual Reality / Augmented Reality Experience: As an Emotional Regulation Tool

Furthermore, interactions made during the virtual reality/augmented reality experience enables its users to put into practice the fine-tuning of emotion, in which reacting to facial expressions, natural movements, and dialogue rhythm, primarily by the human's nervous system rather than algorithmic codes of the avatar, empowers them to deal with emotional triggers in a controlled manner (Bade et al., 2009). Progressively, users accumulate the knowledge and practice to become more self-controlled and emotionally stable in the face of triggering situations. Hence, this provides them with a place to fumble, self-reflect, and attempt once again, which all go hand in hand with self-growth and development. Such repeated recalibration is a key aspect of emotional regulation and maturity, especially when it is performed during reliable and realistic simulations.

4.5 Avatars: New Lens for More Accurate Social Intuition

Additionally, it is deemed true and proven that activating behavioural realism in avatars paves the way for more accurate social intuition for users. When an avatar replicates and reinitiates human behaviour in the real-world context, such as expressions, change of postures, and turn-taking in conversation, the users are involuntarily put their minds into it. They bring their higher attention onto minor incidents that are more likely challenging to fully realize through daily communications, i.e., hesitation, micro-aggressions, sarcasm, or unease. These social cues are highly fundamental to emotional intelligence and managing social interactions successfully. With recurring virtual exposure, they fine-tune them to pick up these cues; accordingly, the users learn patterns of healthy social behaviour through internalization. More importantly, they will be trained to listen more than they talk, to know when to initiate the conversation, and how to respond respectively in an empathetic manner. This is owing to the tentative experience they had that was provided by the virtual environment rather than being induced to act upon some situations (Roth et al., 2019). This amplification of cross-generational interpersonal intelligence not only allows users to be further present and conscious of other people's behaviour but, more importantly, to be engaging and communicative in their daily interactions.

4.6 AR/VR Immersive Experience: A New Tool for Deepening Social Interactions

It is worth mentioning that a key outcome of experiencing such interactions for a lengthy period is Inclusion. Since inclusion does not initially mean that some identities are just visible in their abstract version, but more eloquently guarantees that identities are being seen in depth in various aspects. However, cultural, physical, or psychological nuances are at stake when cartoon-like or generic avatars are utilized, as more realistic ones, when operational, are more relevant to human identities in terms of race and gender, ability, age, etc. This supports diverse types of users, especially marginalized identities, to experience the feeling of being more seen and perceived as realistic, often beyond in the digital world. Consequently, from an empathetic point, people who were sidelined will have a greater chance to be regarded with an extra layer of recognition and dignity, which will counter in return stereotypes and put more weight on treating other people with comprehension and compassion (Arouca et al., 2024).

4.7 Immersive Environments: Triggering Collective Awareness and Global Thinking

Immersive environments generate other important effects besides inclusion, which are Collective Awareness and Global Thinking. As immersive experiences provide extensive engagement with diverse global issues across multiple dimensions and levels ,thereby enhancing awareness and catalyzing paradigm shifts (Campbell & Jackson, 2014). The creation of various settings, such as being trapped in a war zone, experiencing the drawbacks of climate change, or even encountering instability, helps significantly to mend the rift between individual experience and holistic ones. Henceforth, this immersive experience fortifies the importance of taking sustainable and ethical actions while empowering users to make wiser choices in life.

4.8 Immersive Experiences and Setting Long-Term Goals

Furthermore, Immersive experiences potentially enhance intrinsic motivation and long-term goals. The virtual environments offer a professional mechanism where the goal-setting process is definite, progressive, and monitored, which, in turn, can be easily utilized in real life (Tiwari et al., 2020). When users encounter a similar experience as an avatar and begin accomplishing tasks, overcoming challenges, and achieving goals successfully, this augments the confidence levels of users and amplifies their motivation to be more productive in the real world. This self-fulfilling experience is highly influential for the less-motivated users who encountered depressive episodes due to self-doubt. The clarity and form of immersive platforms can also assist users in practising focus, delayed gratification, and persistence, which are essential factors in long-term success.

4.9 Immersive Technologies as a Two-Edged Sword

It is worth stating that anything is like a two-edged sword since immersive technologies provide their users with a very sharp sense of presence. As soon as the users wear a VR headset, they stop being spectators; they become agents. Such freedom can be so appealing, particularly to those who feel constrained, overwhelmed, or unfulfilled with the real world. In the long run, when individuals regularly experience a virtual world in which they feel powerful, popular, or in complete control, their brains can become accustomed to these falsified experiences, prompting them to prioritize virtual life over human life. Consequently, escapism will be their only survival mechanism, which is not simply a way of being distracted but an emotional addiction that has numerous negative effects (Mostovoy, 2018).

5 CONCLUSION

This chapter makes a very valid point that a thoroughly immersive VR experience is not only about the high-fidelity visuals but also an artistic form that will emotionally and psychologically involve the user. This chapter commences by stating that the aesthetic experience in VR is a complicated process, which starts with a state of aesthetic fascination that induces a user into a state of deep concentration, like the flow of mind. This is done by the real immersion, the full sensory experience of a virtual world, and the sense of being there, the user feels that he/she is an active participant of the simulated world. Furthermore, this chapter elucidates the fact that users are active co-producers who construct the virtual arena rather than being passive consumers. The intelligent utilization of metaphoric thinking and visualization in the design is what formulates these interactions as intuitive and sense-making.

Finally, this chapter provides insights into the influential role of colour, which is a fundamental instrument of shaping the mood of the users and the achievability of their cognitive performances. It displays the significance of diverse colours in inducing attention and stimulation capacity of a user, and the difficulty in attaining colour constancy, whereby colours become precise regardless of the change in virtual light conditions to create a more realistic world. Significantly, the part that discusses the avatar design is the cornerstone section of this chapter. It refutes with reliable and intellectual arguments that the key to initiating a robust feeling of first-person embodiment is the ability to make realistic, human-like avatars with nuanced movements and facial expressions. This not only paves the way for experiencing the world through the lenses of virtual reality or an avatar, but, most importantly, also for feeling genuine emotions, which has, in fact, been shown to induce empathy and enhance skills acquisition.

This chapter demonstrates that such realism can serve as an anti-hazardous training environment via fostering practical intelligence, critical thinking skills, and social instincts of the users through practising and rehearsing challenging scenarios and situations. Additionally, it reflects briefly on the inclusion offered and self-awareness promoted by realistic avatars, as users will have their own actions reflected back at them. To conclude, these immersive technologies offer great potential for self-development, even though the same power that makes them so captivating may spawn escapism; the user might enjoy the virtual world more than the real one. To sum up, this chapter emphasizes the complex equilibrium between art and technology that's required to produce the VR content that is not only superb but truly transformative, where VR/AR becomes an evocative space where art, technology, and meaning converge.

REFERENCES

Arouca, M. G., Amorim, A. M., Pestana, M. C., & Vieira, V. (2024). *Towards inclusive avatars: A study on self-representation in virtual environments.* https://doi.org/10.5753/sbsc.2024.238056

Bade, A., Sunar, M. S., & Daman, D. (2009). *A new realistic-believable avatar to enhance user awareness in serious game and virtual environment.* https://www.researchgate.net/publication/265788160_A_new_realistic-believable_avatar_to_enhance_user_awareness_in_serious_game_and_virtual_environment

Buttazzoni, A., Ellard, C., Sadiora, S., & Minaker, L. (2022). Toward conceptualizing "place immersion" as a spatial neuropsychosocial phenomenon: A multidisciplinary meta-review and synthesis. *Journal of Environmental Psychology, 81*, 101810. https://doi.org/10.1016/j.jenvp.2022.101810

Campbell, S., & Jackson, N. (2014). *CHAPTER C6 immersive experiences: An important ecology for lifewide learning and development.* https://scispace.com/pdf/chapter-c6-immersive-experiences-an-important-ecology-for-116jr2sw45.pdf

De Borst, A. W., Sanchez-Vives, M. V., Slater, M., Slater, M., de Gelder, B., & de Gelder, B. (2020). First-person virtual embodiment modulates the cortical network that encodes the bodily self and its surrounding space during the experience of domestic violence. *Eneuro, 7*(3). https://doi.org/10.1523/ENEURO.0263-19.2019

Djokic, V. G., Shutova, E., & Fiebrink, R. (2021). MetaVR: Understanding metaphors in the mind and relation to emotion through immersive, spatial interaction. In *Extended abstracts of the 2021 CHI conference on human factors in computing systems* (Article 185, pp. 1–4). Association for Computing Machinery. https://doi.org/10.1145/3411763.3451565

Elliot, A. J. (2015). Color and psychological functioning: A review of theoretical and empirical work. *Frontiers in Psychology, 6*, 368. https://doi.org/10.3389/fpsyg.2015.00368

Elzie, C. A., & Shaia, J. (2021). A pilot study of the impact of virtually embodying a patient with a terminal illness. *Medical Science Educator, 31*(2), 665–675. https://doi.org/10.1007/s40670-021-01243-9

Finkler, W., Vlietstra, L., Waters, D. L., Zhu, L., Gallagher, S., Walker, R., Forlong, R., & van Heezik, Y. (2025). Virtual nature and well-being: Exploring the potential of 360° VR. *Applied Psychology: Health and Well-Being, 17*(1), e70008. https://doi.org/10.1111/aphw.70008

Fitkin, R. J. (2015). *Effect of an adaptive thinking training methodology on critical thinking disposition using human patient simulators: A catalyst for preparing advanced nursing students.* https://doi.org/10.25777/432P-M221

Fu, X., Zhou, Z., & Zhu, X. (2023). The unique aesthetic experience of VR technology. *Highlights in Science, Engineering and Technology, 44,* 177–188. https://doi.org/10.54097/hset.v44i.7317

Gil Rodríguez, R., Hedjar, L., Toscani, M., Guarnera, D., Guarnera, G. C., & Gegenfurtner, K. R. (2024). Color constancy mechanisms in virtual reality environments. *Journal of Vision, 24*(5), Article 6. https://doi.org/10.1167/jov.24.5.6

Griffith, T. S., Fidopiastis, C. M., Bockelman-Morrow, P., & Johnston, J. H. (2020). *Behavioral indicators of interactions between humans, virtual agent characters and virtual avatars* (pp. 330–342). Springer. https://doi.org/10.1007/978-3-030-59990-4_25

Mostovoy, G. (2018). *United States patent No. US10065113B1.* U.S. Patent and Trademark Office. https://patents.google.com/patent/US10065113B1

Pietrangelo, A. (2020, October 22). *What is the Yerkes–Dodson law?* Healthline. https://www.healthline.com/health/yerkes-dodson-law

Roth, D., Stauffert, J.-P., & Latoschik, M. E. (2019). *Avatar embodiment, behavior replication, and kinematics in virtual reality.* (pp. 321–346). A K Peters/CRC Press. https://doi.org/10.1201/B21598-17

Suk, H. J., & Laine, T. H. (2023). Influence of avatar facial appearance on users' perceived embodiment and presence in immersive virtual reality. *Electronics, 12*(3), 583. https://doi.org/10.3390/electronics12030583

Tiwari, K., Tiwari, K., Kyrki, V., Cheung, A., & Yamamoto, N. (2020). DeFINE: Delayed feedback based immersive navigation environment for studying goal-directed human navigation. *arXiv: Human-Computer Interaction, 53,* 2668. https://doi.org/10.3758/S13428-021-01586-6

Xia, G., Henry, P., Chen, Y., Queiroz, F., Westland, S., & Cheng, Q. (2023). The effects of colour attributes on cognitive performance and intellectual abilities in immersive virtual environments. *Computers in Human Behavior, 148,* 107853. https://doi.org/10.1016/j.chb.2023.107853

Xia, G., Li, M., Henry, P., Westland, S., Queiroz, F., Peng, Q., & Yu, L. (2021). Aroused and impulsive effects of colour stimuli on lateral and logical abilities. *Behavioral Sciences, 11*(2), Article 24. https://doi.org/10.3390/bs11020024

Zibrek, K., Kokkinara, E., & McDonnell, R. (2018). The effect of realistic appearance of virtual characters in immersive environments - Does the character's personality play a role? *IEEE Transactions on Visualization and Computer Graphics, 24*(4), 1681–1690. https://doi.org/10.1109/TVCG.2018.2794638

CHAPTER 5

The Science behind Virtual Reality

Austin Hendy

1 INTRODUCTION

When referring to the science of virtual reality (VR), it distills down to the illusion of being human—the illusion of how we perceive the world through the senses. VR isn't about creating 3D virtual environments (VEs) that the user can walk around in; it's about creating immersion and presence (Fuchs et al., 2011a, 2011b, 2011c, 2011d) where the user truly believes they're in a 3D VE. Immersion can be defined as the user's degree of sensory engagement within the virtual simulation (Kim & Biocca, 2018), while presence is the perceptual illusion of being there (Slater, 2018). Slater identifies the correlation but difference between immersion and presence, where immersion is the objective property of the VR system, while presence is the subjective (Slater, 2018). This immersive presence is not achieved through visuals alone. Although visuals are the most critical component, a cross-modal integration between other senses must be achieved to create a stronger presence for the user (Malpica et al., 2020). A wooden door within a VE should contain visual attributes—scale, depth, and textures—that make it believable, but also auditory—it creaks as the user rotates it open and clicks when it shuts—and tactile—the user operates on its handle and is made aware of their body relative to the space as a result. This sixth sense, known as proprioception, is crucial to VR as the user perceives themself as the center of the VE (Fuchs et al., 2011a, 2011b,

DOI: 10.1201/9781003673538-5

2011c, 2011d), thus making them aware of their position, movement, and action. To understand the science of VR, this chapter will start with the fundamentals. It will describe the anatomical and neurological processes in which we perceive these senses. Research and technology of the visual, auditory, and haptic/proprioception senses for VR have greater development compared to other senses, such as taste and smell. The former will be the focus of this chapter. With a basic understanding of human sensory perception, this chapter will proceed to describe the three levels of VR: non-immersive, semi-immersive, and fully immersive, and provide examples for each category. Using these examples, this chapter will present the technological developments that correspond to the mechanisms of human perception—the science behind VR.

2 HUMAN PERCEPTION

Our perception of reality stems from the interaction of various sensory systems classified as exteroceptors and proprioceptors. Exteroceptors, including the eyes, ears, nose, mouth, and skin, tell us about modifications in our surroundings, while proprioceptors, including the tips of organs, muscles, joints, and the internal ear, provide us with perception related to position and movement (Fuchs et al., 2011a, 2011b, 2011c, 2011d). The science of how we perceive reality must be defined first before uncovering the science behind VR.

2.1 Visual

Vision greatly impacts and shapes how we perceive space and depth, often at times dominating other sensory modalities. When we look at space, our retina converts light rays into neural signals using photoreceptors. The retina contains around 6 million rods, which allow us to see in dim light with no color, while cones, stimulated by bright light, produce color vision (Tortora & Nielsen, 2010). Visual experiences are constructed by the cone system and exit the eyeball through the optic (II) nerves to the optic chiasm as signals (Tortora & Nielsen, 2010). There are two eyeballs sending signals toward the brain, so some cross to the opposite side while others remain (Tortora & Nielsen, 2010). The signals or fibers then enter the brain into the visual cortex, which projects and processes the visuals (Huff et al., 2025). The horizontal separation between the eyes creates image disparities, which the brain processes into one visual, allowing us to perceive depth and three-dimensionality (Gonzalez & Perez, 1998). This phenomenon is known as stereoscopic vision. For instance, if you were to hold out your finger in front of your eyes, then proceed to close the left eye and open the right eye, then switch, the image of the finger will jump. In the same investigation, if you proceed to look at an object behind your finger, two ghost images of the finger will appear, creating a binocular parallax effect (Fuchs et al., 2011a, 2011b, 2011c, 2011d). Objects that are farther away jump less, allowing our brain to perceive depth. The benefits of having two eyes allow for a wider field of view (FOV) and the preservation of sight if one eye is lost (Smith, 2015). To gauge our 3D spaces using monocular sight, our eyes use light and shadows, relative dimensions, occlusions, texture gradients of surfaces, visibility variation (fog), perspective, height, and brightness (eScience Lectures Notes: Human Sight : Depth Cues vs. Stereoscopy, n.d.). These attributes can be designed and implemented within a VE just like you would a level for a 3D platformer. Processing images from our eyeballs to our brain takes approximately 50 milliseconds (van Hateren & Lamb, 2006), depending on the lighting. This time will affect the technological latency of the VR system, which will be elaborated upon in a later section. As we start to move our eyes, our head, and our bodies, images within the environment also begin to move. Several types of eye movements must be mimicked by eye-tracking technology, including saccades, smooth pursuit, vestibulo-ocular reflexive eye movements, and vergence eye movements (Adhanom et al., 2023). Saccades move the eyes from one object to another with velocities of 400–600° per second and are never still when the eye fixates on an object in the environment (Adhanom et al., 2023). Pursuit eye movements stabilize the image while we slowly track movement, while the vestibulo-ocular reflex stabilizes visual rotations (Adhanom et al., 2023). Finally, vergence eye movements are the motions of both eyes, allowing the eyes to change the binocular focal depth and convergence angle (Adhanom et al., 2023). A combination of the convergence angle and retinal disparity defines how we detect stereoscopic depth (Adhanom et al., 2023).

2.2 Auditory

The visual sense is complemented by our two ears to localize horizontal and vertical sound in our 360° environment. At the anatomical level, the auditory system transforms sound waves into messages that are sent to the auditory nerve and brain. Sound waves pass through the ear canal and eardrum, causing both auditory structures to vibrate. These vibrations continue to the ossicles and then the cochlea, which sends messages through its tiny hair cells. The brain then interprets these messages that came from the auditory nerve into sounds (Tortora & Nielsen, 2010). Similar to 3D visual perception, our auditory system also picks up on 3D audio through a series of localization cues to determine the source of a sound in space, thus enhancing our perception. Localization cues utilize both ears, incorporating the interaural time difference, inter-aural level difference, timbre difference, motion parallax, and reverberation of a sound (Berger et al., 2018). Aside from reverberation, these localization cues are indicative of the head, the separation of the ears, and how sound waves can move around objects, unlike light. The inter-aural time difference localizes sounds based on the time it takes for both ears. Since our ears are on average 20 centimeters apart, a left-localized sound will appear 0.006 seconds slower to our right ear. The inter-aural level difference parallels this, only it is the difference of sound level between the ears. Timbre difference represents the frequency of sounds; thus, our auditory system localizes a sound using the head. A sound from the left will be blocked by the head when it reaches the right ear and will have a different frequency that our brain can process. Sounds that move quickly amid both ears are recognized as closer, which is regarded as motion parallax. Reverberation is concerned less with the ears, but rather with the reflective capabilities of objects and spaces. Sound reflecting on a wall to then return to our ears below 50 milliseconds is considered a reverberation, while anything above 50 milliseconds is considered an echo. Visual cues additionally play a role in sound localization, where actions such as moving lips or moving objects can trick the signal to our brain that a sound was produced (Deed, 2024).

2.3 Tactility

Touch functions as the physical interface between the body and the physical world and is largely conducted through the skin. Serving as our largest organ, the skin contains additional receptors that inform our perception, including nociceptors, thermoreceptors, mechanoreceptors, and proprioceptive mechanoreceptors. Nociceptors provide sensations of pain, thermoreceptors enable thermal sensitivity during tactile engagement, mechanoreceptors activate when the skin contacts an object, and proprioceptive mechanoreceptors provide signals in measuring muscle, tendon, and joint tension and the position of our limbs (Fuchs et al., 2011a, 2011b, 2011c, 2011d). When the skin goes from rest to operation, a signal is sent to notify the brain, otherwise known as the action potential. The action potential of the membrane must become positive, thus transforming touch stimuli into electrical impulses (Jenkins & Lumpkin, 2017). VR technology transfers the action potential to the computer to accurately simulate the tactile experience of real-world objects.

3 LEVELS OF IMMERSION

With a fundamental understanding of how humans perceive the world through vision, hearing, and touch, the next section will discuss the science behind VR—how it captures those sensory modalities. A measure of good VR needs to capture the feeling of being there (Scarfe & Glennerster, 2019) with great levels of immersion and presence. VR systems can achieve different levels of immersion depending on case-by-case use. When a user views a computer-generated environment on a monitor or TV and proceeds to interact with the VE via a keyboard, mouse, or game controller, the user is interacting with a non-immersive system (Robertson et al., 1993). An example of this would be a video game. Semi-immersive systems provide better immersion compared to non-immersive systems and typically use large-scale projectors, multi-screen displays, and selective headset use, where the user can partially see the real world. Examples of these systems would include Cave Automatic Virtual Environments (CAVE), dome projectors, and AR headsets. The highest level of immersion entirely engulfs a user's FOV within the VE via a head-mounted display (HMD), thus blocking their view from the physical world. This chapter will briefly touch upon the CAVE systems, but it will examine the science of VR through the exploration of HMDs.

3.1 Cave Automatic Virtual Environments

The CAVE is one of the prominent semi-immersive VR systems, first designed at the University of Illinois (Strickland, 2015). The concept behind CAVE was to create a VR system not limited by poor image resolution, shareability with others, and real-world isolation (Gutiérrez et al., 2008a). CAVE systems use projectors to display images on a series of surfaces within a small room, and users can move around the display wearing specialized glasses to enhance the illusion. A singular plane could have several projectors to increase the resolution and widen the field of vision (Gutiérrez et al., 2008b). CAVE room structures generally follow this configuration but can vary in the number of seats, luminous power, and possibility of displaying stereoscopic projections. Stereoscopic projecting works with special eyewear to mimic our binocular viewing. These images are displayed on a singular plane to which the eyeglasses have two liquid crystal screens that shut 50–60 times per second, while the projections display images at 100 hertz. For two projectors of a plane, a liquid crystal screen is situated in front, enabling the light to polarize at varied moments for each pair of stereoscopic projections. The user then views the picture in relief via the two filters on the eyewear. Tracking the head with cameras aids in calculating the images projected, thus allowing the system to sync up with what the user is looking at, as well as what they hear. CAVE system tracking does add a layer of immersion for a singular user; however, it becomes complicated when having to support multiple people at once. As the user orients themself in a CAVE environment, they can simultaneously see the projection as well as their body. The user's vision of their own body and proportion relative to their space is crucial to presence but becomes complicated with HMD, as the vision is completely obscured. CAVE systems thus allow the user to experience the VE at their own scale. It's one of the most recognized semi-immersive large-projection VR systems, but it's also the most costly and difficult to set up and maintain (Fuchs et al., 2011a, 2011b, 2011c, 2011d) and will likely stay off the mainstream market for the everyday consumer.

3.2 Head-Mounted Displays

HMDs provide users with a fully immersive VR experience by completely enclosing the vision from reality. HMDs include one to two screens equipped with either cathode ray tubes (CRT), liquid crystal on silicon, organic light-emitting diodes (OLED), or, most commonly, liquid crystal displays (LCD) technology. Apart from the visual component, HMDs are equipped with speakers or headphones that present the user with localized audio. Localized audio can be emitted based on the head position of a user via tracking sensors or cameras equipped with the HMD systems (Gutiérrez et al., 2008c). While there is an additional set of features that determine an HMD system, these core components comprise its main structure. The following section will examine HMD features in further detail, thus uncovering the scientific underpinnings of VR immersion and presence.

3.3 Crossmodal Sensory Integration

The immersive power and ability for presence in VR isn't just about engaging the visual sense but rather about the collection of the other senses in correlation with each other. This chapter will focus on the crossmodal relationship between the visual, auditory, and tactile senses, particularly in HMDs, and omit the olfactory and taste senses due to the current lack of development in VR. Each modality will be examined in turn, starting with the visual dimension, where stereoscopic displays, eye-tracking technology, latency minimization, geometric spatial calibration, and convergence-accommodation work in tandem to serve as the basis for the visual VR experience. This will be followed up by the auditory sense, where 3D spatial audio and the head-related transfer function (HRTF) will produce a spatially immersive soundscape that syncs up with the user's point of view. The section will close with the discussion of haptic systems and motion tracking technology that aims to enhance the interactive and proprioceptive experience of VR.

3.4 Stereoscopic Displays

The digital screens found in HMDs use a technique from the 19th-century Brewster stereoscope that presents two stereo video images to each eye that are slightly different (Biocca, 1992) and mimics the binocular disparity that allows humans to perceive 3D depth. Stereoscopic vision works when the two eyes, activated by several coordinated muscles, converge on a singular object. Two synthetic images will be created with a slight offset from the point of view of the VE, which the brain merges into one image (Laplante, 2017). In order to achieve stereopsis in the displays, an HMD can use polarization techniques or time-multiplexed 3D displays. For polarization displays, the image on one side would be invisible to the other eye, whereas the imagery from one eye to the other would switch on and off in the time-multiplexed 3D displays, creating a depth perception not capable of 2D digital displays (Lin & Woldegiorgis, 2015). Graphics and resolution must also be considered to achieve a convincing level of immersion. With the current technology, photorealistic ray tracing is possible, making it nearly impossible for a user to distinguish between the virtual and real. Ray tracing, however, is computationally draining and requires a demanding amount of rendering time as the graphics must render two microdisplays in real time while the user moves their gaze around 360°. This is possible in higher-end HMD products but not in the affordable options. There are techniques to save on computational power that will be explored in the eye-tracking section, but the standardized method of real-time rendering has been through rasterization. Rasterization is less computationally demanding, but it can only approximate the physical behavior of light within a scene. An additional aspect of HMD displays is that they typically sit centimeters from the eyes of the user in order to reduce their size and weight. This becomes an issue because any lack of clarity creates the "screen door" effect, where gaps between pixels become visible (Scarfe & Glennerster, 2019). Not to mention, it would not be possible to view the screen being situated only centimeters from the eyes. To address the close positioning of the screens, HMDs are fitted with optical lenses placed between the eyes and the display to correct and magnify the distortions generated by the microdisplays. Optical lenses used in HMDs include aspherical lenses with smooth curves that change across their surface, Fresnel lenses with a composition of concentric rings, and pancake lenses that offer a compact system that uses the folds of polarized light. These are some of the lens options that can be implemented based on specific purposes. In addition to clarity, the microdisplay must simulate our FOV of at least 240°. Methods have been proposed to expand the current HMD systems, including a module of Fresnel lenses and screens, or in the SpareLightVR system, which expands the FOV through an assembly of LEDs and diffusers at the boundaries of the display (Miyashita et al., 2024). An FOV of 270° has been achieved through these methods and others, but the cost and computational power aren't proportional to its merits. Earlier HMD models utilized CRT displays, but modern products use LCD or OLED microdisplays for high resolution, color saturation, and their lightness (Strickland, 2015). Implementing the stereoscopic microdisplays isn't simply about image disparity for our binocular vision but also the consideration of our optic clarity and FOV. However, reaching visual clarity and FOV isn't enough. The illusion of reality also depends on how the VR system stays aligned with the user's head movements because even a minimal delay will break the illusion.

3.4.1 Latency

Any sense of lag we experience when moving our gaze shatters the presence and makes the user feel disconnected from their visual and vestibular system. HMD systems must minimize this lag or latency to avoid this disparity. Commercial HMDs like the Oculus Rift or HTC Vive output 1,080 × 1,200 pixels per eye at 90 hertz, demanding a data transfer of 5.6 billion bits per second (Scarfe & Glennerster, 2019), but the human eye is exceptionally sensitive to latency, where the difference of 7 milliseconds between the movement of their gaze and the system visuals is detectable. If detected, a user will suffer from what is known as VR motion sickness. Any system with a latency rate of more than 15–20 milliseconds (Clay et al., 2019) will cause the user to suffer severe motion sickness. The same goes for a slow frame rate. This is because the user assumes the VE abides by the same rules of reality, so if they turn their head and the visuals even experience the slowest delay, they would likely experience dizziness and nausea. Scarfe and Glennerster illustrate this best with the visual-to-vestibular disparity of being inside a boat. While looking at a scene within the boat, we see a static space, but the vestibular system experiences movement. The reverse occurs in VR, where the eyes detect movement but the body registers delayed movements or even no movement if the user is moving in VR while being stationary in real life (Scarfe & Glennerster, 2019). For body movement like walking or running, designers have explored the use of virtual teleporting, although this doesn't feel natural, or omnidirectional treadmills, which provide locomotion, but they remain underdeveloped and expensive (Clay et al., 2019). As for latency, Scarfe and Glennerster argue that it's possible to reduce lag to 9 milliseconds in a 60-hertz HMD by taking measurements of the user's pose from the tracking devices at the last moments before the image is displayed (Scarfe & Glennerster, 2019).

3.4.2 Eye Tracking

Human vision can be categorized by fixation and gaze, where fixation remains at the eye at one point of interest, and gaze is the shifting of eyes from target to target (Kowler, 2011). To track the movement of the eyes, many modern VR HMDs rely on video or sensor-based systems. The video-based eye tracking systems integrate noninvasive cameras with high sampling rates, approximately around 2,000 hertz, and an accuracy of 0.15° (Stein et al., 2021). A common method, the Pupil Center Corneal Reflection, directs near-infrared light toward the cornea of the eye, creating reflections that cameras can track to calculate the eye's sight line (Punde et al., 2017). Specialized techniques such as electro-oculography (EOG), scleral search coils, and video-oculography (VOG) exist to provide designers with benefits but also challenges depending on the case use (Adhanom et al., 2023). Adhanom et al. describe how EOG is the only method that allows tracking while the eyes are closed. As a result, the method is less precise because it measures based on positioning electrodes on the surrounding eyeball skin. Scleral search coils track movement through an embedded wire loop found within the contact lens donned by the user. This method is highly precise with a spatial resolution of 0.1° and a temporal resolution greater than 1 kilohertz, because the coils generate a magnetic field based on the head's position. VOG is the most common method, like PCCR, that relies on identifying the shape of the pupil via cameras attached within the HMD. Before running the simulation, the HMD will probe the user to calibrate their eyes to capture the baseline of the eye position. HMDs will calibrate eye tracking through a procedure that shows a series of small points to the user and then asks the user to fixate on each target successively for a couple of seconds. From this, the system can discover a mapping function that aligns the coordinates of the tracked eye to the gaze position in the VE (Adhanom et al., 2023). This tracking requires, however, high computational output and could increase the system latency. In addition, the high-resolution output for 360° would require high demands on an HMD. A technique in eye tracking, recognized as foveated rendering, focuses the computing resources on the foveal region of the visual field and reduces the resolution in the peripheries (Wang et al., 2023). Only for 1°–2° of our central vision do we see imagery in sharp detail; therefore, reducing the workload by cutting back on pixels in our periphery maintains a realistic experience and reduces the latency in an HMD, preserving the illusion of reality.

3.4.3 Convergence and Accommodation

A minor challenge in VR associated with 3D depth perception is the vergence-accommodation conflict. In real life, our binocular vision rotates toward the targeted object, ensuring it falls on the retina (Wang et al., 2025). This would be the process of convergence. While this is happening, our eyes proceed to change shape to guarantee the projected light is sharp accommodation (Wang et al., 2025). For instance, if you were to place yourself roughly 1 meter from an object, place your finger in front of the object, and proceed to move it closer to the object than closer to your eye, the clarity of the object will change, enabling 3D depth perception. Static objects in a still scene will also appear blurrier depending on the distance from the targeted object. VR headsets, however, display the stereoscopic microdisplays at a fixed distance (Wang et al., 2025). While wearing an HMD, the eyes accommodate to a fixed distance, and the discrepancy between the vergence and accommodation interferes with synchronization between the two (Wang et al., 2025). VR systems would make up for this by filtering the convergence-accommodation blur for blur uniformity (Lanman, 2020). Douglas Lanman, director of Display Systems at Facebook Reality Labs, depicts a working solution using a series of electronic varifocal lenses. He describes the module to be a series of six crystal lenses that can be programmed to adjust the focal length. The lenses electronically modify the light-directing characteristics so the eyes can intrinsically focus on an object's 3D depth. This method, however, didn't include eye-tracking technology (Lanman, 2020). With many of the visual and 3D depth cues established, the final step toward the visual illusion of reality would be to align the user to their adjacent space via spatial calibration.

3.4.4 Spatial Calibration

Calibrating the geometry and perspective of our space is critical for the proprioceptive experience of the VR simulation. Calibrating not only the FOV but also the camera, scale, and height should be done to ensure the user can correctly judge distances in VR (Kellner et al., 2012). Mentioned by Kelner et al., many researchers depend on psychophysical calibration methods where users compare the virtual elements with the real-world counterparts. Users were asked to locate and identify virtual markers, allowing the VR system to approximate the angular difference between the proprioceptive outputs and visual indicators. On the more intuitive spectrum, Meta Quest 2 instructs users to calibrate their setup by asking the person to lower the input device or hand controllers to the floor until a virtual grid appears (Meta Quest, 2021). Once the height of the user has been calibrated, the user will then be guided to draw a play boundary with the controller using the pass-through function that lets the person see the real world while covered by the headset. This play boundary notifies the VR system if the user steps outside of the specified space. With the height and boundaries now set up, the user can proceed to visually immerse themselves within the VE.

3.5 3D Spatial Audio

The auditory aspect of VR complements the visual sense with 3D, localized sounds that can be viewed within 360°. 3D spatial audio in VR provides the user with sound cues originating from sources that the HMD would update in real time (Kim et al., 2019). These cues would include the inter-aural time difference, interaural level difference, timbre difference, motion parallax, and reverberation of a sound. To generate 3D audio, techniques such as multichannel audio systems, sound rendering 3D models, and HRTFs are used to achieve this effect (Kim et al., 2019).

3.5.1 Head-Related Transfer Function

HRTFs capture all parameters and sync up the visuals to the audio. This isn't about emulating the physical results of a sound but rather a simulation through the control of the sound cue parameters. For instance, the inter-aural level difference would be controlled from one headphone to the other based on the source of the sound. These sounds can be output in standard headphones, but they need to be hardcoded in real time to display the mono-sound sources in 3D spatial audio (Berger et al., 2018). If the sounds are to be processed in the headphones using an accelerometer, the audio could adjust based on the motion of the head. For this purpose, HRTFs can be generic or individualized (Berger et al., 2018). A generic HRTF is calculated based on average measurements of the head, ear, and torso, thus estimating the sounds for a typical human. While generic HRTFs are easier and cheaper to implement, an individualized HRTF is measured for the specific user, therefore providing highly precise audio output. HRTFs, however, don't account for all of the listed sound cues. Reverberation and its sound propagation are added separately through a room-acoustic simulation engine. For a particular surface, the reverberation can be calculated by applying a filter to where the system either uses the numerical or geometric method to capture its sound propagation (Kim et al., 2019). With this cross-modal interaction between the visuals and audio through the HRTF, the level of immersion and presence will increase. The next layer of touch will solidify the interactivity and proprioception that the user will feel toward the VR simulation.

3.6 Haptic Systems

Touch remains an essential facet for environmental presence and relies on technologies unrelated to the HMD. Technologies such as haptic gloves—CyberGrasp™, Dexmo™, and HaptX—and full-body haptic suits have been integrated to supplement the VR experience with tactile and kinesthetic subject matter (Crofton et al., 2019). How do these suits simulate the feeling of touch in the virtual space if the user isn't touching anything in the real world? As mentioned previously, the skin contains a series of receptors that detect sensations of pain, thermal changes, pressure, vibration, texture, muscle, joint, and tendon tension (Fuchs et al., 2011a, 2011b, 2011c, 2011d). VR haptic systems replicate these feedback mechanisms through tactile sensing devices and force sensors. Described by Tao et al., tactile sensors simulate the function of physical contact between the skin and environment with an option of sensing mechanisms known as piezoresistive sensors, piezoelectric sensors, and triboelectric sensors (Tao et al., 2022). Piezoresistive haptic sensors utilize the transformed resistance in mechanical stimuli, while piezoelectric sensors generate an electric field due to disparity in the stimuli. Triboelectric sensors operate through electrostatic induction, transmuting low-frequency mechanical stimuli into electrical transmissions (Tao et al., 2022). Designers can implement these sensors in devices such as haptic gloves and even touch screens, enabling the user to interact directly with the VE. Therefore, the input force and even sliding trajectory (Bai et al., 2020) can be precisely measured in the touchscreens with force sensors that convert force input into electrical signals (Shi & Shen, 2024), where signals are logged as 0 seconds and 1 second to represent the contact (Tao et al., 2022). Haptic technology, however, isn't just about registering user input but also the mechanical feedback that provides users with an output of sensations. A common method for output is mechanical vibration feedback, which utilizes pneumatic and magnetic actuators to provoke vibration-sensitive receptors found in the skin (Shi & Shen, 2024). Pneumatic actuators depend on the expansion and contraction of air in a soft membrane, leading to a vibration stimulus. On the adverse, magnetic actuators offer designers a fast and controlled flexible approach that relies on the vibration of mini motors to produce sensations of objects moving on the skin. The mechanical vibration feedback approach provides a wide range of controllable frequencies but falters as it brings nonconformal contact touch to the skin (Shi & Shen, 2024). Another option is electrotactile (ET) feedback, which takes advantage of the nervous system's communication strategies through bioelectricity, provoking tactile receptors in the skin with electrical currents. ET devices are manufactured with groupings of anodes and cathodes that generate an electrical current under the skin, making them beneficial for high spatial resolution on a smaller scale. At the same time, differences in skin between individuals can alter the current and make it challenging to get uniform outputs. A third alternative approach, dielectric elastomer actuators, places the elastomer actuators between two compliant electrodes and compresses, thus pushing against the skin when there's a voltage (Shi & Shen, 2024). When implementing these mechanisms back into the haptic gloves and full-body suits, the actuators are scaled up in arrays across the arms, legs, and torso so that the user can feel the simulated tactile sensations. The next leap in VR tactility comes with tracking the motions and input to inform the VR system how the user interacts with the VE.

3.7 Motion Tracking

A new wave of tactical innovation was prompted when VR systems began to track the physical movements of a user and began to translate them in the VE. Innovations such as Zhu et al.'s exoskeleton manipulator capture the arm and finger movements with bidirectional triboelectric sensors and transmit them into a robotic arm or in the VE (Zhu et al., 2021). Motion tracking can be done through inside-out tracking or outside-in tracking. Outside-in tracking uses external sensors or cameras placed in the surrounding space to track the motion of the VR headset and controllers. In contrast, the more commonly used inside-out tracking method involves sensors or cameras placed inside the HMD. Inside-out trackers need to be small enough to fit within the HMD and in the haptic gloves. The emergence of depth cameras, which can be found in Microsoft's Kinect, allows for motion tracking without necessitating markers (Li et al., 2025). The Kinect device mapped the contours and depth of objects and spaces with precision using infrared technology.

4 CONCLUSION

The future for VR remains unprecedented, like most technologies. Will it ever achieve a level of presence and immersion undiscernible from reality or has the field already hit this milestone? It's undeniable that in order to achieve this goal, the technology will need to take steps toward cross-modal sensory integration and not just of the visual, auditory, and tactile but also of the taste and smell senses. It was only through its scientific foundations that VR has been able to become an extension of our reality. Scientific principles such as stereoscopic displays, latency minimization, eye tracking, spatial calibration, and convergence-accommodation for visuals, 3D spatial audio, and HRTFs to sync localized sound cues to the visuals and enhance the proprioceptive experience through haptic suits and motion tracking technology. The science behind VR reveals how technology can engage and simulate our sensory systems, broadening its impact for other fields to come.

REFERENCES

Adhanom, I. B., MacNeilage, P., & Folmer, E. (2023). Eye tracking in virtual reality: A broad review of applications and challenges. *Virtual Reality, 27*(2), 1481–1505. https://doi.org/10.1007/s10055-022-00738-z

Bai, N., Wang, L., Wang, Q., Deng, J., Wang, Y., Lu, P., Huang, J., Li, G., Zhang, Y., Yang, J., Xie, K., Zhao, X., & Guo, C. F. (2020). Graded intrafillable architecture-based iontronic pressure sensor with ultra-broad-range high sensitivity. *Nature Communications, 11*(1), 209. https://doi.org/10.1038/s41467-019-14054-9

Berger, C. C., Gonzalez-Franco, M., Tajadura-Jiménez, A., Florencio, D., & Zhang, Z. (2018). Generic HRTFs may be good enough in virtual reality. Improving source localization through cross-modal plasticity. *Frontiers in Neuroscience, 12*, 21. https://doi.org/10.3389/fnins.2018.00021

Biocca, F. (1992). Virtual reality technology: A tutorial. *Journal of Communication, 42*(4), 23–72. https://doi.org/10.1111/j.1460-2466.1992.tb00811.x

Clay, V., König, P., & König, S. (2019). Eye tracking in virtual reality. *Journal of Eye Movement Research, 12*(1), 1–18. https://doi.org/10.16910/jemr.12.1.3

Crofton, E. C., Botinestean, C., Fenelon, M., & Gallagher, E. (2019). Potential applications for virtual and augmented reality technologies in sensory science. *Innovative Food Science & Emerging Technologies, 56*, 102178. https://doi.org/10.1016/j.ifset.2019.102178

Deed, M. (Director). (2024, December 14). *Spatial Audio for VR and AR* [Video recording]. https://www.youtube.com/watch?v=4lOIRVFM9z4&ab_channel=MikeDeeds

eScience Lectures Notes: Human Sight: Depth Cues vs Stereoscopy. (n.d.). Retrieved 5 September 2025, from https://www.vrarchitect.net/anu/ivr/sight/printCG.en.html

Fuchs, P., Moreau, G., & Guitton, P. (Eds.). (2011a). Human senses. In *Virtual Reality: Concepts and Technologies.* CRC Press.

Fuchs, P., Moreau, G., & Guitton, P. (Eds.). (2011b). Introduction to virtual reality. In *Virtual Reality: Concepts and Technologies.* CRC Press.

Fuchs, P., Moreau, G., & Guitton, P. (Eds.). (2011c). *Virtual reality: Concepts and technologies.* CRC Press. https://doi.org/10.1201/b11612

Fuchs, P., Moreau, G., & Guitton, P. (Eds.). (2011d). Visual interfaces. In *Virtual Reality: Concepts and Technologies.* CRC Press.

Gonzalez, F., & Perez, R. (1998). Neural mechanisms underlying stereoscopic vision. *Progress in Neurobiology, 55*(3), 191–224. https://doi.org/10.1016/S0301-0082(98)00012-4

Gutiérrez, M. A. A., Vexo, F., & Thalmann, D. (Eds.). (2008a). Audition. In *Stepping into Virtual Reality* (pp. 139–146). Springer. https://doi.org/10.1007/978-1-84800-117-6_8

Gutiérrez, M. A. A., Vexo, F., & Thalmann, D. (Eds.). (2008b). Touch. In *Stepping into Virtual Reality* (pp. 147–155). Springer. https://doi.org/10.1007/978-1-84800-117-6_9

Gutiérrez, M. A. A., Vexo, F., & Thalmann, D. (Eds.). (2008c). Vision. In *Stepping into Virtual Reality* (pp. 125–137). Springer. https://doi.org/10.1007/978-1-84800-117-6_7

Huff, T., Mahabadi, N., & Tadi, P. (Eds.). (2025). Neuroanatomy, Visual Cortex. In *StatPearls.* StatPearls Publishing. https://www.ncbi.nlm.nih.gov/books/NBK482504/

Jenkins, B. A., & Lumpkin, E. A. (2017). Developing a sense of touch. *Development (Cambridge, England), 144*(22), 4078–4090. https://doi.org/10.1242/dev.120402

Kellner, F., Bolte, B., Bruder, G., Rautenberg, U., Steinicke, F., Lappe, M., & Koch, R. (2012). Geometric calibration of head-mounted displays and its effects on distance estimation. *IEEE Transactions on Visualization and Computer Graphics, 18*(4), 589–596. https://doi.org/10.1109/TVCG.2012.45

Kim, E., Yun, J., Chung, W., Kim, Y., Kim, C. G., & Park, W.-C. (2019). *A Study of Realistic 3D Sound Rendering Using Sound Tracing for Mobile Virtual Reality.*

Kim, G., & Biocca, F. (2018). Immersion in virtual reality can increase exercise motivation and physical performance. *Virtual, Augmented and Mixed Reality: Applications in Health, Cultural Heritage, and Industry,* 94–102. https://doi.org/10.1007/978-3-319-91584-5_8

Kowler, E. (2011). Eye movements: The past 25 years. *Vision Research, 51*(13), 1457–1483. https://doi.org/10.1016/j.visres.2010.12.014

Lanman, D. (Director). (2020, January 26). *EI 2020 Plenary: Quality Screen Time: Leveraging Computational Displays for Spatial Computing* [Video recording]. https://www.youtube.com/watch?v=LQwMAl9bGNY&ab_channel=IS%26 TElectronicImaging%28EI%29Symposium

Laplante, P. A. (Ed.). (2017). *Encyclopedia of Computer Science and Technology* (2nd ed.). CRC Press. https://doi.org/10.1081/E-ECST

Li, X., Fan, D., Feng, J., Lei, Y., Cheng, C., & Li, X. (2025). Systematic review of motion capture in virtual reality: Enhancing the precision of sports training. *Journal of Ambient Intelligence and Smart Environments, 17*(1), 5–27. https://doi.org/10.3233/AIS-230198

Lin, C. J., & Woldegiorgis, B. H. (2015). Interaction and visual performance in stereoscopic displays: A review. *Journal of the Society for Information Display, 23*(7), 319–332. https://doi.org/10.1002/jsid.378

Malpica, S., Serrano, A., Allue, M., Bedia, M. G., & Masia, B. (2020). Crossmodal perception in virtual reality. *Multimedia Tools and Applications, 79*(5–6), 3311–3331. https://doi.org/10.1007/s11042-019-7331-z

Meta Quest (Director). (2021, November 13). *Quest 2 Setting Up Guardian* [Video recording]. https://www.youtube.com/watch?v=GojevL05Avw&ab_channel=MetaQuest

Miyashita, Y., Harasawa, M., Hara, K., Sawahata, Y., & Komine, K. (2024). Estimation of horizontal spatial specifications for ideal head-mounted displays in practical conditions. *Frontiers in Virtual Reality, 5.* https://doi.org/10.3389/frvir.2024.1485243

Punde, P. A., Jadhav, M. E., & Manza, R. R. (2017). A study of eye tracking technology and its applications. *2017 1st International Conference on Intelligent Systems and Information Management (ICISIM)*, 86–90. https://doi.org/10.1109/ICISIM.2017.8122153

Robertson, G. G., Card, S. K., & Mackinlay, J. D. (1993). Three views of virtual reality: Nonimmersive virtual reality. *Computer, 26*(2), 81. https://doi.org/10.1109/2.192002

Scarfe, P., & Glennerster, A. (2019). The science behind virtual reality displays. *Annual Review of Vision Science, 5*, 529–547. https://doi.org/10.1146/annurev-vision-091718-014942

Shi, Y., & Shen, G. (2024). Haptic sensing and feedback techniques toward virtual reality. *Research, 7*, 333. https://doi.org/10.34133/research.0333

Slater, M. (2018). Immersion and the illusion of presence in virtual reality. *British Journal of Psychology, 109*(3), 431–433. https://doi.org/10.1111/bjop.12305

Smith, A. T. (2015). Binocular vision: Joining up the eyes. *Current Biology, 25*(15), R661–R663. https://doi.org/10.1016/j.cub.2015.06.013

Stein, N., Niehorster, D. C., Watson, T., Steinicke, F., Rifai, K., Wahl, S., & Lappe, M. (2021). A Comparison of eye tracking latencies among several commercial head-mounted displays. *I-Perception, 12*(1), 2041669520983338. https://doi.org/10.1177/2041669520983338

Strickland, J. (2015). *Virtual Reality Immersion.* HowStuffWorks. https://electronics.howstuffworks.com/gadgets/other-gadgets/virtual-reality.htm

Tao, K., Chen, Z., Yu, J., Zeng, H., Wu, J., Wu, Z., Jia, Q., Li, P., Fu, Y., Chang, H., & Yuan, W. (2022). Ultra-sensitive, deformable, and transparent triboelectric tactile sensor based on micro-pyramid patterned ionic hydrogel for interactive human–machine interfaces. *Advanced Science, 9*(10), 2104168. https://doi.org/10.1002/advs.202104168

Tortora, G., & Nielsen, M. (2010). *Principles of Human Anatomy* (12th ed.). John Wiley & Sons, Inc.

van Hateren, J., & Lamb, T. (2006). The photocurrent response of human cones is fast and monophasic. *BMC Neuroscience, 7*(1), 34. https://doi.org/10.1186/1471-2202-7-34

Wang, L., Shi, X., & Liu, Y. (2023). Foveated rendering: A state-of-the-art survey. *Computational Visual Media, 9*(2), 195–228. https://doi.org/10.1007/s41095-022-0306-4

Wang, X. M., Prenevost, M., Tarun, A., Robinson, I., Nitsche, M., Resch, G., Mazalek, A., & Welsh, T. N. (2025). *Investigating A Geometrical Solution to the Vergence-Accommodation Conflict for Targeted Movements in Virtual Reality* (Version 1). arXiv. https://doi.org/10.48550/ARXIV.2505.23310

Zhu, M., Sun, Z., Chen, T., & Lee, C. (2021). Low cost exoskeleton manipulator using bidirectional triboelectric sensors enhanced multiple degree of freedom sensory system. *Nature Communications, 12*(1), 2692. https://doi.org/10.1038/s41467-021-23020-3

CHAPTER 6

Tools and Technologies for Virtual Content Creation

Wael Brahim

1 FROM WIREFRAMES TO PHOTOREALISM: A HISTORICAL COMPRESSION

The early years of the 2000s witnessed a modest but challenging experiment: my attempt to render a simple colored cube using C++ and OpenGL (The OpenGL Architecture Review Board, 1997). Back then, OpenGL was known as the first free cross-platform library that created 2D/3D visuals on the GPU side. This process demanded hundreds of carefully arranged lines of code. Each vertex must be placed with precision. Every transformation matrix must be applied with extreme care. Having a theoretical/technical knowledge of computer vision is key to catch the code logic. The process of compiling complex code without errors felt like a quiet victory. Not to mention, the very few resources and supports that can help with debugging. It was common to be lost for hours or even days trying to figure out an error or to implement an uncharted task.

Today, the same result can be produced within milliseconds. Engines and visual frameworks automate behind a "beginner-friendly interface" what once required hours of concentration. This democratization of tools represents progress, but it also raises a question. If the struggle

DOI: 10.1201/9781003673538-6

with code was part of a learning curve, does the absence of the same struggle decrease the "depth" and the "quality" of our future digital creators' skills?

This section aims to map the path, from those modest beginnings (spinning cube), all the way to the high-poly real-time environment. This is not only a history of techniques. Instead, it is also an examination of the consequences: what has been gained and what may have been lost.

1.1 Early Wireframe Prototypes and Rasterization Limits

If we examine the first attempts at three-dimensional visualization, we can notice that wireframe models were not an aesthetic choice. It was an imposed condition by the existing technology of that time. The very few RAM bytes made filled polygons impossible to handle. What later appeared as minimalism was in fact a survival strategy to render. Each vertex on screen carried a cost. Every polygon added to the scene was a wager that risked slowing performance to a crash. The success of the test depended on a fine balance between your restraint, as a designer, and your machine capacity.

Rasterization pipelines during that period offered limited tolerance to errors. Hardware accelerators were absent or primitive. Creators were compelled to cultivate a discipline where no line was casual and no transformation was arbitrary. Figure 6.1 shows this progress of moving through distinct modes of representation.

As a digital creator, beginning with wireframe mode was never a simple viewport habit. It was a way to comprehend geometry and try to imagine what the final result would be before investing rare and valuable resources in surface or texture.

In a present where abundant GPU power has enabled almost "unrestricted" three-dimensional visualization, many practitioners can now enter directly into material and real-time rendered views, bypassing the skeletal stage altogether.

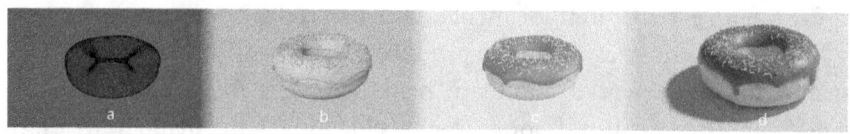

FIGURE 6.1 Wireframe to Realism: Donut (a: Wireframe Mode, b: Solid Mode, c: Material Mode, d: Rendered Mode).

Source: Personal project on Blender.

1.2 The Shift to Physically Based Rendering in 3D Engines

After decades of fake shading, the appearance of a realistic surface that reacts naturally to light revealed the limitations of earlier techniques. This "guesswork" of artistic estimation was replaced by a framework rooted in the physics of light. The arrival of physically based rendering (PBR) was a transformative moment in real-time graphics (Tuliniemi, 2018).

As stated previously, these old shading techniques, such as Phong (1975) and Blinn-Phong (1977), had relied heavily on visual intuition. Surface irregularities were adjusted until they looked somewhat convincing. But these illusions often faltered when the light conditions changed. By contrast, PBR draws from microfacet theory (Pharr et al., 2016). It uses physically measurable parameters, including Albedo, Metallicity, Smoothness, and Roughness. A copper pipe rendered under this model (**Albedo:** R ≈ 0.95, G ≈ 0.64, B ≈ 0.54; **Metallic**: 1.0; **Smoothness**: 0.9 [≈ Roughness 0.1]) retains the quality of copper regardless of illumination conditions (single lamp vs full HDR sky). This is possible because the illumination simulation is guided by the optical properties of the material itself.

This achievement brought both freedom and responsibility. Realism could now be achieved without the frustrating labor of manual tweaking. But this new system called for a richer awareness of how materials interact with their surroundings and to changing light. It was no longer sufficient to adjust a texture until it appeared correctly in one frame. Assets now had to stay consistent and coherent across a wide range of natural conditions, and it is the responsibility of the artist to ensure that. Figure 6.2 compares the Blinn-Phong shading model with PBR, highlighting their visual characteristics.

FIGURE 6.2   Visual Comparison of Blinn-Phong and PBR.

Source: Personal project on Blender.

1.3 The Rise of Real-time Global Illumination and Ray Tracing

"Lighting is the paintbrush of cinematography, it can set the mood and evoke emotions like nothing else" (Bookey, n.d.). These words from Roger Deakins (one of the most influential cinematographers of contemporary cinema) highlight that lighting is not a "mere" technical procedure but an opportunity to strengthen emotional resonance and narrative depth.

Similarly, lighting has long been the invisible architect of immersion in virtual environments. In the early stages of digital environments, scenes depended on static solutions: lighting baked into textures through this intensive calculation procedure called "Offline rendering". This procedure could demand hours or even days of intensive processing. The outcome can be "frustrating" if the resulting frame (fixed and immutable) was incorrect, as the digital creator needs to adjust and "rebake" the whole scene. Therefore, the emergence of real-time global illumination was a "blessing" for digital creators as now light could bounce, scatter, and shift hue and more importantly could be checked in real time which echoed natural behavior and ease of use (Christensen, 1997).

Global illumination models compute indirect light (light that reflects from surrounding surfaces), creating richness and realism. In immersive environments such as virtual reality, these subtle variations become critical. The human visual system uses changing light as a cue for special coherence (Gutteling et al., 2015). Without such visual feedback, even the most detailed objects risk appearing static and lifeless. In the scene without global illumination, the image seems "flat" and "boring". With GI activated, the dynamic interaction of the lights between neighboring surfaces subtles color bleeding and enriches shadowed regions. This moves the experience from a mere visibility to "convincing" realism.

Ray Tracing extends the pursuit of realism by directly simulating the physical paths of light within a scene (Gangar, 2024). Traditional rasterization techniques rely on acceptable approximations to mimic such effects. Reflection probes, shadow maps, transformation matrices, and screen-space conversions can provide very convincing results. But these techniques often collapse under unusual viewing angles or complex lighting conditions. Here, Ray Tracing comes to the rescue. It produces crisp reflections and soft shadows and elevates natural phenomena such as caustics and color bleeding. The outcome is imagery that borders on photorealism. The version rendered with Ray Tracing demonstrates natural light distribution and a striking fidelity to real-world optics. But, of course, this improvement comes at a "confusing" cost. Virtual reality systems, already constrained by the famous "90 Hz or higher" threshold, struggle to integrate Ray Tracing without performance penalty. Even with hardware acceleration, most practical workflows adopt hybrid strategies. Rasterization carries rendering, while Ray Tracing is applied selectively to critical elements (shadows, reflections, or refractions). This tension exposes a more profound design dilemma. The essential question has shifted. The issue is no longer whether the frame can be rendered, but whether it can be rendered in a manner that preserves the "artistic intention" and the "well-being of the user".

2 NEXT-GEN ENGINE ARCHITECTURE

Imagine building an immersive scene where every element is set by hand: 3D models created at the vertex level, PBR coded and adjusted manually, GI and Ray Tracing scripted from scratch. Of course, this is possible, but exhausting. That is why we, content creators, consider the rendering engine as the heartbeat of the whole process. It brings speed, flexibility, ease, portability, and accuracy. It decides how real a world can feel. Early engines were rigid systems, specialized in limited tasks and very constrained. But now, they have matured into modular frameworks. They gather asset management, physics, animation, rendering, and scripting in one single place. These cohesive ecosystems also support multi-disciplinary projects (cinematic storytelling, large-scale simulations, entertainment, virtual reality, etc.). And in the VR context, the choice of the engine's architecture is an even crucial decision, because it can make the difference between "immersion" and "discomfort".

2.1 Rendering Pipelines: Forward+, Deferred, and Hybrid Approaches in VR

Deep in the project settings of your favorite engine, the rendering options appear. Forward. Deferred, Forward+ – the terms seem straightforward, but which one to choose? Forward suggests simplicity, while deferred promises flexibility with lighting. Hybrid seeks to balance the two. The decision is not trivial. It can shape performance, image quality, and even user comfort.

Early forward rendering pipelines are simple: each object is drawn once per light that affects it. So, lighting is calculated during the geometry pass. This approach proved effective for small scenes. However, this technique can struggle with multiple lights (more than four real-time dynamic lights) and the hardware can quickly saturate. Here where deferred rendering came to the rescue. The idea is to separate geometry and lighting into distinct passes (Deering et al., 1988). Geometry is rendered once into multiple buffers (G-buffer: normal, albedo, depth, etc.). And then, lighting is applied as a second pass using this data. This approach is clearly more efficient in handling multiple dynamic lights (supports 100+ dynamic lights). But it introduced other issues related to handling transparency, "appetite" for memory consumption (expensive for VR because you need to fill the G-buffer twice [once per eye]).

Forward+ (Harada et al., 2012) and clustered shading (Olsson et al., 2012) extended traditional pipelines with methods that split space into tiles or clusters. Like forward rendering but divides the screen into a grid or clusters. Each cluster only considers the lights affecting it, reducing per-object lighting cost. More efficient than classic forward in VR and AR, where performance is critical when you have multiple lights (can handle 1,000–4,000 lights). Oculus (Meta) makes its stance clear: deferred rendering is not recommended on mobile VR devices such as the Quest. The reason is simple: resolve operations are costly, and memory usage quickly becomes a "bottleneck". Their guidelines point developers toward forward rendering, which remains, according to Meta, the safer choice for stable performance (Dasch, 2019). At the same time, Forward+ is highlighted as a path with potential when the target is a virtual reality and augmented reality desktop with multiple dynamic lights.

2.2 Advanced Physics: Soft-Body, Fluid, and Cloth Simulations in Immersive Environments

The rendering pipeline is not the only layer that can positively or negatively impact the believability of your immersive experience. The accurate simulation of physics is as important when it comes to realism. Immersivity has moved from a static wireframe cube through the lens of "Sword of Damocles" of Ivan Sutherland (Sutherland, 1968), often referred to as the "parent of virtual reality", to a set of impressive systems capable of modeling elastic deformation, fabric motion, and realistic fluid interaction in real time.

Within Blender, for example, creators can rely on the Soft Body Modifier (Blender Foundation, 2025a) and the Cloth Physics system (Blender Foundation, 2024a). Both systems deploy thousands of vertex-based models to approach natural deformations. Unity offers similar capabilities through Obi Softbody and Obi Cloth (Virtual Method Studio, 2019). Unreal Engine, Chaos Physics, and Nvidia Flex, all combined, can simulate elastic materials and multiphase fluids. The result is so spot on that it can compete with the "Offline Rendering" level (Epic Games, 2025a).

In immersive contexts, the result can be powerful. A cushion that yields beneath a fingertip, or cloth that ripples with "convincing" weight, intensifies the illusion. At the same time, such realism is costly. In other words, the value of these advanced physics should serve the experience, not the realism.

2.3 Performance Profiling

Syntax errors at the compilation phase are not the worst. Logic errors and misconceptions are far worse, especially those related to performance. Debugging these can be really challenging and require patience and perseverance. It does not matter how immersive the graphics or intelligent the non-player characters (NPCs) are. Lag or poor interaction design can quickly destroy the illusion. Fortunately, developers have powerful tools to analyze, optimize, and adapt experiences. A live example comes from Unity's 2025 extended reality (XR) Performance Toolkit. This tool allows developers targeting multiple hardware simulations. After checking, the toolkit suggests upgrades that preserve quality and performance (90+ FPS). In one documented case, Nsight was able to flag redundant post-processing passes, which increased render time by an impressive 35% (Meta Horizon, 2024). Still, these tools cannot replace meticulous hands-on testing. Instead, the best option is to adopt a hybrid approach. Developers should mix metrics with real-user trials.

2.4 Telemetry-Driven Interaction Design

One remarkable aspect of next-gen engines is the use of data-driven strategies to increase performance and accessibility. Tobii Pro VR Analytics, Unreal Insights, and VR Interaction Logger are performance-checker tools that track gaze and hand motion at unprecedented precision. The main goal is simple: helping developers optimize the placement of interactive elements (Tobii, 2025; Epic Games, 2025f). In the same context, Chen and Hou (2022) presented a verified approach. The authors explored gaze-based interaction intention recognition in VR. The system uses data-driven decisions (gaze data) to adapt menus and interaction elements for faster and more intuitive navigation.

3 HIGH-END SOFTWARE ECOSYSTEM

"Diversification is protection against ignorance", Buffett said (Town, 2025). Keeping an eye on each platform's latest innovations can accelerate the workflow, enhance realism, and even open new creative avenues. What follows is a quick overview of what is new with four giants of the virtual creation industry: Blender, Maya, Unity, and Unreal Engine.

3.1 Blender: Procedural Workflows, Geometry Nodes, and VR Scene Inspection

Blender's open-source foundation has long made it a central tool in the 3D community, and the release of version 4.5 demonstrates both its maturity and its ongoing experimentation. This version introduces some artificial intelligence (AI)-assisted features like sculpting and procedural material generation. The intent is to enable artists produce detailed textures and complex models with minimum effort (Sahu, 2024). Cumbersome processes like retopology, UV unwrapping, texture baking, are now partially automated.

The updates integrate Vulkan for faster viewport performance and GPU subdivision. Also, the Geometry Nodes is now more modular and easier to work with (Blender Foundation, 2024b). The EEVEE renderer has improved as well (Blender Foundation, 2025b). A VR developer can visualize their model in VR during the modeling phase. But the gap between preview quality and final renders remains a concern (for those working at cinematic standards). In practice, the system works best for iteration and early validation.

For experienced users, these developments provide valuable tools. For newcomers, however, the abundance of options can be very overwhelming (ThreeDee, 2024).

3.2 Maya: Rigging Automation, Predictive Animation, and Scene Optimization

Another giant of the digital industry is Autodesk Maya. According to Zhang (2024), Maya stands as the industry standard for high-end animation (more particularly when rigging and motion capture are involved). Over the last five years, we have seen how AI is being gradually integrated into many established professional software, and Maya is no exception. For example, predictive animation (Autodesk Media & Entertainment, 2025) and auto-rigging (Autodesk, 2025) are rich research areas where AI can help. These two AI features are already integrated into the latest versions of Maya. This can save hours on complex sequences. Artists can finally focus on refining content instead of wasting time on repetitive labor.

Another important update on the platform is portability. For studios managing complex multi-DCC (Digital Content Creation) workflows, seamless interchange between software is genuinely "liberating". In a typical production pipeline, an asset team might deliver a high-poly spaceship mesh directly from Blender. Then ingest it into Houdini for rigid-body destruction passes and particle FX. Those USD (Universal Scene Description) layers can be non-destructively referenced back into Maya, where supervisors handle shot layout, camera blocking, and animation timing. Finally, the assembled USD scene can be handed off to Unreal Engine for real-time look-dev, ray-traced lighting, and final cinematic renders.

The trade-offs, however, are clear and usually related to the business model of Autodesk. Maya is resource-intensive and financially costly (RocketBrush, 2025). Its subscription-based licensing costs approximately $1,700–$1,800 per year (Juego Studio, 2025). These can be barriers in front of independent creators and smaller studios.

3.3 Unity: XR Interaction Toolkit, Data-Oriented Technology Stack for Performance, and Shader Graph for VR

Unity's dominant strength was its portability and accessibility, which particularly benefited individual creators and small teams. In light of recent policy changes, the accessibility of Unity has shifted. According to a Polygon report (2024), Unity's retracted runtime fee and subsequent price hikes led "some developers" to move toward platforms like Godot, reflecting concerns over unpredictable licensing costs and trust issues. In practice, Unity remains a powerful and flexible environment. The AI Game Designer module introduces automated support for level design, asset placement, and even gameplay mechanics. Also, the new Data-Oriented Technology Stack allows the engine to handle complex simulations (Unity Technologies, 2024).

For immersive media, Unity's Shader Graph removed technical barriers, for "non-programmer" profiles, to produce visually compelling effects (Unity Technologies, 2025a). Meta's Block system (Meta, 2024) adds another "user-friendly" option, allowing drag-and-drop assembly of prebuilt interactive elements. It provides an effective bridge between rapid prototyping and functional design.

Collaboration has also become a defining part of Unity's ecosystem. Unity Reflect Live (Unity Technologies, 2019) supports multi-user review of scenes across devices, removing geographic barriers.

The same flexibility that makes Unity appealing can also be a pitfall. Large scenes with a VR or AR layer can easily break. Developers, in this case, must adopt a modular approach: content broken into smaller sections, unit testing, and carefully assembled.

3.4 Unreal Engine: Nanite for VR, Lumen Lighting, and Live Link for Real-time Animation

Unreal Engine continues to set the pace for real-time graphics. It is ambitious. It is heavy. And it is still the benchmark against which others are measured. Nanite 2.0 manages dense geometry with surprising efficiency (Epic Games, 2025b). Lumen calculates illumination in real time, letting scenes shift and adapt to changing conditions (Epic Games, 2025c). Live Link feeds motion capture straight into the engine, synchronizing animation with little friction (Epic Games, 2025d). The result is a toolkit that makes vast, high-poly environments possible without crashing resources (something that really matters in VR settings).

Character creation has also shifted. MetaHuman Creator (Epic Games, 2025e) allows fully rigged, realistic figures to be built in minutes. The technical barrier drops, but a new trade-off appears. Artists can now spend more time on story and interaction. But they may also find themselves "trapped" in the same set of standardized building blocks. The outcome of this process can lack authenticity.

Similar to Blender, unreal is not welcoming to the unprepared. Its interface is layered, and its features sprawl. Real-time ray tracing and other advanced effects can strain even "high-end" GPUs. Large projects can easily become heavy, unstable, and difficult to control.

4 IMMERSIVE HARDWARE INNOVATION

Algorithms may be the most refined, AI-enabled rendering paths streamlined, physics simulations tuned to perfection. Yet, such sophistication cannot succeed in isolation. Without harmony between the software layer and the hardware layer, the system falters. Many of us remember the first time a smartphone was placed into a simple Google Cardboard headset. The experience was modest but impactful. Even with limited hardware, the sensation was strong as if the body stepped into a parallel world. But this sensation soon dissipates after the first signs of discomfort due to the "bad" VR experience at that time. This simple hardware could not ensure a high refresh rate, high enough not to be flagged as an unnatural event by the brain. Our human brain does not like contradiction, so any VR experience that defies logic will trigger discomfort for the user.

The field has since advanced rapidly. Head-mounted displays (HMDs) are more reliable (good resolution, wider fields of view). Motion-tracking systems are accurate. Together, they give creators the ability to manipulate digital worlds with remarkable precision. The act of creation is less confusing. Iterations are faster, and design decisions are more intuitive.

4.1 HMD Optics and Display Evolution

Modern HMDs are no longer just "screens strapped to your face". The 2025 Meta Quest Pro 2, for example, now features improved pancake optics with reduced chromatic aberration, higher pixel density, and real-time eye-tracking. These upgrades allow foveated rendering (Meta, 2025). This means that only the regions where you look will be fully detailed. The other regions can have low quality, which can improve performance without sacrificing fidelity. The new generation of HMDs comes with advanced wireless protocols like WiGig 60 Hz. According to Kim and Yun (2020), this means you can test immersive experiences anywhere whether in a studio or a client's office without tripping over cables or worrying about latency.

HMDs still have limitations. Even with lighter designs, prolonged use can cause neck strain and fatigue. Field of view and color accuracy vary between models, and real-time eye-tracking requires calibration that may frustrate first-time users.

4.2 Haptics beyond Rumble

Full embodiment in VR cannot be achieved without tactile feedback. That is why haptic simulation has been a dominant research area in the VR community. What follows is a non-exhaustive selection of potential pieces of hardware that can accentuate body ownership in virtual environments.

The sensation of crashing a pillow is different from placing a hand on a table. Force-feedback (Kinesthetic Haptics) systems can somehow simulate that difference. Exoskeleton gloves are the most common implementation. They use articulated structures to restrict or guide motion in ways that mimic the feel of real objects. PalmEx extends this approach by introducing palmar force feedback, creating pressure against the palm to heighten the illusion of contact (Bouzbib et al., 2024). The objective is straightforward yet ambitious: to render object interactions that feel not only visible but physically convincing.

Another way to simulate the touch effect is by using Mid-Air/Spatial Haptics. These systems support the trend of immersive illusion without contact. Ultrasonic phased arrays, like those developed by Ultraleap, can project invisible 3D shapes into the air that our hands can "feel" (Rakkolainen et al., 2021).

Finally, neuro-haptics, largely experimental, represents the state-of-the-art of immersive touch. Advanced brain-computer interfaces (BCIs) aim to "bypass" the body entirely. The sensation of touch is simply projected straight into perception.

Like any invention, these systems present challenges. The major limitation of tactile systems is that they sometimes feel localized or fake. Force-feedback devices are often bulky. Mid-air haptics require cumbersome calibration. Neuro-haptics, meanwhile, demands careful ethical and physiological considerations before they can be safely mainstreamed.

4.3 Hybrid Tracking Architectures

The current motion-tracking systems have reached a level of precision that seemed "unreal" a few years ago. The latest OptiTrack Prime (NaturalPoint, Inc. dba OptiTrack, n.d.) 41 cameras and Vive Tracker 3.0 (VR-Compare, 2021) sensors achieve sub-millimeter accuracy. This progress makes it possible to replicate complex gestures, micro-expressions, and even finger movements in real time.

The real game-changer is this new AI-enhanced motion prediction. Modern systems now integrate Inverse Kinematics powered by machine learning. This technique fills in the gaps when sensors are occluded or when movements are rapid. So, now, these intelligent tracking systems can "interpolate" actions when an actor, for instance, is occluded partially by another actor. Take Vicon Shogun Live (Vicon Motion Systems Ltd., 2022) or Xsens MVN Animate (Movella, n.d.), for example. These systems allow small indie studios to capture "high-fidelity" body motion without a full mocap suit.

5 CONVERGING TECHNOLOGIES IN XR

Among the many forces shaping the future of XR, two technologies stand out for their transformative potential: AI and Blockchain. AI is getting more involved in the immersive world. As Jensen Huang, CEO of NVIDIA, explains: "Virtual reality, all the A.I. work we do, all the robotics work we do — we're as close to realizing science fiction as it gets" (Quotes, n.d.). AI can create intelligent, responsive virtual worlds but is it safe to buy there? This is where Blockchain comes into action. "For a game, you need designers, coders and artists. And people to balance the economy", says Randy Saaf, CEO of Lucid Sight (McQuillan, 2018). This quote highlights how blockchain can balance the virtual world's economy. The nature of blockchain (balance, security, decentralized transactions, trustworthy ownership, etc.) is very much in line with XR, VR, and metaverse concepts.

5.1 Blockchain for Asset Licensing

Beyond dynamic content, XR creators face critical questions: who owns these digital assets? How can ownership be verified? Blockchain provides a solution. Storing licenses, sources, destinations, and transaction history adds a layer of traceability and security to these digital assets. Platforms like Enjin and Tezos NFT standards are being integrated into XR marketplaces. Creators could, for instance, create a virtual sculpture in Blender, mint it as a blockchain-backed asset, and deploy it across multiple XR environments without losing ownership metadata.

Transaction fees (exceeding $1 per operation), latency (approximately eight minutes), and environmental concerns (each transaction consuming over 700 kWh) can be real barriers for XR developers (Pacheco et al., 2022). Also, the learning curve can be intimidating for newcomers.

5.2 AI-Powered Breakthroughs

Procedural AI-driven environments and intelligent NPCs are no longer a luxury; they are becoming standard. The semi-automation of manual/ repetitive labor, like terrain creation and scripting interactive characters with infinite if-else statements, is a game-changer. Now, artists could focus on creative storytelling and engaging gameplay. For those eager to start, Unity's AI Game Design and Procedural Generation tutorials provide a free platform (Unity Technologies, 2025b). In practice, combining procedural terrain with adaptive NPCs can catapult collaborative VR experiences. However, this power comes with challenges as well. This is true for any AI-assisted task, which is about authenticity. Procedurally generated words can risk repetition. And AI-monitored NPCs' behavior can be unpredictable if not constrained. This study, presented by Drachen, Canossa, and Yannakakis (2009), confirms that self-organizing NPC behavior can lead to emergent, sometimes unpredictable patterns if not bounded, which impacts gameplay balance.

6 CONCLUSION

Digital creation has always carried a visionary impulse. Our success depends on our ability to predict tomorrow's technology to make our creative ideas last. Is our system robust toward XR changes? If not, how do we future-proof our pipelines and infrastructure?

Future-proofing pipelines means planning for durability, scalability, interactivity, and portability. Regarding scalability, emerging cloud services like AWS Nimble Studio or Microsoft Azure PlayFab (AWS, 2025; Microsoft, 2025) can help go beyond local hardware and stretch production to meet large audiences. Neural signals and BCIs signal possible breakthroughs in interactivity (Leeb & Pérez-Marcos, 2020). As for portability, existing game engines are already cross-platform environments, but developers must develop good practices related to content versioning, modular asset pipelines, and automatic performance and accessibility testing (Unity, 2025; Epic Games, 2025g).

Seen in this light, the themes of the chapter come together. Tools such as modeling software, game engines, and hardware remain at the center. AI, cloud infrastructures, and mixed reality add new layers of possibility. Some tools speed up iteration, others expand scale, and many demand trade-offs between fidelity and performance.

REFERENCES

Autodesk. (2025). *Create an automatic character rig for a mesh* (Maya Help). In *Maya Help*. Retrieved August 28, 2025, from https://help.autodesk.com/view/MAYAUL/2025/ENU/?guid=GUID-6CAEA6C2-D4F9-422D-8E0F-522171B47C35

Autodesk Media & Entertainment. (2025, June 4). Meet MotionMaker: Maya's new AI animation tool (10 min read). In *Autodesk Media & Entertainment Blog*. Retrieved August 28, 2025, from https://blogs.autodesk.com/media-and-entertainment/2025/06/04/meet-motionmaker/

AWS. (2025). *AWS nimble studio: Cloud-based creative workstations*. https://aws.amazon.com/nimble-studio/

Blender Foundation. (2024a). *Cloth* [Online documentation]. In *Blender Manual*. Retrieved August 13, 2025, from https://docs.blender.org/manual/en/latest/physics/cloth/index.html

Blender Foundation. (2024b). Introduction — Geometry nodes (blender 4.0 manual). In *Blender Manual*. Retrieved August 28, 2025, from https://docs.blender.org/manual/en/4.0/modeling/geometry_nodes/introduction.html

Blender Foundation. (2025a). Soft body modifier [Online documentation]. In *Blender Manual*. Retrieved August 13, 2025, from https://docs.blender.org/manual/en/latest/modeling/modifiers/physics/soft_body.html

Blender Foundation. (2025b). *Introduction — EEVEE* (blender manual). In *Blender Manual*. Retrieved August 28, 2025, from https://docs.blender.org/manual/en/latest/render/eevee/introduction.html

Blinn, J. F. (1977). Models of light reflection for computer synthesized pictures. *International Conference on Computer Graphics and Interactive Techniques*, 11, 192–198. https://doi.org/10.1145/563858.563893

Bookey. (n.d.). 30 best Roger Deakins quotes. In *Bookey*. Retrieved August 31, 2025, from https://www.bookey.app/quote-author/roger-deakins

Bouzbib, E., Teyssier, M., Howard, T., Pacchierotti, C., & Lécuyer, A. (2024). PalmEx: Adding palmar force-feedback for 3D manipulation with haptic exoskeleton gloves. *IEEE Transactions on Visualization and Computer Graphics*, 30(7), 3973–3980. https://doi.org/10.1109/TVCG.2023.3244076

Chen, X.-L., & Hou, W.-J. (2022). Gaze-based interaction intention recognition in virtual reality. *Electronics*, 11(10), 1647. https://doi.org/10.3390/electronics11101647

Christensen, P. H. (1997). Global Illumination for Professional 3D Animation, Visualization, and Special Effects. In: Dorsey, J., Slusallek, P. (eds) *Rendering Techniques '97. EGSR 1997. Eurographics*. Springer, Vienna. https://doi.org/10.1007/978-3-7091-6858-5_29

Dasch, T. (2019, November 19). PC rendering techniques to avoid when developing for mobile VR. In *Meta Horizon Developer Blog*. Retrieved August 29, 2025, from https://developers.meta.com/horizon/blog/pc-rendering-techniques-to-avoid-when-developing-for-mobile-vr/

Deering, M., Winner, S., Schediwy, B., Duffy, C., & Hunt, N. (1988). The triangle processor and normal vector shader. *ACM SIGGRAPH Computer Graphics*, 22(4), 21–30. https://doi.org/10.1145/378456.378468

Drachen, A., Canossa, A., & Yannakakis, G. N. (2009). Player modeling using self-organization in Tomb Raider: Underworld. In *Proceedings of the IEEE Symposium on Computational Intelligence and Games*, 1–8. https://doi.org/10.1109/CIG.2009.5286500

Epic Games. (2025a). *Unreal engine documentation* [Website]. Retrieved August 13, 2025, from https://dev.epicgames.com/documentation/en-us/unreal-engine

Epic Games. (2025b). *Nanite virtualized geometry* (Unreal engine 5.6 documentation). In *Unreal Engine 5.6 Documentation*. Retrieved August 28, 2025, from https://dev.epicgames.com/documentation/en-us/unreal-engine/nanite-virtualized-geometry-in-unreal-engine

Epic Games. (2025c). *Lumen global illumination and reflections* (Unreal engine 5.6 documentation). In *Unreal Engine 5.6 Documentation*. Retrieved August 28, 2025, from https://dev.epicgames.com/documentation/en-us/unreal-engine/lumen-global-illumination-and-reflections-in-unreal-engine

Epic Games. (2025d). *Live link in unreal engine* (Unreal engine documentation). In *Unreal Engine 5.x Documentation*. Retrieved August 28, 2025, from https://dev.epicgames.com/documentation/en-us/unreal-engine/live-link-in-unreal-engine

Epic Games. (2025e). *MetaHuman 5.6 release notes* (MetaHuman documentation). In *MetaHuman Documentation*. Retrieved August 28, 2025, from https://dev.epicgames.com/documentation/en-us/metahuman/metahuman-5-6-release-notes

Epic Games. (2025f). *Unreal Insights: Telemetry for immersive design optimization*. https://dev.epicgames.com/documentation/en-us/unreal-engine/unreal-insights-in-unreal-engine

Epic Games. (2025g). *Unreal engine 6: Cross-platform VR and AR development.* https://www.unrealengine.com/en-US/xr

Gangar, M. (2024). Advancements in ray tracing: From fundamentals to neural innovations and practical applications. *Indian Scientific Journal of Research in Engineering and Management.* https://doi.org/10.55041/ijsrem30137

Gutteling, T. P., Selen, L. P. J., & Medendorp, W. P. (2015). Parallax-sensitive remapping of visual space in occipito-parietal alpha-band activity during whole-body motion. *Journal of Neurophysiology, 113*(5), 1574–1584. https://doi.org/10.1152/JN.00477.2014

Harada, T., McKee, J., & Yang, J. (2012). Forward+: Bringing deferred lighting to the next level. *Eurographics,* 5–8. https://doi.org/10.2312/CONF/EG2012/SHORT/005-008

Juego Studio. (2025, February 20). Maya vs blender: A detailed comparison of 3D modeling software. *Juego Studio.* Retrieved August 29, 2025, from https://www.juegostudio.com/blog/maya-vs-blender

Kim, S., & Yun, J.-H. (2020). Motion-aware interplay between WiGig and WiFi for wireless virtual reality. *Sensors, 20*(23), 6782. https://doi.org/10.3390/s20236782

Leeb, R., & Pérez-Marcos, D. (2020). Brain-computer interfaces and virtual reality for neurorehabilitation. In *Handbook of Clinical Neurology* (Vol. 168, pp. 183–197). Elsevier. https://doi.org/10.1016/B978-0-444-63934-9.00014-7

McQuillan, J. (2018, September 5). *Lucid Sight's Randy Saaf on finding the sweetspot for blockchain's frontier games* [Interview]. In *BlockchainGamer.biz.* Retrieved August 29, 2025, from https://www.blockchaingamer.biz/features/interviews/6019/big-interview-randy-saaf-lucid-sight/

Meta. (2024, August 5). *Explore meta quest features with building blocks* (Meta horizon OS developers). In *Meta Horizon OS Unity documentation.* Retrieved August 28, 2025, from https://developers.meta.com/horizon/documentation/unity/bb-overview/

Meta. (2025, February 18). *Eye tracked foveated rendering* (Meta Horizon OS Unity documentation). In *Meta Horizon OS Unity documentation.* Retrieved August 29, 2025, from https://developers.meta.com/horizon/documentation/unity/unity-eye-tracked-foveated-rendering/

Meta Horizon. (2024). *XR performance toolkit: Optimizing VR experiences across devices.* https://developers.meta.com/horizon/documentation/unity/unity-perf

Microsoft. (2025b). *Azure PlayFab: Scalable backend for live games.* https://playfab.com

Movella. (n.d.). *Xsens animate* [Software product page]. In *Movella – Motion Capture.* Retrieved August 29, 2025, from https://www.movella.com/motion-capture/xsens-mvn-animate

NaturalPoint, Inc. dba OptiTrack. (n.d.). *OptiTrack for VR* (Virtual Reality application). Retrieved August 29, 2025, from https://optitrack.com/applications/virtual-reality/

Olsson, O., Billeter, M., & Assarsson, U. (2012). Clustered deferred and forward shading. *High Performance Graphics*, 87–96. https://dl.acm.org/doi/10.5555/2383795.2383809

Pacheco, M., Oliva, G. A., Rajbahadur, G. K., & Hassan, A. E. (2022). *Is my transaction done yet? An empirical study of transaction processing times in the ethereum blockchain platform* (arXiv preprint arXiv:2206.08959). arXiv. Retrieved from https://arxiv.org/abs/2206.08959

Pharr, M., Jakob, W., & Humphreys, G. (2016). Microfacet models. In *Physically based rendering: From theory to implementation* (3rd ed.). Morgan Kaufmann Publishers. Retrieved August 29, 2025, from https://www.pbr-book.org/3ed-2018/Reflection_Models/Microfacet_Models

Phong, B. T. (1975). Illumination for computer generated pictures. *Communications of The ACM*, *18*(6), 311–317. https://doi.org/10.1145/360825.360839

Polygon. (2024, September 12). *Unity fully revokes maligned runtime fee.* Retrieved August 29, 2025, from Polygon website. https://www.polygon.com/news/450804/unity-runtime-fee-canceled-sept-2024/?utm_source=chatgpt.com

Quotes. (n.d.). Jensen Huang: "Virtual reality, all the A.I. work we do..." In *BrainyQuote.com*. Retrieved August 29, 2025, from https://www.brainyquote.com/quotes/jensen_huang_1101057

Rakkolainen, I., Freeman, E., Sand, A., Raisamo, R., & Brewster, S. A. (2021). A survey of mid-air ultrasound haptics and its applications. *IEEE Transactions on Haptics*. Advance online publication. https://doi.org/10.1109/TOH.2020.3018754

RocketBrush Studio. (2025, May 15). 3ds Max vs Maya: What to choose for your project? In *RocketBrush Studio Blog*. Retrieved August 29, 2025, from https://rocketbrush.com/blog/3ds-max-vs-maya-what-to-choose

Sahu, J. P. (2024). From clay to code: The evolution of 3D sculpting and its impact on virtual realms. *International Journal of Research Publication and Reviews*, *5*(4), 886–900. https://doi.org/10.55248/gengpi.5.0424.0921

Sutherland, I. E. (1968). *A head-mounted three dimensional display.* In *Proceedings of the December 9–11, 1968, Fall Joint Computer Conference, Part I* (AFIPS '68 (Fall, part I), pp. 757–764). ACM. https://doi.org/10.1145/1476589.1476686

The OpenGL Architecture Review Board. (1997). GLUT example programs. In *OpenGL*. Retrieved August 31, 2025, from https://www.opengl.org/archives/resources/code/samples/glut_examples/examples/examples.html

ThreeDee. (2024, March 3). Why Blender is hard to learn for beginners. In *ThreeDee*. Retrieved August 29, 2025, from https://threedee.design/blog/why-does-blender-feel-hard-to-learn

Tobii. (2025). *Pro VR Analytics: Measuring gaze and interaction in immersive environments.* https://www.tobii.com/blog/eye-tracking-in-vr-a-vital-component

Town, P. (2025, April 1). The truth about diversification: What Warren Buffett and top investors really do. In *Rule One Investing*. Retrieved August 29, 2025, from https://www.ruleoneinvesting.com/blog/how-to-invest/why-diversification-is-for-the-ignorant/

Tuliniemi, J. (2018). *Physically based rendering for embedded systems*. https://jultika.oulu.fi/files/nbnfioulu-201805101776.pdf

Unity. (2025). *Unity 2025 LTS: Multi-platform XR development*. https://docs.unity3d.com/6000.2/Documentation/Manual/XR.html

Unity Technologies. (2019, June 5). Unity technologies announces unity reflect – first of its kind product enables real-time BIM collaboration on any device with one click. In *Unity News*. Retrieved August 28, 2025, from https://unity.com/news/unity-technologies-announces-unity-reflect-first-its-kind-product-enables-real

Unity Technologies. (2024, February 22). Start learning data-oriented design in Unity with these … (Unity blog). In *Unity Blog*. Retrieved August 28, 2025, from https://unity.com/blog/engine-platform/dots-bootcamp-resources

Unity Technologies. (2025a). About shader graph – Shader graph (17.3.0 manual). In *Shader Graph Manual*. Retrieved August 28, 2025, from https://docs.unity3d.com/Packages/com.unity.shadergraph@17.3/manual/index.html

Unity Technologies. (2025b). *AI game design and procedural generation*. Unity Learn. https://learn.unity.com/g/procedural-generation

Vicon Motion Systems Ltd. (2022). *Shōgun brochure* [Brochure]. Retrieved August 29, 2025, from https://info.vicon.com/hubfs/entertainment/shogun-brochure.pdf

Virtual Method Studio. (2019). *Obi physics framework [Website]*. Retrieved August 13, 2025, from https://obi.virtualmethodstudio.com/

VR-Compare. (2021). HTC Vive Tracker 3.0. In *VR-Compare*. Retrieved August 29, 2025, from https://vr-compare.com/accessory/htcvivetracker3.0

Zhang, Q. (2024). Cutting-edge techniques in 3D modeling and animation: Leveraging mathematical models and advanced software tools. *Applied and Computational Engineering*, 102, 30–36. https://doi.org/10.54254/2755-2721/102/20240990

CHAPTER 7

Virtual Content Design Principles

Rocío Cifuentes-Albeza and
Elpidio del Campo-Cañizares

1 INTRODUCTION

Virtual spaces are used for a wide range of purposes. According to Levis (2006: 26–27), they can be found in technical fields, such as medicine and health, architecture, urban planning and civil engineering, science, industry and robotics, and also play a role in military and aerospace technology, as well as in everyday activities such as education, art, commerce, finance, telecommunication and entertainment. Virtual reality (VR) technology has influenced how we interact with and perceive information (Zhu and Chen, 2024). As Fencott suggests, "interactive 3D virtual systems will be to the 21st century what the moving image was to the 20th and will significantly change the way we view ourselves and the world around us" (2001: 25). Virtual content has come to be considered a medium of communication of its own (Jerald, 2015; Kuksa and Childs, 2014; Markowitz and Bailenson, 2019), although Fencott (2001) points out that our understanding of VR as a communications medium is not as well developed as VR technology itself. Communication is "an essential component and basis of VR" and "VR design is concerned with the communication of how the virtual world works, how that world and its objects are controlled, and the relationship between user and content"

DOI: 10.1201/9781003673538-7

(Jerald, 2015: 10). Virtual spaces could also be considered a form of art, and interactivity is a new attribute that allows a new way to communicate (Kuksa and Childs, 2014).

Although "some of the promise and popularity of virtual worlds lies in their ability to offer an alternative means to communicate, collaborate, and even to organize economic activity" (Jarvenpaa et al., 2007, quoted by Chaturvedi et al., 2011), there are still many challenges to be tackled in the development of virtual content. As Chong et al. (2021: 8) point out, these challenges include insufficient virtual content and scenarios; the time-consuming nature of 3D graphic creation; the lack of standard file formats; oversimplification of information and lack of originality; limited experience in the field of experimentation; the lack of clarity on design purposes and the poor definition of rules and even problems with the presentation of information.

2 THE FOUNDATIONAL PRINCIPLES OF VIRTUAL CONTENT DESIGN

2.1 Immersiveness, Presence and Immediacy

The aim of designers should be to guide the design of virtual content in accordance with the principle of immersiveness, i.e. the degree of perceived vividness or realism in relation to the virtual content and/or virtual space (Kuksa and Childs, 2014). In addition to the technology, the narrative design and the coherence of the virtual content play a crucial role in fostering immersiveness in a virtual scenario. Both the content and the environment must be able to substitute for the perception of reality through the senses and on the intellectual level: to establish an analogy between the model represented and reality itself. The level of realism enhances the sense of presence in the virtual environment (Welch et al., 1996; Witmer and Singer, 1998). The factors influencing the sense of realism are associated with the connection and continuity of the stimuli experienced by the user rather than the level of realism of the content, although the nature of the scene content, texture, resolution, light sources, field of view etc., also have an influence, as Witmer and Singer (1998: 230) observe. Chong et al. point out that

> users' prior knowledge and experiences hinder the immersion and engagement because of the expectations between the real and virtual spaces. Vice versa, there is no absolute solution to curb learning distraction due to its implementation, especially for new users without prior experience.

(2021: 11)

The visual, auditory and haptic stimuli presented in the virtual environment play a crucial role in establishing connections between what is represented virtually and what users expect. Kuksa and Childs (2014: 7–8) distinguish between two types of immersion: psychological immersion, which is the sense of being submerged in the experience of the environment, and perceptual immersion, referring to the degree to which the senses are dominated by the technology.

Witmer and Singer define presence as "the subjective experience of being in one place or environment, even when one is physically situated in another" (1998: 225). The characteristics of use and of the medium itself have an impact on the sense of presence (Coelho et al., 2006), which depends on the meaning that presence has for the user, as well as the user's previous experience and skill level, motivation, degree of attention and level of credibility, among other factors. Formal characteristics of the medium such as sensorial channels, the level of pictorial realism, system response times, control and field of vision are all aspects that designers need to consider, as are content variables such as body representation and the presence of others (Coelho et al., 2006: 33–35). To elicit a sense of presence, the designer must be able to integrate technological and narrative discourses with the aim of providing the user with a meaningful, real and vivid experience.

A full sense of immediacy influences the degree of immersiveness and the sense of presence. The design of virtual content and environments should facilitate a fluid perception without distractions, free of any barriers that might constrain the experience of users in the environment and their intuitive access to the virtual content, without perceiving any form of mediation. The perception that the technology is mediating the activity (hypermediacy) hinders the experience of a full connection with the virtual space and may even affect the relationships with others in that same space (Kuksa and Childs, 2014).

2.2 Flow

The psychologist Mihaly Csikszentmihalyi developed the theory of flow in the 1970s. Although he first presented the concept of flow in his book *Beyond Boredom and Anxiety: Experiencing Flow in Work and Play* (Csikszentmihalyi, 1975), it was not until the 1990s that the theory gained widespread attention. Flow theory posits that to achieve a level of high concentration and enjoy a truly satisfying optimal experience, the user must enter a state of consciousness referred to as "flow" (Csikszentmihalyi,

1990). Csikszentmihalyi explains that optimal experiences occur in activities that have a goal and a clearly defined set of rules and that require attention and the application of certain skills. According to Modena and Parisi (2021), clear goals and feedback are inherent conditions of flow that cannot be attributed to either presence or immersiveness, although they do share certain characteristics with both. In relation to the skills required for activities in virtual scenarios, there needs to be a balance between the level of difficulty of the actions or tasks to be performed and the capabilities required of users in the virtual experience. Csikszentmihalyi (1975, 1990) argues that a state of focused concentration equates to absolute absorption in an activity. The purpose of this balance is to ensure that users hold their attention on the action in which they are immersed and maintain their engagement, as only in this way will they be able to enjoy an optimal experience. The design of content with flow needs to be intuitive, with the capacity to provide completely clear and regular feedback while also sustaining an experience based on challenges that users are able to take on in keeping with their competence and skill levels.

Modena and Parisi point out that "[o]nly by acting, feedback can be expected. Flow is then the condition that seems highly specific for activities that engage the 'reader' performatively" (2021: 70). Csikszentmihalyi (1990) identifies five characteristics that are necessary to achieve this state of flow: "clarity, centering, choice, commitment and challenge". When combined with the right content, these characteristics will engage the user's interest, continued engagement, motivation and sustained attention. Research on flow has explored a wide range of different contexts. Rodríguez-Ardura and Meseguer-Artola (2017), for example, examine the applicability of flow theory to the online world, particularly e-learning environments. Their findings confirm the benefits of flow states as they facilitate positive emotions, improve academic performance and contribute to effective student retention in the online learning environment. In the context of VR storytelling, Yang and Zhang (2022) find that immersive stories improve users' sense of presence, flow and credibility, as well as enjoyment. In the context of VR and video games, Modena and Parisi (2021) suggest that the achievement of flow depends on the task and occurs through reacting to stimuli.

2.3 Aesthetics: Visual Language and Perception

In the process of creating virtual content, designers need to be guided by the principles of visual language (Wong, 1995: 41) and of perception.

An understanding of these principles is highly advantageous for designers, as it will enable them to ensure that their design takes into account the rules and patterns of observation and perceptual behaviour of users in virtual environments. Arnheim argues that looking at the world requires "an interplay between properties supplied by the object and the nature of the observer subject" and that "vision is not a mechanical recording of elements but rather the apprehension of significant structural patterns" (2004: 6). The Gestalt school of psychology, founded by Max Wertheimer, Wolfgang Köler and Kurt Koffka, developed Gestalt theory in the early 20th century, positing what they refer to as Gestalt laws to explain how we perceive and structure information, thereby revealing our sensory perception mechanisms. The application of these principles turns the task of content creation and development into a predictive act because the designer knows in advance how the target audience's visual perception operates. This approach facilitates the creation of effective experiences that can engage the observing subjects while generating a fluid dialogue between object and subject. The communicative act that occurs between the object (virtual content) and the subject (user) is mediated by the principles of visual perception. In general terms, Gestalt principles such as the law of proximity and the law of similarity focus on explaining certain perceived assortments of objects, while others, such as the law of closure, the law of contrast, figure-ground organisation, the law of invariance and the law of past experience, deal with the perception of figures. Finally, the law of *Prägnanz* combines many of these principles to facilitate memorability and the easy recollection of objects, which in this case relates to virtual content and virtual environments.

Manresa-Yee and Mas Sansó point out that "[t]he appearance of an object outlines characteristics such as its colour and brightness at each point on its surface, while also considering texture, surface structure, lighting and point of view" (2011: 120). Wong articulates a classification of what he calls "elements of design", consisting of "conceptual, visual, relational and practical elements" (1995: 42–44) that highlight different levels of analysis and strata on which the designer should explore the process of content conception, creation and analysis in virtual environments.

Colour creates a degree of complexity due to the very diverse perspectives from which it can be considered: physical, physiological, psychological, cultural, artistic, anthropological, etc. However, there are certain key aspects that should be taken into account in the design of content for virtual environments. Colour can have a direct impact on the usability of virtual content and thus on user engagement, affecting aspects of the user experience such as navigation, interactivity and/or communication, or even imposing barriers to accessibility. From the perspective of its aesthetic functions, colour can contribute to the construction of the aesthetic space of the image and affect the creation of spatial rhythms, composition through contrast, and sensory effects related to "the synaesthetic manifestations of colour" (Villafañe and Mínguez, 1996: 120–121), as well as textures. Among other aspects, designers need to consider the three dimensions of colour: hue, saturation and brightness. Moreover, colour can influence the organisation of visual information: a large number of colours can make it difficult to order content hierarchically, i.e. arranging the information in order to establish different degrees of importance or to identify a logical way of reading it. Arnheim argues that although "we are quite sensitive in distinguishing subtly different shades from one other, […] when it comes to identifying a particular color by memory or at some spatial distance from another, our power of discrimination is severely limited […]" and that "[t]he number of colors we can recognize reliably and with ease hardly exceeds six", namely the primary colours (blue, yellow and red) and the secondary colours (orange, green and violet) (2004: 333).

An image's colour, texture and even degree of synthesis and stylisation, among other elements, contribute to its level of iconicity: they may be perceived as denotative, characteristic and descriptive features that establish an analogy with the reality represented, but they may also possess a symbolic connotation that evokes alternative meanings, or that even becomes a code. In this respect, Schneidermann (1982: 253) suggests that an appropriate physical model of reality can be the key to the creation of a system of direct manipulation. Colour can also evoke a connotative meaning (the subjective dimension of colour) in a particular context and culture, or based on a personal interpretation (González-Solas, 2002: 180; Dondis, 2000: 69; Villafañe and Mínguez, 1996: 119). As Dondis observes, "[c]olour not only has a universally shared meaning through experience, but also has an independent informational value through meanings that are symbolically attached to it" (2000: 69). Individuals from the same cultural background tend to interpret colours in similar ways (Niemi, 2025), and colour and cultural context influence attention and perception of usability (Noiwan and Norcio, 2006). Colour-in-context theory is used to explain the relationship between colour, affect, cognition and behaviour

(Elliot and Maier, 2012), and research carried out by Lipson-Smith et al. (2021) suggests (albeit not conclusively) that the context in which a colour appears can influence the mood and preferences of users.

Colour can also impose barriers to accessibility, for example, among colour-blind users, as "almost one in ten people have some level of color blindness or visual impairment" (Wang et al., 2020: 519). In such cases, in order to consider their view of colour, Aytac (2017) suggests the use of simulators in the process of designing user interfaces, while López and Medina (2021) go further by proposing a colour-blind player-focused inclusive design model with the aim of making video games more inclusive, a model that could be extended to other virtual applications.

2.4 Attention, Emotion, Mood and Arousal

From the perspective of virtual content design, the attention, emotion, mood and level of physiological activation of users determine the stimuli they will apprehend and that will help them retain the information conveyed. Ensuring comprehension and memorability is of vital importance, and in the virtual content design process, both the narrative structure and the structure of visual elements are key to achieving that goal.

John Sweller (1988; Sweller et al., 2019) developed cognitive load theory in the 1980s to explain how cognitive overload in the learning process can affect our ability to transform data into useful information and to build long-term memory. Human cognitive processing is limited by our working memory and its ability to process a limited amount of information at the same time (Sweller et al., 2019). There are three practical implications of cognitive load theory that virtual content designers need to take into account. First of all, intrinsic load, referring to the level of complexity of the information presented, can be managed by introducing key concepts and symbols, segmenting information into short blocks and splitting up long tasks into shorter jobs. Second, extraneous load, which is associated with the way content is presented, can be reduced by synthesising and stylising the visual and narrative information hierarchically to establish and direct the user's attention in an orderly way based on order of importance, while avoiding stimuli that are unnecessary or that undermine clarity. Finally, germane load, referring to the mental effort made by the user to integrate new content into the long-term memory structure, can be enhanced through visual examples and comparisons based on active learning, through tasks that encourage reflection and stimulate information processing and also by emotional and motivational connections.

Research conducted by Debue and Van de Leemput (2014) measuring cognitive load in a hypermedia context reveals the existence of a positive association between germane load and cognitive absorption.

3 USABILITY AND ACCESSIBILITY

Both usability and accessibility are key aspects to be considered in the design of virtual content, and by combining them, designers will be able to create accessible, barrier-free content and an intuitive design that can facilitate the user experience and make it more enjoyable. There are a number of international standards detailing usability and accessibility criteria that can help guide designers. These include the International Organization for Standardization's "Ergonomics of human-system interaction" standard (ISO 9241), which defines usability as the "extent to which a system, product or service can be used by specified users to achieve specified goals with effectiveness, efficiency and satisfaction in a specific context of use" (ISO 9241-20:2021), and the Web Content Accessibility Guidelines 2.2 (WCAG) (W3C WAI, 2023), which provides a set of technical standards for making content accessible.

The term "usability" was popularised by interface engineer Jakob Nielsen in the 1990s. A pioneer in the field of usability, Nielsen published a book titled *Usability Engineering*, which focuses on the design of web user interfaces. Nielsen (1994: 16) identifies five components of usability to evaluate the user's relationship with the system: (1) it is easy to understand and learn how to use (learnability); (2) it can be used efficiently to ensure productivity (efficiency); (3) it is easy to remember how to use it (memorability); (4) it has a low error rate and errors are easy to correct (errors) and (5) it is pleasant and even enjoyable to use (satisfaction). Usability is associated with human–computer interaction, user satisfaction, user interaction and user immersion, among others (Chong et al., 2021). The key attributes of the system that designers need to ensure are a clear and well-defined content and information structure, simplicity of interactions, continuous and immediate feedback, adaptability between devices and contexts of application.

The aim of accessibility is to ensure universal access to digital content, taking into account the skills of different user profiles, including users with cognitive or motor function limitations (disabilities). Accessibility is the "extent to which products, systems, services, environments and facilities can be used by people from a population with the widest range of user needs, characteristics and capabilities to achieve identified goals in identified contexts of use" (ISO 9241-20: 2021). The World Wide Web

Consortium's Web Accessibility Initiative (W3C WAI, n.d.) highlights a number of important questions that designers should consider in relation to user interface design and accessible visual design for people with disabilities. These include the need for sufficient contrast between text and background, not relying solely on colour to provide information, making interactive elements easily identifiable, providing clear and consistent navigation options, including labels associated with form elements, providing easily identifiable feedback, using appropriate headings and spacing to visually identify groups of content, using different display sizes for content or information, including images and alternative media in the design and providing controls for content that starts automatically.

4 INTERACTION USER DESIGN AND ENGAGEMENT

4.1 Interaction User Design

The user experience involves questions of human–computer interaction, usability, user satisfaction and immersiveness, among others. As Chaturvedi et al. observe, "virtual alternate realities carry the potential to change dramatically the ways in which we interact with one another in both the real world and the virtual" (2011: 674). The person (or groups of people), the computer and the interaction are essential elements of the human–computer interaction (Manresa-Yee and Mas Sansó, 2011: 115). Cognitive and perceptual skills, physical abilities, tasks to be performed and context of use are all key to determining the profile of the user interacting in a given situation; the computer is governed by the system or technology used and by properties such as the operating system and the mobility of the device, while interaction refers to all the exchanges occurring between the user and the computer (2011: 115). According to Sundar et al., "mediated communication involves transmission of information from one entity to another" (2010: 2248). In this regard, Shneidermann (1982: 237) stresses the need to validate designs through pilot tests in order to acquire a better understanding of user skills and capabilities and to seek maximum user interaction not only in the design phase but also in the development process and throughout the system life-cycle.

Shneidermann (1982: 239–242) also points out various aspects of interface design that should be considered in relation to human–computer interaction: menu selection versus command language; response times and display rates; wording of system messages; user support materials (online tutorials, explanations and help messages) and hardware devices.

When choosing between menu selection and the use of command language, designers should consider the advantages and disadvantages of both. On the one hand, the language used in menu systems must be easy to understand, and their design should minimise information overload and visual noise, with an appropriate length and a reasonable load time. It is also advisable to include shortcuts and numbering systems in order to meet the needs of experienced users. Menu selection eliminates the need for memorisation, which is an advantage for novice users. It also limits the options or actions available and guides the process by defining intermediate steps, while also serving for information retrieval. On the other hand, command languages have the advantage of speeding up task completion, which is useful for expert users. Their design requires a coherent and well-defined hierarchical content structure, congruent command names and uniform syntax and abbreviations.

The response times and display rates of menus and interfaces are other factors for designers to consider. The form and characteristics of system response messages also have an impact on interaction. As Sundar et al. explain, "[t]he contingency principle—the idea that a given message is contingent upon user reception of the previous message and the ones preceding that—can be used to explain the underlying theoretical mechanism of interactivity as a message feature" (2010: 2253). The wording should have a positive tone, include specific instructions in accessible language, and contain sufficient information for users to perceive they are in control of the situation. The messages should guide and direct users' actions and help locate them in a specific context; they should therefore include definitions and statements that serve to trigger an action, help answer questions or solve problems. These messages constitute a vital element of human–system interaction as they provide the user with feedback.

The choice of the right hardware in the design process is another essential task that designers have to perform. Ultimately, users need to have plenty of room to choose, control, categorise and even create content, as this will facilitate an individual experience that reinforces their identity with customised options adaptable to each user profile. These are the challenges posed by interactive design according to Sundar et al. (2010: 2253).

4.2 Engagement

Engagement can be described as "a category of user experience characterized by attributes of challenge, positive affect, endurability, aesthetic and sensory appeal, attention, feedback, variety/novelty, interactivity, and perceived user control" (O'Brien and Toms, 2008: 941). According to Sutcliffe, "design for user engagement and experience will depend on the domain and details of who the users are and their goals" (2016: 116). Sutcliffe points out various principles of user experience design, including immersion and presence, flow, aesthetics, attention, mood and arousal and emotion. O'Brien and Toms (2008) understand engagement as a process operating on a continuum, involving various different stages: a point of engagement, a period of sustained engagement and disengagement, and also including the possibility of re-engagement (another point of engagement after disengagement, which may be short- or long-term depending on different variables). As O'Brien and Toms explain:

> The experience of being engaged was perpetuated by the interactivity of the computer environment—sometimes physical, social, or cognitive—and the usability of the interface as they matched the users' attention, motivation, interest, and need for aesthetic and sensory appeal, novelty, control, and challenge.
>
> *(2008: 950)*

5 USER-CENTRIC DESIGN THROUGH INTUITIVE AND INTERACTION DESIGN

User-centric design (UCD) is a design approach aimed at creating intuitive environments with meaning and clear responses between users. According to Tromp et al. (2024: 1), the user-guided development framework in VR environments is oriented towards users, placing them at the centre of the process, while also iteratively defining the objects used by the system according to user characteristics and organisational needs. At the same time, this approach is associated with technologies, interfaces and procedures that ensure time and cost efficiency. The user is at the centre of every stage of the process: from conception to development and evaluation of the virtual environments. User satisfaction is associated with efficient task performance and workflow. Virtual environments "should enhance the physical, cognitive, and perceptual capabilities of the user, allowing them to do things that are impossible in the real world" (Bowman and Hodges, 1999).

The interactive design should explore all avenues in order to ensure that interaction is intuitive, predictable, accurate and clear, and that the design has basic and precise instructions on the navigation process, while also meeting user expectations. Gabbard et al. identify two distinct domains of interactive system development: behavioural and constructional. The behavioural domain is associated with the user's point of view and interaction with the application, while the constructional domain is related to software development and the overall system (2002: 51). Psychological, physiological and contextual factors all play a role.

Icons, text, graphics, audio, video and devices through which a user communicates with an interactive system are all user interaction components, along with locomotion, layout and content (Gabbard et al., 2002: 51). Virtual content should be meaningful, easy to understand and useful in a wide range of ways.

Bowman and Hodges (1999) propose a methodology for the design, evaluation and application of interaction techniques in immersive virtual environments. These authors present a classification of basic, universal interaction tasks in the virtual world: viewpoint motion control, which describes how users orient and position their point of view; selection, which involves picking one or more virtual objects for a given purpose (feedback, indication of object and indication to select); manipulation, which refers to the orienting or positioning of virtual objects (feedback, object attachment, position and orientation, indication to drop and final position of the object); and system control, which refers to other commands given by the user to perform other tasks in the application (1999: 38). Bowman and Hodges propose a model for evaluating the correct choice of interaction techniques based on the interactions to be performed by users. They also point out that the choice of interactive techniques must involve the establishment of a taxonomic classification of the techniques themselves, the evaluation of certain external characteristics of the user, the environment and the system related to the tasks that the user will perform and the inclusion of performance metrics to analyse the speed or time that users need to perform a task, the degree of accuracy, ease of use, ease of learning and user comfort, among other elements.

6 NARRATIVE IN VIRTUAL EXPERIENCES

Narratives in the context of virtual content are characterised by non-linear structures, as users guide the development of the story through their decisions and actions. In contrast to conventional narrative structures, it is the user's interactions that serve as the basic building blocks. The active role of the user, who is provided with the opportunity to make decisions, abandons the passive attitude characterised by traditional narrative and replaces the conventional narrator. The immersion is greatly enhanced by the user's sense of presence and direct interaction. Multimodality is another feature of narratives in virtual environments, with the intrinsic expansion and combination of different media formats to create the immersive experience even on different platforms. This opens up the possibility of offering a personalised experience in which the user's decisions redirect the narrative in real time.

VR should be recognised as a narrative medium of its own, with specific narrative forms, means of communication and displays of content in relation to story (Aylett and Louchart, 2003). In their discussion of the characteristics of VR, Aylett and Louchart stress the visual nature of the narrative representation and also point out features such as interactivity and immersion in terms of non-physical but immersive presence, as well as believability. These are inherent qualities of VR narrative that favour an active role for the user, who forms part of and constructs the resulting VR experience. Other aspects of VR to be considered include narrative intensity, which is necessarily interactive and at the same time multiple.

7 CONCLUSIONS

Designers of virtual content need to consider a highly complex range of interconnected aspects, especially given that virtual environments constitute both a medium of communication and a form of expression and of human relations. The human–computer interaction is defined not only by aspects of technology but also by the human component. This chapter has offered an overview of a wide range of questions with the aim of reflecting the implicit complexity of this interaction and the dimensions that designers need to take into account in order to achieve their work effectively.

Designers need to understand the virtual environment as a means of communication of its own that not only relies on technological advances but also depends on key aspects of the human experience. The user, positioned in the centre, has to be the axis for the conception and creation of virtual content, imposing some kind of meaning on the development of that content from the very diverse perspectives entailed in its complexity. As has been explained in this chapter, it is the designer who needs to understand, master and apply the foundational principles of virtual content design (immersiveness, presence and immediacy; flow; aesthetics; attention, emotion, mood and arousal), as well as the principles of usability and accessibility; interaction user design and engagement; UCD through intuitive and interaction design and narrative in virtual experiences.

REFERENCES

Arnheim, R. (2004). *Art and visual perception: A psychology of the creative eye.* University of California Press. (Original book published in 1954).

Aylett, R., & Louchart, S. (2003). Towards a narrative theory of virtual reality. *Virtual Reality, 7*(1), 2–9. https://doi.org/10.1007/s10055-003-0114-9

Aytac, S. (2017). Using color blindness simulator during user interface development for accelerator control room applications. In *International Conference on Accelerator and Large Experimental Control Systems* (pp. 1958–1968). https://doi.org/10.18429/JACoW-ICALEPCS2017-THSH103

Bowman, D. A., & Hodges, L. F. (1999). Formalizing the design, evaluation, and application of interaction techniques for immersive virtual environments. *Journal of Visual Languages & Computing, 10*(1), 37–53. https://doi.org/10.1006/jvlc.1998.0111

Chaturvedi, A. R., Dolk, D. R., & Drnevich, P. L. (2011). Design principles for virtual worlds. *MIS Quarterly, 35*(3), 673–684. https://doi.org/10.2307/23042803

Chong, H. T., Lim, C. K., Ahmed, M. F., Tan, K. L., & Mokhtar, M. B. (2021). Virtual reality usability and accessibility for cultural heritage practices: Challenges mapping and recommendations. *Electronics, 10*(12), 1430. https://doi.org/10.3390/electronics10121430

Coelho, C., Tichon, J., Hine, T. J., Wallis, G., & Riva, G. (2006). Media presence and inner presence: The sense of presence in virtual reality technologies. *From Communication to Presence: Cognition, Emotions and Culture towards the Ultimate Communicative Experience, 11*, 25–45.

Csikszentmihalyi, M. (1975). *Beyond boredom and anxiety: Experiencing flow in work and play.* Jossey-Bass.

Csikszentmihalyi, M. (1990). *Flow: The psychology of optimal experience* (Vol. 1990, p. 1). Harper & Row.

Debue, N., & Van de Leemput, C. (2014). What does germane load mean? An empirical contribution to the cognitive load theory. *Frontiers in Psychology, 5*, 1099. https://doi.org/10.3389/fpsyg.2014.01099

Dondis, D. A. (2000). *La sintaxis de la imagen. Introducción al alfabeto visual.* (J. G. Beramendi Trad.). Gustavo Gili. (Original book published in 1973).

Elliot, A. J., & Maier, M. A. (2012). Color-in-context theory. In *Advances in experimental social psychology* (Vol. 45, pp. 61–125). Academic Press. https://doi.org/10.1016/B978-0-12-394286-9.00002-0

Fencott, C. (2001). Comparative content analysis of virtual environments using perceptual opportunities. In: R. Earnshaw, & J. Vince (Eds.), *Digital content creation* (pp. 25–51). Springer. https://doi.org/10.1007/978-1-4471-0293-9_4

Gabbard, J. L., Hix, D., & Swan, J. E. (2002). User-centered design and evaluation of virtual environments. *IEEE Computer Graphics and Applications, 19*(6), 51–59. https://doi.org/10.1109/38.799740

González Solas, J. (2002). *Identidad visual corporativa. La imagen de nuestro tiempo.* Síntesis.

International Organization for Standarization. (2021). *ISO 9241: Ergonomics of Human–System Interaction - An Ergonomic Approach to Accessibility. Terms and Definitions. (ISO 9241:20)*. Retrieved: https://www.iso.org/obp/ui/es/#iso:std:iso:9241:-20:ed-2:v1:en

Jarvenpaa, S., Leidner, D., Teigland, R., and Wasko, M. (2007). New ventures in virtual worlds. *MIS Quartely, 32*(2), 461–462.

Jerald, J. (2015). *The VR book: Human-centered design for virtual reality.* Morgan & Claypool.

Kuksa, I., & Childs, M. (2014). *Making sense of space: The design and experience of virtual spaces as a tool for communication.* Elsevier Science & Technology.

Levis, D. (2006). *¿Qué es la realidad virtual?* Retrieved: https://www.academia.edu/2449000/_Qu%C3%A9_es_la_realidad_virtual_ (accessed July 15, 2025).

Lipson-Smith, R., Bernhardt, J., Zamuner, E., Churilov, L., Busietta, N., & Moratti, D. (2021). Exploring colour in context using virtual reality: Does a room change how you feel? *Virtual Reality, 25*(3), 631–645. https://doi.org/10.1007/s10055-020-00479-x

López, J. M., & Medina, N. M. (2021). Un enfoque para el diseño inclusivo de videojuegos centrado en jugadores daltónicos. *Revista de la Asociación Interacción Persona Ordenador (AIPO), 2*(1), 25–37.

Manresa-Yee, C., & Mas Sansó, R. (2011). Introducción a las interfaces basadas en visión. En: M. J. Abásolo Guerrero, C. Manresa Yee, R. Mas Sansó, & M. Vénere (Eds.), *Realidad virtual y realidad aumentada* (pp. 111–139). Universidad Nacional del Litoral. https://doi.org/10.35537/10915/18399

Markowitz, D., & Bailenson, J. (2019). Virtual reality and communication. *Human Communication Research, 34*, 287–318. https://doi.org/10.1093/OBO/9780199756841-0222

Modena, E., & Parisi, F. (2021). Exploring stories, reading environments: Flow, immersion, and presence as processes of becoming. *CINERGIE, 19*, 69–82. https://doi.org/10.6092/issn.2280-9481/12399

Nielsen, J. (1994). *Usability engineering.* Morgan Kaufmann.

Niemi, H. (2025). Colour in Human-Centred Interface Design—A Systematic Literature Review. [Bachelor's Thesis, Aalto University, Helsinki]. Aaltodoc. https://aaltodoc.aalto.fi/items/b8ce95e9-2318-4aab-ad4e-f5d6c5af9200

Noiwan, J., & Norcio, A. F. (2006). Cultural differences on attention and perceived usability: Investigating color combinations of animated graphics. *International Journal of Human-Computer Studies, 64*(2), 103–122. https://doi.org/10.1016/j.ijhcs.2005.06.004

O'Brien, H. L., & Toms, E. G. (2008). What is user engagement? A conceptual framework for defining user engagement with technology. *Journal of the American Society for Information Science and Technology, 59*(6), 938–955.

Rodríguez-Ardura, I., & Meseguer-Artola, A. (2017). Flow in e-learning: What drives it and why it matters. *British Journal of Educational Technology, 48*, 899–915. https://doi.org/10.1111/bjet.12480

Shneiderman, B. (1982). The future of interactive systems and the emergence of direct manipulation. *Behaviour & Information Technology*, *1*(3), 237–256. https://doi.org/10.1080/01449298208914450

Sundar, S. S., Xu, Q., & Bellur, S. (2010, April). Designing interactivity in media interfaces: A communications perspective. In *Proceedings of the SIGCHI Conference on Human Factors in Computing Systems* (pp. 2247–2256). https://doi.org/10.1145/1753326.1753666

Sutcliffe, A. (2016). Designing for user experience and engagement. In: H. O'Brien & P. Cairns (Eds.), *Why engagement matters: Cross-disciplinary perspectives of user engagement in digital media* (pp. 105–126). Springer International Publishing. https://doi.org/10.1007/978-3-319-27446-1_5

Sweller, J. (1988). Cognitive load during problem solving: Effects on learning. *Cognitive Science*, *12*(2), 257–285. https://doi.org/10.1016/0364-0213(88)90023-7

Sweller, J., van Merriënboer, J. J. G., & Paas, F. (2019). Cognitive architecture and instructional design: 20 years later. *Educational Psychology Review, 31*, 261–292 . https://doi.org/10.1007/s10648-019-09465-5

Tromp, J. G., Le, C. V., & Nguyen, T. L. (2024). User-centered design and evaluation methodology for virtual environments. In *Encyclopedia of computer graphics and games* (pp. 1955–1960). Springer International Publishing.

Villafañe Gallego, J., & Mínguez Arranz, N. (1996). *Principios de Teoría General de la Imagen*. Pirámide.

Wang, Z., Liu, H., Pan, Y., & Mousas, C. (2020, March). Color blindness bartender: An embodied VR game experience. In *2020 IEEE Conference on Virtual Reality and 3D User Interfaces Abstracts and Workshops (VRW)* (pp. 519–520). IEEE. https://doi.org/10.1109/VRW50115.2020.00111

Welch, R. B., Blackmon, T. T., Liu, A., Mellers, B. A., & Stark, L. W. (1996). The effects of pictorial realism, delay of visual feedback, and observer interactivity on the subjective sense of presence. *Presence: Teleoperators & Virtual Environments*, *5*(3), 263–273. https://doi.org/10.1162/pres.1996.5.3.263

Witmer, B. G., & Singer, M. J. (1998). Measuring presence in virtual environments: A presence questionnaire. *Presence*, *7*(3), 225–240. https://doi.org/10.1162/105474698565686

Wong, W. (1995). *Fundamentos del diseño*. (H. Alsina Thevenet, & E. Rosell i Miralles Trad.). Gustavo Gili. (Original book published in 1993).

World Wide Web Consortium & 3C's Web Accessibility Initiative. (n.d.). *Designing for Web Accessibility*. Retrieved: https://www.w3.org/WAI/tips/designing/

World Wide Web Consortium & 3C's Web Accessibility Initiative. (2023). *Web Content Accessibility Guidelines 2.2*. (WCAG 2.2). Retrieved: https://www.w3.org/WAI/standards-guidelines/wcag/

Yang, S., & Zhang, W. (2022). Presence and flow in the context of virtual reality storytelling: What influences enjoyment in virtual environments? *Cyberpsychology, Behavior, and Social Networking*, *25*(2), 101–109. https://doi.org/10.1089/cyber.2021.0037

Zhu, H., & Chen, B. (2024). Enhancing visual communication through experience design in virtual. *Journal of Electrical Systems*, *20*(6s), 254–260. https://doi.org/10.52783/jes.2635

CHAPTER 8

Virtual Storytelling Techniques

Begoña Ivars Nicolás

1 INTRODUCTION

You put on a head-mounted display (HMD) and controllers. You open your eyes, and you find yourself in the middle of a leafy forest. It is a realistic image. The sun filters through the leaves of ancient trees, creating an interplay of light and shadows all around you. The trunks are more than 5 metres in diameter. You can hear the song of birds as they fly back and forth, the crunch of leaves beneath your feet and a stream babbling to your right. You explore this environment as you turn around. You can see how the controllers have turned into hands. You hear a group of children approaching you. They are playing with a ball. You hear: "Hey!!!" You turn in that direction and see a child. He looks you in the eye and calls again: "Come and play with us!" And he throws a ball at another boy's back. This one catches the ball and throws it at a third child who dodges it and runs towards you, going around you to your right. The ball lands near your feet. Without knowing how, you take a step forward, bend down and pick up the ball. The children run and hide in the trees before you have time to react. You try to follow them with your eyes as you turn around. The sound of the children's laughter guides you in your search. You take a few steps forward and throw the ball to one of the children. The ball bounces off one of the trunks, and another child picks it up and carries on with the game. You suddenly hear the wind picking up and leaves fly all around

DOI: 10.1201/9781003673538-8

you and prevent you from seeing anything for a few moments. After the leaves touch your body, they sway as they fall to the ground. Some of them even brush the palms of your hands, and you feel them brush against you as they do so. When everything returns to normal, you look around again and you discover two paths among the trees. The children come running back. As they pass by, the first one gestures with his hands and shouts for you to follow him and takes the path to the left. At almost the same time, another boy who also passes very close to you tells you to follow him, but this one takes the path to the right. What are you going to do?

This experience not only shows you a forest, but it also takes you inside it and makes you an active participant in a game, while possibly evoking memories of your childhood. Stories have connected people throughout history. They influence our opinions and behaviours and shape us as individuals. Every technological transformation drives humanity's evolution.

Storytelling in virtual environments (VE) has become an innovative and powerful tool that provides unparalleled opportunities for communicating and interacting with people. Virtual content creators must think immersively, spatially and natively when creating these environments. The story is no longer being told to an audience, but instead the story becomes an experience in which the audience is immersed (Riggs, 2019) and experiences it as if it were real. The opportunities and challenges of this immersive medium, which as Murray (2017) argues, gives the audience control, must be understood and used to achieve this.

Writers must attract and guide the audience into these sensory and emotional experiences and construct narratives that meet their expectations. They must therefore include the potential offered by their most outstanding features and promote them in their narratives: the disappearance of frames, the active role of the viewer-user and interactivity (Ivars-Nicolás & Santos-Gonçalves, 2023, pp. 165–167).

This chapter provides a meaningful context for understanding the spatial and immersive narratives of these virtual experiences. It explains fundamental techniques and tools and provides keys to creating a spatial narrative design that captivates the audience and provokes deep emotions, blurring the boundaries between reality and virtuality.

2 IMMERSIVE STORYTELLING TECHNIQUES AND TOOLS

This short story is provided as an example in an introduction to the basic techniques that virtual content creators use to write successful immersive experiences for VEs. These environments can offer the user a spatial narrative in which they participate in the diegesis, see the narrative world from their own perspective and are able to interact with it.

We begin with access to these VEs. It must take place by body-mounted displays or room-scale VR. These devices foster immersiveness because, technologically, they isolate one or more of your senses so that they focus on what is taking place in the virtual world. With VR glasses, you are unable to perceive your real surroundings, and your sense of sight is focused exclusively on the images that appear on the display built into the glasses. The device's audio system or headphones also mean that you can only hear what is happening in the VE. Similarly, haptic tools are linked to the sense of touch and recreate physical sensations, such as touching and interacting with objects. In the experience presented here, you can feel a vibration that simulates the light brushes off the leaves when they touch the controllers, which are represented by hands. The HMDs also have sensors for head tracking in VR and adjusting the VE to your orientation and position.

During these first few seconds, you begin to turn around without realizing it and move your head in different directions, exploring all around. One characteristic of VE is that no frame defines the composition of the image, and there is free access to a 360° view without any compartmentalization (Gödde et al., 2018). You realize that if you turn and look up, you will be able to see those birds fluttering from one side to the other, as well as the rest of the landscape. You hear sounds in much the same way as you would in the real world. This is simulated by spatial audio, which creates a more realistic experience. It helps you to determine which direction a sound is coming from and even to distinguish whether something is moving, such as birds.

Psychologically, you have the feeling that what is around you is real, that you are present in that place and that you are turning around, even though you know this is not the case. This kind of sense of presence (Slater, 2009) in the VE is called place illusion (Slater & Sanchez-Vives, 2016) and is reinforced with the help of the technological immersion discussed above. Technological breakthroughs mean that image and audio can be reconstructed with sufficient levels of quality and speed so that you do not perceive any latency or distortion when you turn, thereby creating continuous experiences that are very similar to reality.

What happens if you don't turn around to see the child who is talking to you? One of the challenges faced by the content creator is how to direct user's attention towards the point of interest (POI) within the spatial experience to ensure that the story develops. There are various diegetic devices that do not run counter to the sense of presence or limit exploration of the environment

(Nielsen et al., 2016, p. 229). On the one hand, the construction of spatial audio provides spatial orientation and directs your attention (Biocca and Delany, 1995, p. 81), e.g., towards the children when they talk. This device encourages you to look at them and triggers other events and sensations. Planning the movements of characters or objects is equally useful. Examples include their movements or gestures when a character moves from side to side, points or looks in a specific direction. At the end of the experience, the creator is trying to attract your attention and suggest which path to follow. In addition to contributing to the creation of a specific atmosphere and realism, lighting is crucial in guiding your attention. An example of this is when the sun's rays illuminate the paths so that you can discover them.

In short, the aim is to integrate visual signals by means of some of the production's visual and sound elements. The less obvious the signal, the more likely the natural attraction (Brillhart, 2016). A factor to consider is that, for neuronal and psychological reasons, when it sees the movement of a person or an object, the human eye will follow the person. When you see a person who is moving and talking and another one who is only moving, the former will attract your sensory attention (Otero-Millan et al., 2014).

As the experience progresses, your psychological presence is not limited to the feeling of being present in the environment, but instead it is expanded as you realize that the environment is aware of you. When the characters in the story look you in the eye while addressing you or move around you in order to avoid colliding with you, expectations of what would happen in the real world are being fulfilled. This feeling that what is happening really is happening is related to your interaction and expectations and is called the Plausibility Illusion (Slater & Sanchez-Vives, 2016).

In the diegesis, you adopt a first-person perspective. You are positioned inside of the simulated narrative world and experience what happens there with either a represented body or an invisible avatar (Laurel, 2014, p. 184). You are part of what happens there, to a greater or lesser extent. You are the focus for the narrative and action, with varying degrees of interactivity. As Flavián et al. point out, users "see themselves as components of the virtual environment, feeling that the VR devices (HMD, gloves, etc.) belong to their own bodies" (Flavián et al., 2019, p. 550). This is the sense of embodiment, which occurs when you perceive yourself physically, whether corporeal or not, within the VE and interact with the characters and events. If you look down in this story, you look for your body, and you are unable to find it, but that does not break down the illusion of presence. Dooley (2024, p. 43) defines embodiment as the feeling of being present as a body in a VE.

This perception, which is mediated by VR devices (Bolter et al., 2021, p. 72), contributes to maintaining and reinforcing the sense of presence discussed above. By placing you in the diegesis from a first-person point of view, the experience, what happens and the interaction that takes place evoke emotions in you. At this point, an emotional connection between you and the story-characters is taking place. If this also leads to memories, feelings or changes of attitudes creating a deep and lasting impact, then emotional resonance occurs (Riva & Vettraino, 2015).

This immersive experience could be in a 360° pre-rendered video format until this point. This type of content, which is the result of recording real-world moving images, limits the user's power of action to choosing the point of view and provides a fixed and predefined narrative. The user, who is at the centre of the environment, is unable to move or to interact with characters or objects. This type of movement is referred to as 3 degrees of freedom (3DoF) and is limited to rotation about the user's vertical axis. This same pattern is followed by computer-generated imagery (CGI) pieces, also linear. Moreover, the feeling that the environment recognizes the user is merely an illusion generated by the narrative design, because, technologically, the environment generated by the video cannot recognize the user.

However, in this experience, you can walk forward, bend down, pick up the ball and throw it. It is CGI content and can offer up to 6 degrees of freedom (6DoF). This motion permits rotation of the head in all directions (3DoF), as well as movement forwards and backwards (Z-axis), left and right (X-axis) and up and down (Y-axis). It is complemented by controllers for picking up and interacting with simulated objects and characters, like the ball and the child you're throwing it to. These technological possibilities for movement are often offered in video games and serious games.

The narrative and action in immersive experiences must be directed towards you and make you a participant in the story. The children talk to you, look at you and respect your virtual interpersonal space. You are no longer a spectator and have become a participant. Dolan and Parets (2016) define four types of users depending on how their existence and/or their ability to influence the story are combined: observant vs. participant and passive vs. active. These immersive environments involve the roles of passive participant and active participant. In the first, the user exists in the story, as either a character or as a device. A feeling that the environment recognizes you for the construction of the narrative is created, but the story makes no demands on you, and you are unable to influence how it develops. These are the linear immersive experiences discussed above. However, in this experience, you do exist in the story; you explore it and influence it with your choices and actions, e.g., when you decide to participate in the game, the children hide from you when you pick up the ball. You take on the role of an active participant, influencing what happens next. However, Dolan and Parets (2016) point out that this role does not necessarily imply 6DoF of movement. Furthermore, you are subject to certain laws, and the story evolves according to the parameters established by the content creator.

At this point, you are fully immersed in the experience and driven by your expectations, which have been fulfilled, and you continue to explore the capacity for freedom of movement that the audiovisual piece offers you. You take a step forward, and the scene is reconstructed in your new location. As you make the movements to catch the ball, you see that your hands are simulated in the environment. You can catch the ball and throw it with varying degrees of strength to change the distance it travels. And when everything fills up with leaves, you can feel them rubbing against your hands if you have a haptic feedback device. Everything happens as expected, just as it would in the real world, reinforcing your Plausibility Illusion.

The role of active participant that the content creator has narratively assigned to you is combined with the technology so that your interaction lets you choose where to look, move, pick up objects and interact with them. The three ways of interacting set out by Bowman and Hodges (1999) are as follows: viewpoint motion control by being able to change the position or orientation, selecting objects and/or manipulating them. And these interactions take place when sensors in glasses and controllers are activated.

Your opportunities for interacting with the environment are related to the role assigned to the user. Ryan (2015, p. 162) identifies four forms of interactivity which combine position and impact. The first binary is internal or external, which depends on the user's position in the narrative world, as either a character in development (internal) or adopting an external perspective from which they may even control events (external). The second is exploratory or ontological, which depends on the interaction's impact on the narrative world. The user can observe their environment but is unable to influence how the story develops (exploratory) or influence it with their actions and decisions (ontological), in both their own narrative experience and that of other user-players. So far, your level of interaction in this experience is internal and exploratory, thanks to the interactive storytelling provided by the creator.

But what happens if you decide not to throw the ball? Or not to take any of the paths? The decisions you make and what you want to do are crucial to the fulfilment of the story in the VE. This ranges from where you decide to focus your attention to whether and how you choose to interact. The narrative does not progress without your full participation. For the first challenge, the content creator has diegetic devices discussed above to guide your attention. The second challenge faces the narrative paradox (Riggs, 2019) of having to give you the freedom to influence the story but without losing control of the dramatic structure. This paradox is related to your agency in the virtual world. It concerns your satisfaction regarding whether your decisions and actions are significant in the development or outcome of the story (Murray, 2017, p. 159). Complex and branching narratives entail a greater degree of agency, which in turn fosters stronger connections with the story-characters and engagement, but a balance between agency and narrative must be sought.

The story can follow three narrative constructions. A fixed narrative maintains the chronological sequence of events, without any possible and continuous change, and is associated with a user who is a passive participant (Dolan & Parets, 2016) with very limited agency (Pausch et al., 1996). In contrast, branching narratives may involve diverging plots and/or alternative endings, and the story's development depends on your decisions (Pausch et al., 1996). In this case, branching refers to the narrative's potential to take alternative paths depending on your interaction (Egenfeldt-Nielsen et al., 2019, pp. 213–214). If the experience is repeated, then you can experience different narratives. Imagine that you choose one path the first time, and you choose the other path the second time. This offers autonomy and participation, personalizing the story and giving you a higher level of agency, but to a limited extent. This is because the branching narratives are predefined by the creator, and sooner or later, the choices available either come from or lead back to the predefined content. Fixed and branching narratives are what Ryan (2009, pp. 51–52) calls top-down systems, in which you can choose where to look, or, at a more intense level, choose options within the branching structure, but in a controlled way. An interactive fixed narrative model could be included in this category. This narrative also has a chronological sequence, but your interaction is required at key points to trigger the next event. This can lead to greater engagement than a fixed narrative as you notice you have an impact on the story, even if you do not influence it to a significant extent. Interactive fixed and branching narratives are examples of gamification in VR and involve devices such as rewards, challenges and levels to increase participation and motivation. The third category is the highly complex emergent rule-based narrative (Spierling, 2007; Riggs, 2019), which has a high level of agency and is linked to artificial intelligence (AI). Ryan (2009, pp. 51–52) defines them as bottom-up emergent systems, which allow you to create the story as it unfolds.

Returning to our story, the content creator has given you freedom of movement, motion and interaction with objects and the environment, such as with the ball. Now, after a moment full of multisensory experiences, you are placed in the position of choosing between one of the two paths without knowing what awaits you… And to convince you that meeting the challenge and staying where you are is not a positive option, this location becomes dim and flattened, containing no actions or interesting features. What are you going to do?

Spatial storytelling is created using multisensory clues and signals which are strategically organized in time and space so that the plot, characters, objects, lighting and sound converge in a game of persuasion so that the story unfolds. Some experiences offer greater freedom of choice, but this is usually in the direction that the content creator has defined for your existence in the experience, seeking a balance between dramatic development and agency. In addition to a coherent and credible world, you must be motivated to participate and continue within the story. This involves engagement and is related to how you feel attracted to and become involved with what is happening. Your engagement may be sought in entertaining ways involving challenges, rewards, choices, etc., or emotionally, through the narrative.

Professionals work together on this task to leverage the foundations of audiovisual communication, design, psychology and narrative to make these experiences attractive and meaningful (Murray, 1997).

3 CASE STUDY

Let us turn to how these narrative techniques have been applied in examples available in VR glasses with acknowledged high levels of technical and artistic quality:

3.1 Henry (Oculus Story Studio, 2015)

This is a 3D animation short film for a spherical screen. The story opens with a contextualizing voice-over narration. Henry is a lonely hedgehog who wants to make friends. The animation style is detailed and expressive, creating a believable and engaging fantasy world which generates an illusion of place, enhanced by spatial audio.

It has a linear and predetermined structure (a fixed beginning, development and ending). The interaction is limited to choosing the point of view for exploring the environment, discovering details and the characters' reactions. Your role is as an observer of events, a witness, but one that is not recognized by the environment, so there is no illusion of plausibility. Henry sometimes looks you in the eye, which is confusing because there is no chair or plate for you. Even when the balloons float past, they pass through the space reserved for your body, as if you were a ghost. This plot also cannot support the recognizable presence of any other character at the party. This affects your sense of embodiment, which is not enhanced.

Rather than seeking to generate agency, the story wants you to empathize with Henry, and your engagement is obtained through the narrative. By sharing a space with him, Henry's sadness and joy are more personal and create a deep emotional engagement.

3.2 Invasion! (Darnell, 2016)

In this animated short film, two aliens arrive to take over Earth and meet two little white rabbits (one of which is you).

As in Henry, the narrative structure is linear and predetermined and is limited to a 3DoF movement. At the beginning, you are outside the narrative world while a voice-over provides the context. In the next scene, you see yourself with your hands represented as those of a rabbit, with a feeling of some degree of embodiment. Unlike in Henry, your role is one of a passive participant, who is the co-protagonist of the story and recognized by the characters, which creates an illusion of plausibility.

In this piece, the spatial audio invites you to explore the environment meticulously to find the other rabbit and the other characters. The rabbit makes eye contact with you and guides your attention with his gestures and movements for the rest of the story. He also becomes your partner and saves you.

There is no agency, and your engagement with the story is based on your curiosity about what the rabbit is going to do and its relationship with you, which is reinforced by its knowing wink of an eye when it saves you.

3.3 Baba Yaga (Darnell, 2021)

You and your sister Magda must go into the forest and face the witch Baba Yaga to obtain the cure which will save your sick mother. The aesthetics give you the feeling of being inside a fairy tale.

This is an interactive story with a branching narrative structure. Your role is that of an active participant, as a co-protagonist in the story. You have 6DoF movement, and you can pick up and manipulate objects. The narrative lets you choose your fate in the story at two key points, making you more involved and changing the ending. At certain points, the narrative also asks you to participate to resolve conflicts, such as putting out a fire. At other times, the interaction is not essential, such as when you grasp the bars of the cage. This all contributes to creating a sense of plausibility. However, this feeling falters because there are no clear blinks which identify interactive elements, and you have to try them out. The story tells you when to act and what to do through the voices of Magda and the Forest, but it does not continue without your participation. This is a gamified experience with challenges that you can experience several times, creating different plots and/or endings.

The lighting is vital for focusing your attention. Spatial audio also plays a role. However, the primary device to prevent you from being diverted from the plot is Magda, who establishes eye contact. Her direct gaze into your eyes, her dialogue, gestures and movements focus your attention and guide your actions throughout a large proportion of the story.

Your decisions influence how the story progresses and develops, resulting in a guided agency, but which is limited as there are a limited number of endings. Meanwhile, your interaction at key points aiming to provide help or salvation makes you feel like an important part of the story and fosters your narrative and emotional engagement.

3.4 Bogo (Oculus, 2019)

Bogo is a pet dragon who you must feed and take care of. This piece is a game with a very simple plot, and the focus is on your interaction with Bogo and how he responds to you.

It is raining. With the spatial audio, you hear some moaning and turn around to find Bogo. A drawing of a fruit appears above his head. If you explore your surroundings, you see some bright and colourful fruit. You pick a piece of fruit up and offer it to him. Bogo comes over and eats it out of your hand. The fruit appears inside a heart above his head to show his gratitude. These blinks, organized in a spatial narrative, are used by the content creator to guide your attention, tell you where the interactive elements are and instruct you on which actions to take. You can give him one or more pieces of fruit, put them in his mouth, throw them to him or eat them yourself. Every action and movement you make has a direct and visible consequence on Bogo's behaviour, creating a strong illusion of plausibility. This is because, Bogo is a virtual agent controlled by AI. His tracking capabilities are enhanced by your behaviour, and he has his own personality and credible reactions. If you offer him fruit, he comes closer. If you pick up a brush, he lies down so that you can pet him. You are an active participant and co-protagonist, recognized by Bogo, the objects and environment, which gives you 6DoF movement and allows you to select and manipulate objects.

Bogo has a predetermined interactive narrative structure. The story is a sequence of fixed events that require your participation. You cannot go from event to event until Bogo is satisfied and until he asks you to play, for example. The story fails to progress if you do not do what he asks.

You feel that your actions are valuable for moving from one event to another, creating agency based on the relationship you establish with Bogo. However, your influence on the story is subject to the parameters established by the content creator. A type of guided agency also takes place, as Bogo asks you for actions to progress.

The level of engagement is very high. The interaction with Bogo and his facial expressions is crucial. And you also feel responsible for him. Bogo sees you, recognizes you, asks you for things and responds to you in a meaningful way. This new layer of interactions makes the emotional bond with the character more believable and stronger. And Bogo's reactions create curiosity, which encourages you to move on to the next event, reinforcing this engagement.

4 CREATING COMPELLING VIRTUAL STORYTELLING

There is no single solution for designing compelling virtual storytelling. Each project involves different challenges, entailing specific needs and solutions. It is essential to take the characteristics of the medium into account and to ensure that the idea can be adapted to it.

This is a technologically immersive and interactive medium, which can represent spherical images in motion, without frames. This means that the viewer is located in the centre of the environment, with a first-person perspective. This in turn means they are present in the diegesis. These parameters determine the need for a spatial narrative that involves the viewer and makes them a participant in the story.

What is the aim of your story? Entertainment, education, training, changing behaviours, raising awareness… What technology are you going to use to develop the piece, panoramic video or CGI? This will depend on which one you have access to or the type of movement and interaction you want to offer. What role do you want to give the user and how much agency will you offer? This establishes the level of interaction and their relationship to events within the story. If you are sure of the answers to these questions, keep these recommendations in mind:

- **Enhance the user's role as a character in the story, recognized by the environment (characters and objects).** The narrative and action must be directed towards the user, making them a character in the story, with or without a represented avatar. Define the relationship between the user and the characters/environment: a witness, participant or protagonist. Assign them an active-participant role in branching, interactive or open narratives, or a participant-passive/observer role in linear narratives.

- **Enhance the spherical environment as a means of conveying the plot.** On the one hand, the environment (characters or objects) must recognize the user within the diegesis. On the other, the user must discover the narrative features (the arrangement of characters or objects, lighting and sound) as they explore the space. Use these features to reveal crucial plot points and provide clues in the diegesis that direct the user's attention towards the POI, ensuring continuity in the story. Consider the pace and make the scene long enough to encourage full and leisurely exploration. In addition, control the synchronization of events and avoid displaying several points of interest at the same time and/or points that make frequent rotation necessary in order to avoid overwhelming the user or creating a sense of information anxiety. Remember that the spatial or environmental narrative must unfold as the user moves around and interacts with the environment and should feel as natural as possible.

- **Create meaning and balance between the dramatic structure and agency.** Develop a meaningful interactive narrative structure, focused on the evolution of the dramatic structure and based on the position assigned to the user. Remember that users' agency do not depend on the number of interactions but instead on their choices having a significant impact on the story.

  Bear in mind that panoramic video is used to transport the user to real places or situations that they cannot access and where the environment is relevant. It is not a question of escaping from reality but rather of immersing oneself in a distant or inaccessible reality. On the other hand, CGI can represent whatever we imagine, regardless of whether it is similar to reality. Some narratives simply involve a linear consumption. Others require higher levels of interactivity and/or agency to achieve their objectives. These may range from a 360° video documentary about a refugee camp or a short film about dinosaurs using CGI, which are both linear and limited to 3DoF, to a serious game or a video game with 6DoF and body-mounted displays.

Both the role you give the user and the way in which the environment recognizes them contribute to creating, maintaining and reinforcing immersiveness and a sense of presence. Imagine that you are the user when checking that your expectations related to being in the place and what is happening there are really happening and are being met. Can they be reinforced further? Finally, ensure the story has a logical fulfilment while also achieving narrative immersion.

This all contributes to creating more meaningful experiences and improving the user's level of interest and involvement, leading to increased engagement.

REFERENCES

Biocca, F. & Delaney, B. (1995). Immersive virtual reality technology. In Biocca, F. & Levy, M. R. (Eds.), *Communication in the age of virtual reality* (pp. 57–126). Routledge.

Biocca, F. & Levy, M. R. (1995). *Communication in the age of virtual reality*. Routledge.

Bolter, J. D., Engberg, M. & MacIntyre, B. (2021). *Reality media: Augmented and virtual reality*. MIT Press.

Bowman, D. & Hodges, L. (1999). Formalizing the design, evaluation and application of interaction techniques for immersive virtual environments. *Journal of Visual Languages & Computing 10*(1), 37–53. https://doi.org/10.1006/jvlc.1998.0111

Brillhart, J. (2016). *In the blink of a mind attention*. Medium.com. https://medium.com/the-language-of-vr/all?topic=editing

Darnell, E. (2016). *Invasion!* Vr content. https://www.meta.com/es-es/experiences/invasion-anniversary-edition/3323166227771391/

Darnell, E. (2021). *Baba Yaga*. Vr content. https://www.meta.com/es-es/experiences/baba-yaga/3727135290647922/

Dolan, D. & Parets, M. (2016). *Redefining the axiom of story: The VR and 360 video complex*. Tech Crunch. https://techcrunch.com/2016/01/14/redefining-the-axiom-of-story-the-vr-and-360-video-complex/

Dooley, K. (2024). *Virtual reality narratives: Embodied encounters in space*. Palgrave Macmillan.

Egenfeldt-Nielsen, S., Smith, J. H. & Pajares Tosca, S. (2019). *Understanding video games: The essential introduction*. Routledge.

Flavián, C., Ibáñez-Sánchez, S. & Orús, C. (2019). The impact of virtual, augmented and mixed reality technologies on the customer experience. *Journal of Business Research 100*, 547–560.

Gödde, M., Gabler, F., Siegmund, D. & Braun, A. (2018). Cinematic narration in VR–rethinking film conventions for 360 degrees. In *Virtual, Augmented and Mixed Reality: Applications in Health, Cultural Heritage, and Industry: 10th International Conference, VAMR 2018, Held as Part of HCI International 2018, Las Vegas, NV, USA, July 15–20, 2018, Proceedings, Part II* 10 (pp. 184–201). Springer International Publishing.

Ivars-Nicolás, B. & Santos-Gonçalves, T. (2023). El reportaje inmersivo prosocial en vídeo 360° para promover conductas positivas. In T. Hidalgo-Marí & J. Herrero-Gutiérrez (Eds.), *Nuevas pesquisas: Los rumbos de la investigación en comunicación* (pp. 163–168). Dykinson.

Laurel, B. (2014). *Computers as theatre* (2nd edition.). Addison-Wesley.

Murray, J. H. (1997). *Hamlet on the holodeck: The future of narrative in cyberspace* (Updated edition). MIT Press.

Murray, J. H. (2017). How close are we to the Holodeck. In *Clash of Realities 2015/16: On the Art, Technology and Theory of Digital Games. Proceedings of the 6th and 7th Conference 5* (pp. 29–43). Transcript Verlag.

Nielsen, L. T., Møller, M. B., Hartmeyer, S. D., Ljung, T. C., Nilsson, N. C., Nordahland, R. & Serafin, S. (2016). Missing the point: An explo-ration of how to guide users' attention during cinematic virtual reality. In *Proceedings of the 22nd ACM Conference on Virtual Reality Software and Technology* (pp. 229–232). Association for Computing Machinery.

Oculus (2019). *Bogo.* Vr content. https://www.meta.com/es-es/experiences/?utm_content=53192

Oculus Story Studio (2015). *Henry.* Vr content. https://www.meta.com/es-es/experiences/henry/2404437756348346/

Otero-Millan, J., Macknik, S. L. & Martinez-Conde, S. (2014). Fixational eye movements and binocular vision. *Frontiers in Integrative Neuroscience 8*, 52. https://www.frontiersin.org/journals/integrative-neuroscience/articles/10.3389/fnint.2014.00052/full

Pausch, R., Snoddy, J., Taylor, R., Watson, S. & Haseltine, E. (1996). Disney's Aladdin: First steps toward storytelling in virtual reality. In *Proceedings of the 23rd Annual Conference on Computer Graphics and Interactive Techniques (SIGGRAPH '96). Association for Computing Machinery New York* (pp. 193–203). https://doi.org/10.1145/237170.237257

Riggs, S. (2019). *The end of storytelling: The future of narrative in the storyplex.* Beat Media Group.

Riva, G. & Vettraino, M. (2015). The emotional side of virtual reality: From feelings of fear to the promotion of compassion. *Virtual Reality 19*(3–4), 163–173.

Ryan, M. L. (2009). From narrative games to playable stories: Toward a poetics of interactive narrative. *Storyworlds: A Journal of Narrative Studies 1*, 43–59.

Ryan, M. L. (2015). *Narrative as virtual reality 2: Revisiting immersion and interactivity in literature and electronic media.* JHU Press.

Slater, M. (2009). Place illusion and plausibility can lead to realistic behaviour in immersive virtual environments. *Philosophical Transactions of the Royal Society B: Biological Sciences, 364*(1535), 3549–3557.

Slater, M. & Sanchez-Vives, M. V. (2016). Enhancing our lives with immersive virtual reality. *Frontiers in Robotics and AI 3*, 74.

Spierling, U. (2007). Adding aspects of "implicit creation" to the authoring process in interactive storytelling. In Cavazza, M. & Donikian, S. (Eds.), *4th Virtual Storytelling: Using Virtual Reality Technologies for Storytelling. International Conference, ICVS* (pp. 13–25). Springer, Berlin.

CHAPTER 9

Virtual Content Distribution Channels

Erkan Saka and Berna Çelikkaya

1 INTRODUCTION: THE TRANSFORMATION OF DIGITAL CONTENT DISTRIBUTION

The proliferation of virtual content has fundamentally transformed media consumption patterns, establishing new paradigms for how immersive experiences reach audiences. This chapter examines the multifaceted landscape of virtual content distribution, analyzing how technological infrastructures, social dynamics, and economic models intersect to shape contemporary digital ecosystems. As platforms such as SteamVR, Oculus Store, and PlayStation VR emerge as primary gatekeepers, they not only provide access to immersive experiences but also constitute sites of cultural production where communities engage with content through novel modalities (Wulf et al., 2018; García & Losada-Fernández, 2023; Johnson & Woodcock, 2017).

The evolution from traditional to virtual content distribution represents more than a technological shift; it embodies a reconfiguration of power relationships between creators, platforms, and consumers. This analysis employs an interdisciplinary approach, integrating critical theory with ethnographic sensibilities to illuminate how distribution channels function as socially embedded phenomena that both reflect and reproduce existing hierarchies while simultaneously opening spaces for resistance and innovation.

DOI: 10.1201/9781003673538-9

1.1 The Multifaceted Distribution Landscape

This chapter on Virtual Content Distribution Channels delves into the multifaceted landscape of how immersive media reaches audiences, emphasizing the various platforms and strategies that facilitate this process. The proliferation of virtual content has transformed the way media is consumed, with platforms such as SteamVR, Oculus Store, and PlayStation VR serving as primary distribution channels. These platforms not only provide access to immersive experiences but also foster communities that engage with content in unique ways. The role of social media networks, online marketplaces, and app stores is significant, as they serve as vital conduits for content discovery and audience engagement, creating interconnected ecosystems where traditional boundaries between production, distribution, and consumption become increasingly blurred.

1.2 Emerging Technological Paradigms

Emerging trends in virtual content distribution, such as cloud gaming, are reshaping the landscape fundamentally. Cloud gaming allows users to stream games directly from the cloud, eliminating the need for high-end hardware and making immersive experiences more accessible to a broader audience. This trend is supported by the increasing capabilities of internet infrastructure and the growing acceptance of subscription-based models, which provide users with a library of games for a fixed monthly fee (Mangili et al., 2016). The democratization potential of cloud-based distribution challenges traditional hardware-dependent models while simultaneously raising questions about digital sovereignty and infrastructure dependency.

Additionally, platforms like YouTube and Twitch have become essential for virtual content sharing, enabling users to create, share, and engage with content in real time. The interactive nature of these platforms enhances user engagement, as viewers can participate in live chats and share their experiences, creating a communal atmosphere around gaming and immersive media (Balakrishnan & Griffiths, 2017; Švelch & Švelch, 2020). These streaming platforms represent a paradigmatic shift where content distribution becomes inseparable from social interaction and community formation, transforming passive consumption into active participation.

1.3 Digital Marketing and Authentic Engagement

Digital marketing plays a crucial role in promoting virtual content across these distribution channels, yet it operates within complex tensions between commercial imperatives and authentic community building. Influencer marketing, particularly on platforms like Twitch and YouTube, has emerged as a powerful strategy for reaching target audiences. Streamers and content creators often act as brand ambassadors, leveraging their established communities to promote games and immersive experiences (Pollack et al., 2021; Coates et al., 2019).

In addition to functioning as brand ambassadors, influencers on platforms such as YouTube and Twitch simultaneously perform while playing these video games live. This performative dimension brings the experience to life for viewers who not only witness but may also actively participate in the unfolding dynamics of live (video game) streaming. As a result, the act of distribution becomes inseparable from performance, as audiences engage with both the promoted content and the embodied practices of the influencer in real time. The effectiveness of this approach is evident in the way content creators engage their audiences through authentic interactions, which can lead to increased visibility and sales for the products they endorse (Rashid, 2023).

Furthermore, the integration of user-generated content (UGC) into marketing strategies allows for a more organic promotion of virtual content, as users share their experiences and recommendations within their networks (Törhönen et al., 2019). This organic distribution model challenges traditional advertising paradigms by prioritizing authentic peer-to-peer recommendations over corporate messaging, yet it simultaneously raises questions about the commodification of social relationships and the boundaries between genuine community engagement and market-driven promotion.

1.4 Structural Challenges and Barriers

However, the virtual content distribution landscape faces significant challenges that threaten its democratic potential. Platform exclusivity can create barriers for both creators and consumers, limiting access to certain games or experiences based on the platform used. This exclusivity can hinder audience growth and engagement, as users may be reluctant to invest in multiple platforms to access their desired content (Törhönen et al., 2020). Moreover, the reluctance to subscribe to multiple platforms may not only stem from practical considerations but also from economic constraints or ideological preferences shaping user choices.

Additionally, issues of accessibility remain paramount, as not all users have equal access to the necessary technology or internet bandwidth to engage with immersive media fully. This digital divide can exacerbate existing inequalities in media consumption and participation (Mangili et al., 2016). The promise of democratized access through virtual content distribution remains unrealized for many communities, particularly those facing economic disadvantages or inadequate technological infrastructure.

1.5 Strategic Framework and Navigation Strategies

To navigate these challenges, this chapter outlines several strategies for successful distribution and audience engagement that balance commercial viability with social equity. First, fostering strong community ties through interactive content and regular engagement can enhance user loyalty and encourage word-of-mouth promotion (Wulf et al., 2018; Švelch & Švelch, 2020). This approach recognizes that sustainable distribution models must prioritize authentic community building over short-term profit maximization.

Second, leveraging data analytics to understand audience preferences and behaviors can inform targeted marketing strategies, ensuring that content reaches the right audiences at the right time (Mangili et al., 2016). However, this data-driven approach must be balanced against privacy concerns and the risk of creating algorithmic filter bubbles that limit exposure to diverse content.

Lastly, collaboration between platforms and content creators can lead to innovative distribution methods that enhance user experience and broaden access to immersive media (Rashid, 2023). Such collaborations require careful consideration of power dynamics and revenue sharing to ensure that creators maintain agency while platforms provide necessary infrastructure and reach.

1.6 Chapter Overview and Analytical Framework

In conclusion, this comprehensive examination of Virtual Content Distribution Channels provides an overview of the current landscape, highlighting the importance of various platforms, emerging trends, and effective marketing strategies. By addressing the challenges of exclusivity and accessibility, and by leveraging community engagement and data-driven insights, stakeholders in the virtual content ecosystem can optimize their distribution efforts and enhance audience engagement.

This chapter employs critical theoretical frameworks to analyze how distribution channels function as more than neutral conduits for content delivery. Instead, these channels embody complex sociotechnical systems that actively shape cultural production, social interaction, and economic possibility within immersive media ecosystems. By maintaining critical perspectives while embracing technological possibilities, this analysis seeks to illuminate pathways toward distribution models that expand access, support creativity, and foster meaningful human connection within virtual spaces, while remaining vigilant about the reproduction of existing power structures and inequalities in digital domains.

2 PRIMARY DISTRIBUTION PLATFORMS: ARCHITECTURE OF DIGITAL GATEKEEPING

2.1 Platform Ecosystems and Technical Specifications

The landscape of virtual content distribution is dominated by several key platforms, each constructing distinct ecosystems through technical requirements, curation processes, and business models. SteamVR, developed by Valve Corporation, exemplifies the PC-based distribution model, supporting diverse VR headsets while maintaining relatively open submission processes that rely on community feedback for quality control (Valve Corporation, 2023a, 2023b, 2023c). This approach reflects assumptions about technological democratization and user agency.

SteamVR's technical architecture demonstrates a commitment to hardware agnosticism that distinguishes it from competitors. The platform supports an extensive range of headsets including HTC VIVE, Oculus Rift, Windows Mixed Reality devices, and Valve's own Index system, requiring developers to optimize for multiple hardware configurations rather than a single target device. This technical flexibility comes with trade-offs: while it maximizes potential audience reach, it also complicates development processes and can result in suboptimal performance on specific hardware configurations. The platform's SteamVR runtime serves as a crucial intermediary layer, translating universal VR commands into device-specific instructions, effectively abstracting hardware differences for developers while maintaining compatibility across manufacturers.

The competitive dynamics among these platforms reflect broader shifts in the technology industry toward platform-based business models. North America dominated the virtual reality content creation market, driven by strong investments in immersive technologies and the rapid adoption of VR across entertainment, education, and healthcare sectors. This regional concentration influences platform strategies, as developers often prioritize markets with established infrastructure and higher purchasing power, creating feedback loops that reinforce existing technological inequalities between regions.

In contrast, Meta's Oculus Store implements strict curation processes, particularly for Quest devices, where developers must navigate multiple approval stages including concept approval and technical review (Meta, 2023a, 2023b). This gatekeeping mechanism reveals how platform control extends beyond technical specifications to shape the very possibilities of creative expression within virtual spaces. Meta's approach prioritizes user experience consistency and technical optimization for specific hardware, reflecting a philosophy that values curated quality over open access. The Quest platform's mobile-based architecture imposes significant computational constraints, requiring developers to optimize graphics, reduce polygon counts, and implement efficient rendering techniques that often compromise visual fidelity in favor of performance stability.

The curation process itself embodies ideological assumptions about content quality and user safety. Meta's content guidelines emphasize family-friendly experiences, technical polish, and commercial viability, effectively filtering out experimental, artistic, or politically challenging content that might not align with mainstream consumer expectations. This curatorial approach shapes not only what content reaches users but also influences what developers choose to create, as the prospect of rejection can deter innovative or unconventional projects that might push the boundaries of virtual reality as an artistic medium.

Sony's PlayStation VR platform demonstrates yet another model, tightly integrated with existing console ecosystems and leveraging established quality control processes (Sony Interactive Entertainment, 2023a, 2023b). Sony's approach benefits from decades of experience in console game development, applying proven quality assurance methodologies to virtual reality content. The platform's integration with PlayStation infrastructure provides developers with established development tools, debugging systems, and distribution mechanisms, reducing barriers to entry for traditional game developers while maintaining high technical standards.

Platform technical specifications extend beyond hardware compatibility to encompass entire ecosystems of development tools, content standards, and user experience paradigms. SteamVR's approach emphasizes backward compatibility and cross-device functionality, supporting headsets from multiple manufacturers including HTC, Oculus, and Windows Mixed Reality devices. This technical openness contrasts sharply with Meta's Quest ecosystem, which prioritizes optimization for specific hardware configurations to deliver consistent performance across its device portfolio. The technical implications of these different approaches are profound: SteamVR developers must account for varying display resolutions, tracking systems, and input methods, while Quest developers can optimize for known hardware specifications but face limitations in computational power and thermal management.

2.2 Beyond Consumer Platforms: Professional and Enterprise Distribution

The distribution landscape extends beyond consumer-oriented platforms to include specialized channels serving professional and enterprise markets. VIVEPORT caters specifically to HTC VIVE Focus headsets for commercial applications in training and simulation (Start Beyond, 2024). These enterprise-focused platforms operate under fundamentally different assumptions about user needs, content requirements, and business models compared to consumer-oriented services.

Enterprise virtual reality distribution channels prioritize reliability, security, and integration with existing business systems over entertainment value or broad consumer appeal. VIVEPORT's enterprise offerings include content management systems that allow organizations to deploy, monitor, and update virtual reality applications across multiple devices simultaneously. This capability proves essential for large-scale training programs where consistent content delivery and progress tracking become critical operational requirements. The platform's enterprise features include user analytics, session monitoring, and integration with learning management systems, transforming virtual reality from an entertainment medium into a measurable business tool.

Varjo XR-4 series targets high-stakes professional contexts—astronaut training, nuclear power plant operations—revealing how distribution channels segment according to risk tolerance and capital investment (Varjo Technologies, 2023). Varjo's distribution model operates on enterprise licensing agreements rather than individual content purchases, reflecting the specialized nature of professional virtual reality applications. These high-end systems require custom content development, extensive quality assurance testing, and ongoing technical support that justify premium pricing structures. The platform's technical specifications—including human-eye resolution displays and precise hand tracking—enable applications that would be impossible on consumer hardware, demonstrating how distribution channels and technical capabilities co-evolve to serve specific market segments.

The segmentation between consumer and professional markets creates distinct technological and social ecosystems within virtual reality distribution. Professional platforms often implement features that would be unnecessary or intrusive in consumer contexts: detailed usage analytics, administrative controls, and integration with enterprise security systems. These technical differences reflect deeper assumptions about user agency, privacy, and the purpose of virtual reality experiences. While consumer platforms prioritize user choice and entertainment value, professional platforms emphasize measurable outcomes, compliance with organizational policies, and integration with existing business processes.

NVIDIA Omniverse occupies an interstitial position, providing toolsets for content creation and cross-platform compatibility that blur boundaries between creation and distribution (NVIDIA Corporation, 2023). Omniverse represents a hybrid approach that combines content creation tools with distribution capabilities, enabling real-time collaboration between developers using different software packages and targeting multiple platforms simultaneously. This convergence of creation and distribution tools reflects broader trends toward platform consolidation, where single companies attempt to control multiple layers of the technology stack from content creation through final delivery to users.

Similarly, platforms like Spatial and Virbela focus on enterprise collaboration, with Virbela's "metaverse-as-a-service" model exemplifying how distribution increasingly encompasses entire virtual environments rather than discrete content packages (TechTarget, 2025). These platforms represent a fundamental shift from distributing individual applications to providing persistent virtual spaces where users can access multiple experiences without transitioning between different software environments. This model requires substantial infrastructure investment to maintain persistent worlds, user identity management, and cross-platform compatibility, representing a significant departure from traditional software distribution models.

2.3 Platform Business Models and Economic Implications

All major platforms typically employ a 70/30 revenue split with developers, though variations exist based on sales volume or promotional arrangements. This standardization masks significant differences in how platforms extract value through exclusivity agreements, with Oculus and PlayStation frequently securing exclusive content to drive hardware sales while SteamVR generally maintains platform agnosticism (Lanier et al., 2019). These economic arrangements shape not only developer incentives but also the broader political economy of virtual content production.

The apparent standardization of the 70/30 revenue split obscures more complex economic relationships between platforms, developers, and users. While this percentage split has become industry standard, platforms differentiate themselves through additional services, promotional opportunities, and development support that can significantly impact developer revenues beyond simple percentage calculations. SteamVR offers extensive community features, user review systems, and discovery mechanisms that can drive sales for successful titles, while Meta provides development funding, marketing support, and technical assistance for exclusive content, effectively subsidizing development costs in exchange for platform exclusivity.

Revenue sharing models also vary significantly based on content type, distribution method, and target market. Enterprise platforms like VIVEPORT often operate on flat licensing fees or subscription models rather than percentage-based revenue sharing, reflecting the different value propositions and cost structures of professional content. Educational content may receive preferential revenue terms or promotional support, while experimental or artistic projects might face reduced discovery opportunities despite identical revenue-sharing percentages. These variations demonstrate how platform business models shape not only economic outcomes but also influence what types of content get developed and promoted.

Platform exclusivity agreements represent a particularly contentious aspect of virtual reality distribution economics. While exclusive content can drive hardware adoption and provide platforms with competitive advantages, these arrangements can limit content accessibility and fragment audiences across incompatible ecosystems. The economic logic of exclusivity creates tensions between platform growth and user choice: platforms benefit from exclusive content that differentiates their offerings, but users face increased costs and reduced options when content remains locked to specific hardware platforms.

The economics of platform exclusivity extend beyond simple hardware sales to encompass broader ecosystem development strategies. Platforms invest in exclusive content not only to drive immediate hardware sales but also to establish developer relationships, demonstrate platform capabilities, and create network effects that encourage further ecosystem growth. Successful exclusive titles can establish platforms as viable development targets, attracting additional developers and creating virtuous cycles of content growth. However, exclusivity agreements can also create artificial scarcity that limits market growth and user adoption, particularly when

TABLE 9.1   Major Virtual Content Distribution Platforms—Comparative Analysis

Platform	Owner	Revenue Split	Content Curation	Hardware Focus	Key Characteristics
SteamVR	Valve corporation	70/30 (developer/platform)	Community-driven feedback	PC-based, multi-headset	Open submission, democratic quality control
Oculus Store	Meta	70/30	Strict multi-stage approval	Quest devices primarily	Closed ecosystem, high-quality standards
PlayStation VR	Sony interactive	70/30	Console-integrated QC	PlayStation console integration	Established quality processes
VIVEPORT	HTC/start beyond	Variable	Professional curation	HTC VIVE Focus	Enterprise and commercial applications
NVIDIA Omniverse	NVIDIA	Freemium/subscription	Developer tools focus	Cross-platform	Creation-distribution hybrid

exclusive content represents significant technical or creative achievements that showcase platform capabilities.

The global virtual reality content creation market, valued at USD 33.82 billion in 2024 and projected to reach USD 737.51 billion by 2032 (Gupta, 2024, June), demonstrates the significant economic stakes involved in platform positioning and content distribution strategies. The video segment dominated the market with the largest revenue share in 2024, driven by the growing demand for immersive storytelling in advertising, training, and educational applications. This market growth creates opportunities for new platform entrants while also intensifying competition among established players, potentially leading to more aggressive exclusivity strategies or alternative differentiation approaches.

Platform business models must also account for the high costs of virtual reality content development, which often exceed traditional software development expenses due to specialized technical requirements, testing across multiple hardware configurations, and the need for innovative user experience design. These development costs influence platform strategies toward supporting larger development studios or providing significant financial assistance to smaller developers, creating dependencies that can affect creative autonomy and content diversity. The economic pressures of virtual reality development tend to favor safe, commercially viable projects over experimental or artistic endeavors, potentially limiting the medium's creative potential (Table 9.1).

3 SOCIAL- AND COMMUNITY-BASED DISTRIBUTION: REIMAGINING DIGITAL SOCIALITY

Social VR platforms such as Meta's Horizon Worlds and VRChat represent a fundamental shift in distribution paradigms, where users simultaneously function as creators, distributors, and consumers. This collapse of traditional roles facilitates what might be termed "experiential distribution" content spreads through embodied social interactions rather than discrete download transactions.

The integration of virtual content within traditional social networks further complicates distribution dynamics. Users no longer perceive themselves solely as content consumers but as active community members whose authentic experiences strengthen collective bonds. This participatory framework enables sustainable community formation while raising questions about labor, ownership, and value extraction within platform capitalism. UGC becomes both the product and the medium of distribution, creating recursive loops where community engagement drives platform growth (Törhönen et al., 2019).

3.1 The Collapse of Traditional Distribution Roles

The dissolution of distinct producer-distributor-consumer categories within social virtual reality environments represents a fundamental challenge to established media economics and cultural production theories. Traditional distribution models assume clear demarcations between content creators who produce experiences, distributors who facilitate access, and consumers who purchase and engage with final products. Social VR platforms disrupt this linear progression by enabling users to simultaneously occupy multiple roles within single interactions, creating complex networks of value creation and exchange that resist conventional economic analysis.

Within platforms like VRChat, users create virtual spaces, develop interactive experiences, and share content through their embodied presence and social interactions, effectively functioning as creators, curators, and distributors simultaneously. This role convergence extends beyond simple UGC to encompass collaborative creation processes where multiple users contribute to evolving virtual experiences in real time. A single virtual space might begin as one user's creation but transform through collaborative modification, social interaction, and community input into something that reflects collective creativity rather than individual authorship.

The economic implications of this collapse challenge traditional intellectual property frameworks and revenue distribution models. When users create content within platform-controlled environments, questions arise about ownership, attribution, and compensation that existing legal and economic structures struggle to address adequately. Platforms benefit from UGC that drives engagement and retention, but the creators of this content often receive no direct financial compensation, raising concerns about digital labor exploitation and the appropriation of user creativity for corporate profit.

Social virtual reality distribution also enables new forms of cultural transmission that bypass traditional gatekeeping mechanisms. Users can share experiences, knowledge, and creative expressions directly through embodied interactions without requiring approval from platform administrators or content reviewers. This disintermediation potentially democratizes access to audiences while simultaneously creating new challenges for content quality, safety, and community standards enforcement.

3.2 Community-Driven Content Ecosystems

Community-driven distribution within social virtual reality environments operates through complex networks of social relationships, shared interests, and collaborative creation that transcend individual platform boundaries. These ecosystems emerge organically from user interactions rather than being imposed by platform designers, creating bottom-up distribution networks that can be more responsive to community needs and preferences than top-down algorithmic systems.

The viral propagation of content within virtual communities follows different mechanics than traditional social media sharing, as experiences must be discovered through embodied exploration and social recommendation rather than algorithmic feeds or search functions. Users learn about new virtual spaces, experiences, and events primarily through direct social interactions with other community members, creating word-of-mouth distribution networks that privilege authentic personal recommendations over sponsored or promoted content.

Community moderation and governance within these spaces present unique challenges as traditional content moderation techniques designed for text and images prove inadequate for three-dimensional, real-time social interactions. Virtual communities often develop their own informal governance structures, social norms, and enforcement mechanisms that operate alongside or sometimes in tension with platform-wide policies. These community-driven governance systems can be more responsive to local context and cultural specificity than universal platform rules, but they can also create inconsistent user experiences and potential conflicts between different community standards.

The sustainability of community-driven distribution models depends heavily on volunteer labor from community moderators, event organizers, and content creators who contribute significant unpaid work to maintain vibrant virtual spaces. This reliance on unpaid community labor raises questions about the long-term viability of community-driven distribution and the potential for burnout among key community contributors who enable these ecosystems to function effectively.

Economic models for supporting community-driven content creation remain underdeveloped, as traditional advertising and subscription models often conflict with the social and collaborative nature of community spaces. Some platforms experiment with user-to-user payment systems, virtual goods economies, and creator support programs, but these mechanisms have yet to mature into comprehensive economic frameworks that can adequately compensate community contributors for their essential role in content distribution and platform growth.

3.3 Embodied Social Interaction as Distribution Medium

The embodied nature of social virtual reality transforms content distribution from information transmission to experiential sharing, where the medium of communication becomes inseparable from the message being conveyed. Unlike traditional digital platforms where content exists as discrete objects that can be shared, copied, or redistributed independently of social context, virtual reality content often requires embodied presence and social interaction to be fully experienced and understood.

Embodied social interaction enables new forms of tacit knowledge transmission that cannot be easily replicated through traditional media channels. Skills, techniques, and cultural practices can be shared through demonstration, imitation, and collaborative practice within virtual environments, creating distribution mechanisms that preserve the experiential and contextual dimensions of knowledge that are often lost in formal documentation or instructional content.

The presence of avatar bodies and spatial relationships within virtual environments creates additional layers of meaning and communication that influence how content is received and interpreted by users. Gestures, proximity, eye contact, and spatial positioning all contribute to the social dynamics of content sharing, making virtual reality distribution inherently more complex and contextually dependent than traditional digital distribution methods.

Social presence within virtual environments also enables new forms of collective experience and shared meaning-making that can amplify the impact and reach of content beyond what individual consumption would achieve. When users experience content together in virtual spaces, they create shared memories and social bonds that can motivate them to recommend experiences to others, effectively turning every social interaction into a potential distribution event.

The synchronous nature of embodied social interaction within virtual environments creates both opportunities and limitations for content distribution. While real-time social sharing can create powerful emotional connections and memorable experiences, it also limits the scalability of distribution compared to asynchronous platforms where content can reach unlimited audiences simultaneously. This tension between intimacy and scale represents a fundamental challenge for social virtual reality platforms seeking to balance authentic community experiences with platform growth and commercial viability.

The emergence of virtual influencers and social leaders within VR communities creates new hierarchies and power structures that shape content distribution patterns in ways that differ significantly from traditional social media influence. Virtual reality influence often depends more on embodied charisma, spatial design skills, and community-building abilities than on follower counts or engagement metrics, creating opportunities for different types of creators to gain influence and distribute content effectively within virtual communities.

4 EMERGING DISTRIBUTION TECHNOLOGIES: INFRASTRUCTURE AND ACCESSIBILITY

4.1 Cloud Gaming and Streaming Architectures

Cloud gaming infrastructure represents a paradigmatic shift in distribution logic, with the global market projected to reach USD 18.71 billion by 2027 (ARED Group, 2023). By leveraging edge computing to reduce latency, platforms like NVIDIA's GeForce NOW and Meta's cloud gaming infrastructure bring processing closer to users, addressing the critical challenge of responsive gameplay (Engineering at Meta, 2022). This technological reconfiguration potentially democratizes access by eliminating hardware barriers while simultaneously concentrating power within cloud infrastructure providers.

Streaming platforms have evolved to accommodate immersive content's bandwidth demands. YouTube VR leverages sophisticated recommendation algorithms to promote VR content, while Twitch's real-time interaction model aligns with VR's immersive nature (Steel Series, 2023). These platforms function not merely as distribution channels but as sites of cultural production where new forms of digital performance emerge.

4.2 5G Networks and Edge Computing Synergies

The convergence of 5G networks and edge computing enables ultra-low latency experiences crucial for augmented reality (AR) and virtual reality (VR) applications. With 2.6 billion 5G subscriptions projected by 2025 (Bron, 2023), this infrastructure promises to reshape distribution possibilities.

Edge computing delivered over 5G networks facilitates real-time processing of complex applications, potentially enabling new forms of synchronous, multi-user virtual experiences (Akamai, 2024).

4.3 Subscription Models and Content Bundling Strategies

Subscription-based models reflect broader shifts in digital capitalism toward recurring revenue streams. Research by Buschow and Wellbrock (2024) demonstrates how comprehensive, cross-publisher bundles can stimulate engagement among diverse consumer groups, including those typically resistant to digital media consumption. These findings align with information goods economics principles suggesting that maximizing bundle size often optimizes profitability. Logic is increasingly applied to virtual content distribution.

5 DIGITAL MARKETING AND COMMUNITY ENGAGEMENT IN VIRTUAL SPACES

5.1 Influencer Ecosystems and Authenticity Paradoxes

Digital marketing within virtual content distribution reveals tensions between authentic community building and commercialized promotion. Influencer partnerships on platforms like Twitch and YouTube demonstrate how streamers function as cultural intermediaries, leveraging established communities to promote immersive experiences (Pollack et al., 2021; Coates et al., 2019). This influencer economy raises critical questions about standardization and homogenization, as marketing strategies converge around proven formulas (Rashid, 2023).

The integration of UGC into marketing strategies attempts to preserve authenticity while extracting promotional value. Users share experiences within their networks, creating organic promotion that circumvents traditional advertising's credibility deficit (Törhönen et al., 2019). Yet, this approach risks commodifying social relationships, transforming community bonds into marketing channels.

5.2 Data-Driven Targeting and Algorithmic Curation

Virtual content marketing increasingly relies on sophisticated analytics to understand audience preferences and behaviors (Mangili et al., 2016). While data-driven targeting promises personalized experiences, it simultaneously creates filter bubbles where users encounter repetitive content reinforcing existing preferences. This algorithmic curation shapes not only what content reaches audiences but also what content gets created, as developers optimize platform recommendation systems.

6 CHALLENGES AND BARRIERS: THE POLITICAL ECONOMY OF ACCESS

6.1 Platform Exclusivity and Market Fragmentation

Platform-exclusive agreements create artificial scarcity that fragments audiences and limits content accessibility. This strategy, while potentially lucrative for platforms seeking hardware sales, ultimately constrains market growth and user engagement (Törhönen et al., 2020). The proliferation of platform-specific content libraries forces consumers to invest in multiple ecosystems, exacerbating economic barriers to participation.

6.2 Digital Divides and Infrastructural Inequalities

Accessibility challenges extend beyond platform policies to encompass fundamental infrastructural inequalities. Not all users possess equal access to high-bandwidth internet connections or powerful hardware required for immersive experiences. This digital divide reproduces existing social hierarchies within virtual spaces, as economic capital determines participation possibilities (Mangili et al., 2016). Addressing these disparities requires systemic interventions beyond individual platform initiatives.

7 REGULATORY FRAMEWORKS AND GOVERNANCE CHALLENGES

7.1 Content Moderation in Embodied Virtual Spaces

Content moderation within virtual environments presents unique challenges as embodied interactions blur traditional content boundaries. Unlike traditional digital platforms where content exists such as text, images, or videos that can be algorithmically analyzed, virtual reality environments encompass real-time embodied interactions, spatial relationships, and behavioral patterns that resist conventional moderation approaches. The immersive nature of virtual reality means that harmful content can manifest through avatar movements, spatial positioning, voice interactions, and environmental manipulations that traditional content filtering systems cannot easily detect or categorize.

The complexity of virtual reality content moderation extends beyond identifying explicit material to encompass subtle forms of harassment that exploit the medium's unique characteristics. Virtual reality harassment can include unwanted physical proximity, aggressive gesture replication, virtual stalking through persistent world environments, and the creation of disturbing or threatening virtual scenarios that may not contain traditionally flaggable content but can cause significant psychological distress to users. These behaviors challenge existing content moderation frameworks that rely primarily on keyword detection, image recognition, and user reporting systems designed for two-dimensional digital interactions.

Platform approaches to virtual reality content moderation vary significantly in their technical implementation and philosophical orientation. Some platforms employ real-time behavioral analysis systems that monitor user interactions for patterns associated with harassment or abuse, while others rely primarily on post-incident reporting and human review processes. The technical challenges of implementing effective moderation in three-dimensional, real-time environments require sophisticated machine learning systems capable of understanding spatial relationships, gesture recognition, and contextual behavioral analysis that current technology can only partially address.

7.2 Age Verification and Dynamic Content Classification

Age restrictions and rating systems struggle to account for user-generated experiences that evolve dynamically. Traditional content rating systems such as the Entertainment Software Rating Board or Pan European Game Information operate on the assumption that content remains static after initial classification, but virtual reality platforms increasingly feature UGC that can transform fundamental aspects of the experience after official review. A virtual space initially rated as appropriate for general audiences might later host user-created content involving violence, sexual themes, or other mature content that would alter its appropriate age classification.

The challenge of dynamic content classification becomes particularly acute in social virtual reality platforms where user interactions create emergent narratives and experiences that cannot be predetermined during initial content review. Educational virtual reality applications might be infiltrated by inappropriate user behavior, while gaming environments can evolve to include user-generated modifications that introduce content elements do not present in the original experience. These dynamic transformations challenge the basic premises of age-based content classification systems and require new approaches to real-time content assessment and parental control mechanisms.

Emerging regulatory approaches attempt to address dynamic content through persistent monitoring and adaptive classification systems, but these solutions raise additional concerns about privacy, computational overhead, and the potential for false positives that could inappropriately restrict legitimate user activities. Some jurisdictions have begun developing regulatory frameworks that require platforms to implement real-time content analysis capabilities, while others focus on enhancing user-control mechanisms that allow individuals and parents to customize content filtering according to personal preferences and values.

7.3 Biometric Data Collection and Surveillance Capitalism

Privacy concerns intensify as platforms collect biometric data through VR headsets, raising questions about surveillance capitalism's expansion into intimate bodily experiences. Virtual reality systems necessarily collect unprecedented amounts of biometric and behavioral data, including head movement patterns, eye-tracking information, hand and finger movements, spatial positioning data, reaction times, and physiological responses such as heart rate variability. This data collection occurs continuously during virtual reality sessions and can reveal intimate details about users' psychological states, physical capabilities, behavioral preferences, and even medical conditions.

The scope of biometric data collection in virtual reality environments extends far beyond what traditional digital platforms can access. Eye-tracking data can reveal cognitive load, attention patterns, and emotional responses; hand-tracking information can indicate motor skills, tremors, or coordination issues; head movement patterns can suggest vestibular disorders or psychological states; and interaction patterns can reveal personality traits, social preferences, and behavioral tendencies. This comprehensive biological and behavioral profiling creates unprecedented opportunities for both beneficial applications and potential surveillance overreach.

Current regulatory frameworks struggle to address the unique privacy implications of immersive biometric data collection. The European Union's General Data Protection Regulation provides some protection for biometric data as a special category of personal information, but its application to virtual reality environments raises complex questions about consent, data minimization, and the purposes for which such intimate biological information can be collected and processed. Similar challenges arise under the California Consumer Privacy Act and other emerging privacy regulations that must grapple with virtual reality's unprecedented access to biological and behavioral information.

The commodification of biometric data within virtual reality platforms reflects broader trends toward surveillance capitalism, where intimate human experiences become raw material for computational products and predictive algorithms. Virtual reality platforms can potentially develop detailed psychological and physiological profiles of users that could be valuable for advertising, insurance, employment, or other commercial purposes that users may not have explicitly consented to support. The integration of artificial intelligence and machine learning systems with biometric data collection creates possibilities for inferential analytics that can derive sensitive information about users' health, relationships, financial status, and other private matters from their virtual reality interactions.

7.4 Jurisdictional Complexity and Cross-Border Governance

Regional compliance requirements further complicate distribution strategies, as platforms must navigate diverse regulatory landscapes while maintaining global user bases. Virtual reality platforms typically operate across multiple jurisdictions simultaneously, creating complex compliance challenges when different regions impose contradictory requirements for content standards, data handling practices, or platform governance mechanisms. What constitutes acceptable content in one jurisdiction may be prohibited in another, creating impossible situations for platforms seeking to maintain unified global experiences while respecting local legal requirements.

The jurisdictional complexity of virtual reality regulation becomes particularly apparent in areas such as content standards, where different cultural and legal traditions produce divergent expectations about appropriate material. European regulations may emphasize data protection and user privacy, while authoritarian regimes may prioritize content censorship and social control mechanisms. Democratic societies might focus on transparency and user agency, while other jurisdictions may require extensive government oversight and control over virtual reality experiences.

Emerging international frameworks attempt to address cross-border virtual reality governance through multilateral agreements and standardization efforts, but these initiatives face significant challenges in reconciling fundamentally different approaches to digital rights, content regulation, and platform governance. The Internet Corporation for Assigned Names and Numbers model of multi-stakeholder governance has been proposed as a potential framework for virtual reality regulation, but the immersive and embodied nature of virtual reality experiences raises new questions about sovereignty, jurisdiction, and cultural autonomy that traditional internet governance models were not designed to address.

7.5 Platform Sovereignty and Quasi-jurisdictional Authority

These governance challenges reveal tensions between platform sovereignty and state authority, with virtual spaces increasingly functioning as quasi-jurisdictional territories. Virtual reality platforms exercise unprecedented control over user experiences, implementing their own governance systems, dispute resolution mechanisms, content standards, and enforcement procedures that can significantly impact users' access to information, social interactions, and economic opportunities. This platform governance extends beyond simple content moderation to encompass complex social and economic systems that mirror governmental functions in their scope and impact.

The concept of platform sovereignty becomes particularly complex in virtual reality environments where platforms control not only access to content but also the fundamental parameters of social interaction, spatial navigation, and sensory experience. Users entering virtual reality environments must accept platform-defined terms of service that can be modified unilaterally and may include provisions for data collection, content moderation, account termination, and dispute resolution that significantly limit traditional legal protections and procedural rights.

Virtual reality platforms increasingly function as quasi-jurisdictional territories where platform policies carry more practical weight than formal legal frameworks. Users may spend significant portions of their social and economic lives within virtual environments governed by platform rules rather than democratic institutions, creating new forms of corporate authority that challenge traditional concepts of citizenship, rights, and political participation. The concentration of power within major virtual reality platforms raises concerns about democratic accountability, due process, and the protection of minority interests within platform-governed virtual spaces.

7.6 Emerging Governance Models and Regulatory Innovation

Regulatory innovation in virtual reality governance increasingly focuses on developing new institutional mechanisms that can address the unique challenges of immersive digital environments while preserving user rights and democratic values. Some proposals advocate for virtual reality-specific regulatory agencies with technical expertise and specialized enforcement capabilities, while others suggest adapting existing regulatory frameworks through targeted amendments and interpretive guidance. Hybrid approaches combine governmental oversight with industry self-regulation and user empowerment mechanisms to create multi-layered governance systems that can respond flexibly to rapidly evolving technological capabilities.

Experimental governance models include user-controlled moderation systems where communities can establish their own content standards and enforcement mechanisms, blockchain-based governance systems that distribute platform control among users and stakeholders, and algorithmic transparency requirements that mandate disclosure of automated decision-making processes affecting user experiences. These innovative approaches attempt to balance the need for effective governance with respect for user autonomy and platform innovation, but their effectiveness remains largely untested at scale.

The development of virtual reality governance frameworks also requires consideration of emerging technologies such as artificial intelligence, blockchain systems, and augmented reality that may further complicate regulatory challenges. As virtual reality platforms integrate with broader digital ecosystems and real-world infrastructure, governance frameworks must address not only virtual experiences but also their implications for physical spaces, economic systems, and social institutions. This convergence of virtual and physical governance creates new opportunities for regulatory innovation while also multiplying the potential consequences of governance failures or regulatory gaps.

8 FUTURE TRAJECTORIES: TOWARD PHYGITAL CONVERGENCE

The concept of "phygital" merging physical and digital spaces offers compelling narratives for future distribution models. These hybrid experiences create new possibilities for content dissemination that transcend traditional platform boundaries. The characterization of digital technologies as dramaturgically influential underscores how distribution channels shape not merely access, but the fundamental nature of creative expression.

Emerging distribution models must grapple with questions of preservation and cultural heritage as VR/AR reshape museum contexts and archival practices. Early collaborations between cultural institutions and technology companies suggest pathways for integrating immersive technologies while maintaining critical perspectives on commercialization and access.

9 STRATEGIC RECOMMENDATIONS FOR EQUITABLE DISTRIBUTION

9.1 Community-Centered Design Principles

Successful distribution strategies must prioritize community engagement through interactive content and regular participation. Strong community ties enhance user loyalty and encourage organic promotion through word-of-mouth networks (Wulf et al., 2018; Švelch & Švelch, 2020). Platforms should facilitate user agency in content curation while providing tools for meaningful social interaction.

9.2 Addressing Structural Barriers

Reducing accessibility barriers requires coordinated efforts addressing both technological and economic constraints. This includes developing lightweight content options for lower end hardware, implementing flexible pricing models, and advocating for infrastructural investments in underserved communities. Cross-platform compatibility standards could mitigate fragmentation while preserving platform differentiation (Rashid, 2023).

9.3 Ethical Distribution Frameworks

As virtual content distribution evolves, ethical considerations must inform platform design and policy. This includes transparent data practices, fair revenue sharing with creators, and commitment to preserving cultural diversity within virtual spaces. Platforms should resist tendencies toward algorithmic homogenization while supporting experimental and non-commercial content.

10 CONCLUSION: TOWARD CRITICAL DISTRIBUTION STUDIES

Virtual Content Distribution Channels constitute more than neutral conduits for digital experiences; they embody complex sociotechnical systems that shape cultural production, social interaction, and economic possibility within immersive media ecosystems. As distribution platforms proliferate and evolve, critical analysis must examine not only their technical capabilities but also their role in reproducing or challenging existing power structures.

The future of virtual content distribution depends on navigating tensions between democratization and control, standardization and diversity, commercial imperatives and cultural values. By maintaining critical perspectives while embracing technological possibilities, stakeholders can work toward distribution models that expand access, support creativity, and foster meaningful human connection within virtual spaces. The challenge lies not in perfecting distribution efficiency but in ensuring that these powerful channels serve broader social goods beyond platform profitability.

REFERENCES

Akamai. (August 20, 2024). *Edge computing and 5G: Emerging technology shaping the future of IT*. Retrieved from https://www.akamai.com/blog/edge/edge-computing-5g-emerging-technology-shaping-future-it

ARED Group. (2023). *How to build a cloud gaming infrastructure*. Retrieved from https://aredgroup.com/how-to-build-a-cloud-gaming-infrastructure/

Balakrishnan, J., & Griffiths, M. (2017). Social media addiction: What is the role of content in YouTube? *Journal of Behavioral Addictions*, 6(3), 364–377. https://doi.org/10.1556/2006.6.2017.058

Bron, D. (2023). *The impact of 5G and edge computing*. LinkedIn. Retrieved from https://www.linkedin.com/pulse/impact-5g-edge-computing-powering-next-generation-digital-daniel-bron

Buschow, C., & Wellbrock, C. M. (2024). Bundling digital journalism: Exploring the potential of subscription-based product bundles. *Media and Communication*, 12(1). https://www.cogitatiopress.com/mediaandcommunication/article/view/7442

Coates, A., Hardman, C., Halford, J., Christiansen, P., & Boyland, E. (2019). Food and beverage cues featured in YouTube videos of social media influencers popular with children: An exploratory study. *Frontiers in Psychology*, 10. https://doi.org/10.3389/fpsyg.2019.02142

Engineering at Meta. (2022). *Under the hood: Meta's cloud gaming infrastructure*. Retrieved from https://engineering.fb.com/2022/06/09/web/cloud-gaming-infrastructure/

García, J., & Losada-Fernández, D. (2023). Spanish Twitch streamers: Personal influence in a broadcast model akin to television. *Convergence: The International Journal of Research into New Media Technologies*, 29(3), 713–729. https://doi.org/10.1177/13548565221149892

Gupta, M. (June, 2024). *Virtual reality content creation market – Global market size, share, and trends analysis report – Industry overview and forecast to 2032*. Data Bridge Market Research. https://www.databridgemarketresearch.com/reports/global-virtual-reality-content-creation-market

Johnson, M., & Woodcock, J. (2017). 'It's like the gold rush': The lives and careers of professional video game streamers on Twitch.tv. *Information, Communication & Society*, 22(3), 336–351. https://doi.org/10.1080/1369118x.2017.1386229

Lanier, M., Waddell, T. F., Elson, M., Tamul, D. J., Ivory, J. D., & Przybylski, A. (2019). Virtual reality check: Statistical power, reported results, and the validity of research on the psychology of virtual reality and immersive environments. *Computers in Human Behavior*, 100, 70–78.

Mangili, M., Elias, J., Martignon, F., & Capone, A. (2016). Optimal planning of virtual content delivery networks under uncertain traffic demands. *Computer Networks*, 106, 186–195. https://doi.org/10.1016/j.comnet.2016.06.035

Meta. (2023a). *Oculus app submission guidelines*. Retrieved from https://developer.oculus.com/distribute/latest/concepts/publish-content-guidelines/

Meta. (2023b). *Oculus store*. Retrieved from https://www.oculus.com/experiences/quest/

NVIDIA Corporation. (2023). *Nvidia omniverse*. Retrieved from https://www.nvidia.com/en-us/omniverse/

Pollack, C., Gilbert-Diamond, D., Emond, J., Eschholz, A., Evans, R., Boyland, E., ... & Masterson, T. (2021). Twitch user perceptions, attitudes and behaviours in relation to food and beverage marketing on Twitch compared with YouTube. *Journal of Nutritional Science*, 10. https://doi.org/10.1017/jns.2021.22

Rashid, H. (2023). Collaborative music production via live streaming. *IASPM Journal*, 13(3), 66–75. https://doi.org/10.5429/2079-3871(2023)v13i3.6en

Sony Interactive Entertainment. (2023a). *PlayStation partners*. Retrieved from https://partners.playstation.net/

Sony Interactive Entertainment. (2023b). *PlayStation VR*. Retrieved from https://www.playstation.com/en-us/ps-vr/

Start Beyond. (2024). *VIVEPORT*. Retrieved from https://www.startbeyond.co/media/viveport

Steel Series. (2023). *Twitch vs YouTube: Which platform is right for your game stream?* Retrieved from https://steelseries.com/blog/twitch-vs-youtube-which-platform-is-right-for-your-game-stream-1018

Švelch, J., & Švelch, J. (2020). "Definitive playthrough": Behind-the-scenes narratives in let's plays and streaming content by video game voice actors. *New Media & Society*, 24(5), 1097–1115. https://doi.org/10.1177/1461444820971778

TechTarget. (2025). *Top metaverse platforms to know about*. Retrieved from https://www.techtarget.com/searchcio/tip/Top-metaverse-platforms-to-know-about

Törhönen, M., Sjöblom, M., Hassan, L., & Hamari, J. (2019). Fame and fortune, or just fun? A study on why people create content on video platforms. *Internet Research*, 30(1), 165–190. https://doi.org/10.1108/intr-06-2018-0270

Törhönen, M., Sjöblom, M., Vahlo, J., & Hamari, J. (2020). *View, play and pay? – The relationship between consumption of gaming video content and video game playing and buying*. Retrieved from https://doi.org/10.24251/hicss.2020.332

Valve Corporation. (2023a). *Steam direct*. Retrieved from https://partner.steamgames.com/steamdirect

Valve Corporation. (2023b). *Steam VR*. Retrieved from https://store.steampowered.com/steamvr

Valve Corporation. (2023c). *SteamVR system requirements*. Retrieved from https://store.steampowered.com/app/250820/SteamVR/

Varjo Technologies. (2023). *Varjo XR-4 series*. Retrieved from https://varjo.com/products/xr-4/

Wulf, T., Schneider, F., & Beckert, S. (2018). Watching players: An exploration of media enjoyment on Twitch. *Games and Culture*, 15(3), 328–346. https://doi.org/10.1177/1555412018788161

The Ethics of Social Representations in the Age of Virtual and Augmented Reality

Galo Vásconez Merino and
Antonella Carpio Arias

1 INTRODUCTION

The expansion of virtual reality (VR) and augmented reality (AR) opens up a new audiovisual landscape, where narratives are configured in interactive and immersive digital environments. In this context, social representation takes on a new dimension by placing itself in spaces where interaction and perception are intensified through the illusion of presence.

Unlike traditional media, where the recipient plays a fundamentally passive role, VR and AR experiences can turn them into active participants, capable of modifying their narrative journey, making decisions or interacting with elements of the plot (Non-Linear Storytelling, Interactive Storytelling). This shift in the role of the viewer becomes a cultural and ethical shift that transforms the way collective imaginaries are constructed, negotiated and consumed.

The potential of these technologies to generate empathy, recreate highly emotional situations or give visibility to invisible realities has been

DOI: 10.1201/9781003673538-10

demonstrated in productions such as Carne y Arena of Alejandro González Iñárritu (2017) and Notes on Blindness (Middleton & Spinney, 2016).

However, the same power of immersion that enables a closer link between narrative and audience also carries risks such as the aestheticisation of trauma, symbolic manipulation, the reinforcement of stereotypes and the misappropriation of cultural experiences. Hence, ethical reflection is essential to understanding how social representations are reconfigured in immersive environments.

This chapter proposes to critically examine the role of VR and AR in the reformulation of social representations, addressing both their innovative potential and the ethical dilemmas they entail. The analysis will focus on four interrelated axes: the transformation of audiovisual narrative and its impact on social perception; the reformulation of gender, race and class stereotypes; the risks of symbolic manipulation in immersive environments and the problems of privacy and data use in experiences with social content.

Using a theoretical-critical approach, the aim is to articulate a framework for reflection that can serve to guide the production and consumption of immersive content. The intention is to contribute to an urgent debate on how to ensure that narrative and technological innovations enhance social understanding without violating rights or reproducing inequalities.

2 REPRODUCTION OF SOCIAL IMAGINARIES AND THEIR INFLUENCE ON THE PERCEPTION OF REALITY

Social representations are systems of values, beliefs and practices that enable us to interpret reality and communicate within a community (Moscovici, 1984, p. 3). Constructed through symbols, narratives and discourses, they function as frameworks that guide our perception of social, political and cultural phenomena. In the immersive audiovisual field, they take on a performative character, as they not only describe reality but also shape it through the active interaction of the viewer.

Immersive technologies such as VR and AR transform the construction and circulation of representations. VR creates immersive environments that generate an illusion of presence, the feeling of being inside the environment (Slater & Sánchez-Vives, 2016). AR superimposes digital elements onto the physical world, integrating information and characters in real time, which enhances the convergence between the real and the virtual.

One of the most significant changes introduced by these technologies is the shift from linear narratives to interactive experiences, or Non-Linear

Storytelling, where the user can influence not only the development of the plot but also the rhythm, perspective and degree of immersion in the story world, thereby actively participating in the construction of its social meaning (Ryan, 2020, p. 175). This transformation challenges traditional notions of authorship and reception, as the narrative becomes a co-created process in which meaning emerges through the interplay between designer intention and user agency.

In Social VR environments, these interactions take on a collective dimension, as participants can exchange points of view, create collaborative narratives and even co-create cultural representations. This not only opens up the possibility of multiplying the voices and perspectives present in a story but also raises challenges around veracity, content moderation and bias prevention.

Fully Body Immersion intensifies this experience by allowing the user's body movements to be replicated in their avatar or digital representation, amplifying the sense of agency and of "being there" (Kilteni et al., 2012). However, this level of physical and emotional involvement can also influence the way in which messages or stereotypes present in the immersive environment are internalised, reinforcing certain social imaginaries.

At the same time, the use of Behaviour Biometrics in VR/AR experiences, such as eye-tracking, gesture analysis or body movement pattern detection, allows the narrative to be personalised and the level of difficulty or type of content to be adapted dynamically according to the user's responses (Clay et al., 2019).

This capacity for continuous adjustment not only enhances immersion but also creates the possibility of tailoring experiences to individual emotional states, learning curves or accessibility needs. While such adaptability can enrich engagement and inclusivity, it also raises ethical questions regarding the extent to which behavioural data should be collected, stored and interpreted, particularly when it concerns sensitive aspects of human cognition and emotion.

While this improves the Quality of Experience, it also raises important ethical challenges, particularly with regard to ethics, since the collection and storage of sensitive biometric data involves privacy risks and potential misuse (Madary & Metzinger, 2016) (Table 10.1).

The incorporation of these technologies into film and art reconfigures the production of meaning. Works such as Carne y Arena (Gonzalez Iñárritu, 2017) and Notes on Blindness (Middleton & Spinney, 2016) convey extreme experiences from a sensory perspective, generating embodied

TABLE 10.1   Immersive Technologies and Their Impact on Social Representations

Technology/ Concept	Key Features	Impact on Social Representation	Ethical Challenges
VR	Immersive 3D environments, illusion of presence	Embodied empathy, strong emotional involvement	Risk of trauma aestheticisation, manipulation
AR	Digital overlays on physical world	Convergence of real and virtual, contextualised narratives	Data use, authenticity of overlays
Full body immersion	Motion tracking, embodied avatars	Enhanced agency, "being there" effect	Reinforcement of stereotypes through embodiment
Behaviour biometrics	Eye-tracking, gesture analysis, movement data	Personalised, adaptive narratives	Privacy risks, consent, data exploitation

empathy that is difficult to achieve in traditional media. However, they can also lead to the aestheticisation of trauma, where the pain of others becomes an object of aesthetic consumption and loses its political or social dimension (Nichols, 2016).

Metaverse Ethics is key to defining regulatory frameworks and responsible practices in the design and dissemination of immersive content, ensuring inclusive, truthful and respectful representations. It also involves considering the responsibility of creators, producers and platforms in Multi-User VR/AR environments, where discourses can reproduce stereotypes or encourage discriminatory dynamics without adequate filters or codes (Schroeder, 2021).

The combination of VR/AR immersion with the social interaction of the metaverse creates a privileged but vulnerable space for collective narratives. The challenge is twofold: to harness its potential to make realities visible and generate empathy, while at the same time establishing mechanisms to prevent manipulation, misinformation and unethical use of data and content.

3 TRANSFORMATIONS IN THE REPRESENTATION OF SOCIAL EXPERIENCES

Immersive technologies transform storytelling by replacing linear, passive narratives with interactive experiences where the user is an active agent. With immersive experiences and devices, such as head-mounted displays (HMDs) or haptic suits, the narrative becomes physical and emotional. This shift towards intervention is linked to Murray's narrative agency (1998), where the user co-creates the environment.

A paradigmatic example is Carne y Arena (González Iñárritu, 2017), a VR installation that immerses the viewer in the experience of migrants crossing the Mexico-United States of America border. Through hyper-realistic images, surround sound and Full Body Immersion, it seeks to generate empathy by recreating the tension of the moment. Users walk on real sand, reinforcing the illusion of presence to reduce the emotional distance from the issue.

However, it is worth asking: to what extent can the viewer truly understand the suffering of others without reducing it to an emotional spectacle? The aestheticisation of trauma in immersive environments can pose an ethical risk by turning pain into an intense sensory experience without necessarily offering tools for critical reflection, as indicated by the experimental study by Baptie et al. (2021) named Virtually renovating the Trauma Film Paradigm: Comparing VR with on-screen presentation of an analogue trauma, where the use of VR intensified emotional vividness without increasing discomfort, demonstrating that aesthetic forms can alter the perception of suffering.

The aestheticisation of trauma can end up trivialising the events represented or reinforcing unequal power relations between those who represent and those who are represented. In the case of Carne y Arena, there has been debate as to whether the experience fosters genuine awareness or whether it offers a safe and symbolic version of real suffering, accessible from the comfort of a museum.

Similarly, Notes on Blindness: Into Darkness (Middleton & Spinney, 2016) places the user in the perceptual world of John Hull, an academic who documented his blindness. Through sound, voice-over and an abstract visual environment, it offers an introspective immersion that does not seek to reconstruct trauma, but rather to share another way of perceiving the world. The subjective narrative balances emotion, rhythm and sensorially to avoid sensationalism.

The Key (Tricart, 2019) addresses exile and loss from an allegorical perspective. Through a dreamlike metaphor, the user makes decisions that affect the character, deploying the resource of Interactive Storytelling. The emotional connection is achieved without explicitly showing pain, since, as Tricart points out, the intention was to offer a symbolic narrative that invites reflection based on empathy and choice.

These cases show not only the potential of VR/AR for participatory and empathetic social narratives, but also the risk of simplifying complex conflicts into individual experiences that, without critical design, can lead to the gamification of suffering or symbolic appropriation. Hence, the need for an ethical framework is based on respect, authenticity and community participation (Sora-Domenjó, 2022).

In addition, the emotional personalisation enabled by technologies such as Behaviour Biometrics, which adjust narrative stimuli according to the user's response, adds a new layer of complexity to the ethical debate. Its use allows the experience to be refined, improves its emotional impact and can exploit the viewer's sensitivity to achieve specific effects without fully informed consent (Madary & Metzinger, 2016).

4 THE ROLE OF VR AND AR IN THE REFORMULATION OF GENDER, RACE AND CLASS STEREOTYPES

Immersive environments designed with VR/AR technologies are amplified reflections of the sociocultural systems that produce them. This means that just as traditional media have reinforced exclusionary narratives for decades, virtual spaces can also perpetuate biased representations of gender, race or class. The aesthetics of immersion and interactivity do not eliminate these risks; rather, they can even intensify them when they are hidden under the guise of creative freedom, personalised choice or technological neutrality.

One study revealed that, even in contemporary video games, male and white characters continue to be the most represented, while women and people of other ethnicities appear less frequently and, assiduously, in stereotypical or hypersexualised roles.

This phenomenon is not limited to the entertainment industry but also occurs in professional and educational settings where dynamics have been observed that reflect and reproduce pre-existing social hierarchies, such as in virtual laboratories designed without an inclusive perspective that render the experiences of ethnic and gender minorities invisible (Gallardo-Williams & Dunnagan, 2022).

Similarly, VR opens unprecedented possibilities for rethinking identities through a logic of bodily experimentation. The creation and customisation of avatars enable individuals to play with categories, such as gender, race or age, offering opportunities for self-exploration and the embodiment of perspectives different from their own.

Such practices can foster empathy and challenge conventional boundaries of identity by allowing users to experience alternative subject positions within immersive environments. At the same time, this potential for exploration raises important questions about authenticity, appropriation and the reproduction of stereotypes, highlighting the need for critical awareness in both design and use.

Crone and Kallen (2022) report that when users embody avatars of a different gender than their own, their attitudes and decisions regarding job roles are significantly altered, as occurred in hiring simulations in STEM fields, where men embodying women showed greater openness towards female candidates.

Extreme avatar customisation can also encourage subtle forms of cultural appropriation or symbolic erasure. For example, when white people adopt avatars with diverse ethnic features without understanding their historical significance, they can trivialise experiences of structural oppression.

Added to this is the danger of reinforcing visual stereotypes by representing certain identities only from the perspective of the exotic, the marginal or the violent. An analysis of the representation of migrants in search engines and digital platforms revealed that racial and gender biases present in algorithms end up consolidating standardised images that reduce diversity to visual clichés (Urman et al., 2022).

Given this scenario, it is essential to rethink the construction of identities in immersive environments as an ethical-political process. Avatar design, personalisation, visual narrative and interaction environments must be governed by criteria of equity and critical representation, integrating historically marginalised communities into the definition of aesthetic standards and ethical frameworks of production.

5 THE TRANSFORMATION OF THE SPECTATOR FROM PASSIVE SUBJECT TO INTERACTIVE AGENT IN VIRTUAL ENVIRONMENTS

The transition from passive viewer to active participant has been one of the dominant narratives surrounding immersive media. However, beyond the enthusiasm for interactivity, what is at stake is an ethical reconfiguration of the user's role within virtual environments. Agency must be understood from the user's capacity for action, but also from their space of responsibility in relation to the discourses, characters and conflicts that are established digitally.

In contexts of Full Body Immersion and Social VR, the experience involves the sensory, spatial and relational. Dooley (2024) points out that the design, or absence, of virtual bodies is not a minor technical aspect, but a narrative resource that modulates the user's relationship with the represented world, especially in stories with sensitive social representations, where the immersed body becomes an involved body.

The agency of these environments can induce an illusion of control, since the user decides, explores and modifies environments, but in most cases within pre-established margins. This pseudo-freedom can turn the narrative into a fiction of participation, where justice, commitment or empathy is simulated without altering the structural frameworks that reproduce inequalities outside the virtual experience.

On the other hand, there are VR experiences that seek to turn this agency into a critical turning point. Fawzy (2024) analyses how narratives such as Baba Yaga shape the user as a global citizen in the making, proposing interactions that challenge values such as empathy, climate activism or intercultural responsibility. In these cases, the goal is to recognise one's own ethical involvement in globalised power structures.

The shift towards a more conscious agency requires a narrative design that places the user in a position of active reflection. An example of this is ReCapture, which uses perspective selection mechanics in the reconstruction of memories to invite moral introspection on the part of the participant, rather than imposing a preconfigured emotional path, which avoids emotional overstimulation and fosters a more authentic connection with the experience (Avendano et al., 2022).

This model of agency allows us to reconsider the conditions of production of these narratives by questioning who creates these experiences and from what symbolic position. The inclusion of represented communities in the development phase can transform user agency into a channel for intercultural co-creation, turning interactivity into a political device.

6 THE RISK OF SYMBOLIC MANIPULATION IN VIRTUAL ENVIRONMENTS: ETHICAL AND NARRATIVE DILEMMAS

Symbolic manipulation in immersive experiences is one of the most critical tensions in VR/AR cinema, especially when representing historical events or social conflicts. In the realm of collective memory, these formats modify how events are remembered and interpreted. Although they can generate educational and empathetic effects, they raise ethical dilemmas about narrative fidelity, the aestheticisation of trauma, and the construction of truth.

Immersive cinema, by placing the user within the narrative, modifies the traditional viewer experience. Unlike linear cinema, where the point of view is mediated by the camera, in VR, the user becomes a virtual presence within the diegetic environment.

Being there intensifies sensory and emotional reception, giving new symbolic power to narrative elements. In this context, symbols, spaces and objects are representations as well as activators of memory and emotion. This is what is often referred to as symbolic hyperpresence, where cultural symbols in virtual environments are constantly regenerated and re-signified through user interaction.

Several recent studies propose VR as a memory machine, highlighting its role in the construction and transmission of personal and collective memories. Immersion allows us to embody the perspective of victims, witnesses or perpetrators, overcoming the distancing effect of other media. However, this power requires narrative responsibility to ensure critical, inclusive and ethical memories (Gruenewald & Chen, 2025).

A significant example of these dynamics is The Book of Distance (2020), where the user relives the memory of the forced exile of Japanese people in Canada. In this work, interaction enhances an emotional reinterpretation of history. Similarly, Dobosz (1920), a Polish project, was criticised for using VR as a nationalist tool, shaping the memory of the past according to present political interests (Kazlauskaitė, 2023).

Regarding the boundary between fiction and truth, it should be noted from the outset that it becomes blurred in immersive environments. Unlike traditional documentaries, where voice-overs or archive footage lend authority, in VR, verisimilitude is constructed sensorially. This opens up a space for manipulating historical discourse through staging strategies, which can lead to symbolic distortions.

The project Their Memory (Donald & Scott-Brown, 2019) establishes a collaboration with represented communities, such as war veterans in Scotland, which allows for the reconstruction of an ethical and commemorative narrative. However, without these co-creation processes, VR runs the risk of spectacularising suffering and simplifying complex realities.

Another work, entitled Clouds Over Sidra, allows the user to experience life in a refugee camp, a work that has generated intense debate about whether these representations promote empathy or trivialise tragedy. Without a critical distance or an interpretative framework to contextualise the experience, a kind of tourist empathy can be fostered that functions more as entertainment than as a means of forming critical awareness.

This dilemma is accentuated when VR productions are used for political, commercial or ideological purposes, as in the aforementioned case of the productions sponsored by the Polish Ministry of Culture, since by manipulating the conditions of immersion, such as the viewing angle, ambient sound or avatar, the viewer's perception can be directed towards a partial or instrumentalised view of the facts.

The creation of immersive worlds requires a specific narrative ethic, as design decisions, from interactive elements to character representation, involve the inclusion or exclusion of perspectives and, therefore, the reproduction or subversion of dominant discourses (Martindale et al., 2025). In this sense, immersive experiences must consider what they represent, in the sense of how they do so, to avoid falling into simplifications or symbolic manipulations.

Therefore, the integration of represented communities, the transparent use of fiction and historical contextualisation are fundamental. Immersive narrative must certainly be understood from its artistic and technological perspective but also as a tool for cultural representation with profound emotional and social impacts.

7 PRIVACY, SURVEILLANCE AND USE OF DATA IN IMMERSIVE NARRATIVES WITH SOCIAL CONTENT

Immersive technologies use headsets, haptic sensors and tracking systems that collect large amounts of biometric and behavioural data. This collection raises ethical and regulatory challenges, making privacy a priority concern. Hence, the need to critically reflect on its risks and possibilities in relation to digital sovereignty, surveillance and the misuse of sensitive data.

Immersive devices capture unique data from each user, such as eye movements, breathing rate, facial gestures, emotional reactions, voice, dwell time and navigation trajectories. This collection far exceeds traditional online tracking models, such as cookies or click analytics, generating a kind of emotional digital footprint that can be used to predict and manipulate behaviour.

Warin and Reinhardt (2022) point out that extended reality environments collect data that serves to improve the user experience and could be exploited for commercial, political or even coercive purposes, without the user perceiving or understanding it. From this perspective, technology becomes a form of invisible surveillance that does not consider privacy as a personal issue, but rather as a form of storage.

The integration of AI into VR/AR platforms maximises the risks, as algorithms can identify behaviour patterns that can classify users, personalise content to an extreme degree or modify environments in real time to induce decisions. In games or interactive experiences, this manipulation may go unnoticed, but in educational, political or commercial contexts, the impact can be profound.

A study by Guo et al. (2024) found that many popular VR applications violated their own privacy policies and collected biometric data without explicit consent, including facial and eye movements. The opacity of the algorithmic system, coupled with the lack of control mechanisms on the part of users, creates a scenario of permanent vulnerability.

In response to this situation, regulatory frameworks are emerging that attempt to protect privacy in immersive environments. The General Data Protection Regulation (GDPR) in Europe and legislation such as the California Consumer Privacy Act have begun to include specific provisions on biometric data, although the pace of technological advancement often outstrips the ability of the law to respond.

Xynogalas and Leiser (2024) highlight Meta's challenges in complying with the GDPR due to the use of sensitive data such as eye-tracking, pointing to the lack of specific regulation for the metaverse. Along the same lines, Al-kfairy et al. (2024) emphasise the urgency of governance frameworks that integrate human rights, digital sovereignty and algorithmic transparency.

One of the most complex ethical issues lies in consent, since it is essential to ensure that users fully understand what data they are sharing, how it will be processed and for what purposes. In highly immersive environments, traditional mechanisms of consent, such as dialogue boxes or lengthy contractual agreements, become largely ineffective, as they interrupt the flow of the experience and are often disregarded.

Moreover, the sheer volume and sensitivity of data collected, including biometric, behavioural and emotional information, makes informed consent not only a legal requirement but also a profound ethical challenge. Designing new models of consent that are transparent, accessible and seamlessly integrated into the immersive environment is therefore crucial to safeguarding user autonomy and trust.

Dynamic consent systems and interfaces that clearly visualise data flows and processing could be used. Digital sovereignty means that users retain control over their identity and data at any point in the immersive experience, including the right to be forgotten, to revoke consent or to transfer data to other platforms.

8 ETHICAL REFLECTIONS AND PROPOSALS

The deployment of VR/AR as narrative media has opened up fertile ground for social representation. These technologies, capable of placing the user at the centre of the experience, enable unprecedented forms of immersion, interaction and empathy. However, their transformative potential faces a central dilemma: the same power they have to bring complex realities closer can be used to distort, trivialise or exploit them. This calls for deep ethical reflection on how works that use these resources should be conceived, produced and distributed.

In the history of the media, each new technology has generated a period of initial fascination followed by critical questioning. In the case of VR/AR, the speed of their expansion and the sensory intensity they produce require ethics to be a fundamental pillar. It is not enough to respond to incidents or criticism after the fact; it is necessary to design with clear ethical principles from the very conception of the work.

A comprehensive ethical framework must address three dimensions: the content represented, the user experience and the socio-economic ecosystem that supports production. This means that it is necessary not only to think about what is represented but also to understand how it is experienced and for whom it is produced. In this way, ethics becomes a continuous and cross-cutting practice that accompanies all stages, from preliminary research to final interaction.

Within the realm of respect and authenticity, stories involving real communities or events should be constructed in dialogue with their protagonists. This implies avoiding symbolic appropriation and ensuring that the voices represented actively participate in creative decisions. Respect does not have an aesthetic connotation, since it is relational and measured by the degree of involvement and consent of those who will be represented.

In terms of contextualisation and complexity, immersive experiences tend to condense realities to adapt them to the narrative time and the user's capacity for interaction, with the risk of simplifying to the point of distorting that reality. A key ethical principle is to preserve complexity by integrating contextual information that allows for an understanding of the nuances of the conflict or phenomenon portrayed.

In addition, sensory and emotional immersion can have profound psychological impacts. Ethical design involves providing mechanisms for containment and exit, clear warnings about content and options for modulating the intensity of the experience to ensure that it does not leave any lasting effects.

In environments where the line between fiction and reality is blurred, transparency is essential. The user must know whether what they are experiencing is a documentary reconstruction, a fiction based on facts or a purely imaginary work. Concealing this information can erode trust and manipulate interpretation.

Ethical responsibility in VR/AR is shared. Creators such as scriptwriters and designers define content and interaction, but within an industrial framework that conditions their possibilities. Producers decide on financing, audiences and timing, while platforms control access and visibility, often prioritising entertainment over critical proposals.

This means that the ethical framework is not solely a matter of the creator's individual conscience. It is therefore necessary to establish collective codes, cross-sector agreements and clear policies that align creative, commercial and social interests. Otherwise, ethical decisions will be subordinated to market pressure and the potential of VR/AR for social change will be contingent on its immediate profitability.

Even with clear principles, difficult tensions remain about how much realism to sacrifice to protect the user, how to balance fidelity to the experience with its comprehension by distant audiences or whether to prioritise the voice of the community even if it means giving up narrative resources that enhance immersion.

These tensions have no universal solution, but they do require an ethical framework to guide decisions on a case-by-case basis. The key is a deliberative process that consults all parties involved. Such a framework should involve creators, producers, academics, communities, legislators and platforms, being flexible in the face of cultural and technological diversity, but firm in limiting exploitation, manipulation or violation of rights.

A good starting point could be the creation of interdisciplinary ethics committees to accompany the development of immersive works. These committees could assess risks, propose adjustments and validate that the project meets minimum standards before its launch. Another measure would be to promote ethical distribution licences, which grant visible certification to works that meet certain responsibility criteria.

It would also be essential to promote immersive media literacy so that the public can identify when a work is ethical, when it manipulates representation and how to exercise control over their experience. A critical user is the best defence against abuse, but to do so, they need analytical tools and an environment that encourages reflection.

The ethical challenge of VR/AR in social representation is structural, as these technologies will continue to evolve, integrating artificial intelligence, mixed reality and persistent worlds in the metaverse. Therefore, thinking about ethics is a task of anticipation that allows us to foresee how today's decisions will shape tomorrow's practices.

The opportunity is enormous: with responsibility, VR/AR can amplify marginalised voices, preserve collective memories and foster active empathy. But if warnings are ignored, they can also reinforce inequalities, manipulate perceptions and turn immersion into an instrument of control.

The choice will ultimately depend on the ability of all stakeholders to recognise that ethics is a framework that gives meaning to creativity, because creating virtual worlds involves creating the rules that govern them, and those rules will determine whether these worlds will be spaces for encounter or distortion.

9 CONCLUSIONS

The journey taken throughout this chapter shows that VR/AR are technological innovations with new narrative languages capable of transforming the way we perceive, represent and understand social realities. From the potential to foster empathy to the risks of symbolic manipulation, these tools present unprecedented opportunities and far-reaching ethical dilemmas.

The sensory immersion they offer is not neutral, as it places the user in an active role that, while amplifying participation, also exposes them to subtle or explicit influences on their interpretation of events. This condition makes agency a central focus of the debate as a decision-making power and as a narrative and social responsibility.

The analysis shows that social representation in VR/AR faces tensions between truthfulness and fiction, memory and aestheticisation and interactivity and manipulation. These must be managed with ethical frameworks that ensure respect for communities, privacy and narrative transparency. Otherwise, immersive narrative can reproduce exclusion, simplify realities or aestheticise trauma.

The risks of unregulated use of these technologies are serious: manipulation of collective memory with historical distortions, exploitation of biometric data without informed consent and reproduction of biases in avatars and environments. Without robust ethical oversight, they can favour control and exploitation rather than democratisation and dialogue.

However, the positive potential of VR/AR should not be underestimated, as when well designed and managed, these technologies can become a laboratory for social participation, a space for building collaborative narratives, preserving historical memories, and strengthening intercultural dialogue.

Their ability to offer multisensory, interactive and emotionally meaningful experiences opens not only opportunities for communities to tell their own stories but also to reclaim narrative spaces from which they have historically been excluded. Through immersive environments, marginalised voices can articulate their perspectives in ways that transcend the limitations of traditional media, fostering greater visibility and cultural recognition.

At the same time, the public is no longer positioned as a distant or passive audience, but as an active participant whose presence and decisions shape the unfolding of the narrative. This shift encourages more conscious engagement, deepens empathy and invites critical reflection on the social realities being represented. In this sense, immersive technologies become powerful cultural tools for democratising storytelling, strengthening collective memory and cultivating a more inclusive public sphere.

The future of these technologies will depend on balancing innovation and responsibility. Advances will increase immersion, but it remains to be seen whether they will serve to democratise voices or reinforce control and consumption. That decision rests with creators, producers, platforms, legislators and users in a shared commitment.

The challenge, therefore, is to integrate VR/AR within a shared ethical framework that places authenticity, diversity, privacy and inclusion at its core. Only under such conditions can immersive narratives move beyond the status of mere sensory spectacle to realise their potential as instruments of critical reflection and social transformation.

This requires a collective commitment from creators, producers, platforms, policymakers and audiences alike, ensuring that the values embedded in immersive design and storytelling reflect principles of equity and respect. In doing so, VR/AR can contribute not only to the expansion of aesthetic possibilities but also to the strengthening of democratic participation and the preservation of cultural memory.

REFERENCES

Al-Kfairy, M., Alrabaee, S., & Alfandi, O. (2024). Ethical pathways in VR and the metaverse: Frameworks for responsible innovation. In *Proceedings of the 2024 2nd International Conference on Intelligent Metaverse Technologies & Applications (iMETA 2024)* (pp. 9–17). IEEE. https://doi.org/10.1109/iMETA62882.2024.10807903

Avendano, I., Carnell, S., & Cruz-Neira, C. (2022). ReCapture: A VR interactive narrative experience concerning perspectives and self-reflection. In *Proceedings of the IS&T International Symposium on Electronic Imaging: Engineering Reality of Virtual Reality* (pp. 270-1–270-6). Society for Imaging Science and Technology. https://doi.org/10.2352/EI.2022.34.12.ERVR-270

Baptie, G., Andrade, J., Bacon, A. M., & Norman, A. (2021). Virtually renovating the trauma film paradigm: Comparing virtual reality with on-screen presentation of an analogue trauma. *Cyberpsychology: Journal of Psychosocial Research on Cyberspace, 15*(1). https://doi.org/10.5817/CP2021-1-6

Clay, V., König, P., & König, S. (2019). Eye tracking in virtual reality. *Journal of Eye Movement Research, 12*(1), 1–18. https://doi.org/10.16910/jemr.12.1.3

Crone, C. L., & Kallen, R. W. (2022) Interview with an avatar: Comparing online and virtual reality perspective taking for gender bias in STEM hiring decisions. *PLoS One, 17*(6), e0269430. https://doi.org/10.1371/journal.pone.0269430

Dobosz, T. (Director & Writer). (2020). *Wiktoria 1920* [Virtual reality film]. Biuro Programu „Niepodległa"; Narodowe Centrum Kultury.

Donald, I., & Scott-Brown, K. (2019). Their memory: Exploring veterans. *Journal for Virtual Worlds Research, 12*(2). https://jvwr-ojs-utexas.tdl.org/jvwr/article/view/7360

Dooley, K. (2024). Exploring virtual bodies and invisible avatars as storytelling tools in contemporary narrative-based virtual reality projects. *Interactive Film & Media Journal, 4*(1–2). https://doi.org/10.32920/ifmj.v4i1-2.2061

Fawzy, R. M. (2024). VR as a metaleptic possible world of global citizenship embodiment: A cognitive stylistic approach. *Digital Scholarship in the Humanities, 39*(1), 124–141. https://doi.org/10.1093/llc/fqad078

Gallardo-Williams, M. T., & Dunnagan, C. L. (2022). Designing diverse virtual reality laboratories as a vehicle for inclusion of underrepresented minorities in organic Chemistry. *Journal of Chemical Education, 99*(1), 500–503. https://doi.org/10.1021/acs.jchemed.1c00321

Gruenewald, T., & Chen, C. (2025). Narrative virtual reality as a memory machine. *Convergence, 31*(4), 1306–1326. https://doi.org/10.1177/13548565251320727

Gonzalez Iñárritu, A. (Director). (2017). *Carne y Arena* (Virtually present, physically invisible) [Virtual reality experience]. ILMxLAB/Legendary Entertainment / Fondazione Prada.

Guo, H., Dai, H., Luo, X., Zheng, Z., Xu, G., & He, F. (2024). An empirical study on Oculus virtual reality applications: Security and privacy perspectives. In *Proceedings of the 2024 IEEE/ACM 46th International Conference on Software Engineering (ICSE '24)* (pp. 159:1–159:13). ACM. https://doi.org/10.1145/3597503.3639082

Kazlauskaitė, R. (2023). Virtual reality as a technology of memory: Immersive presence in polish politics of memory. *Memory, Mind & Media, 2*, e7. https://doi.org/10.1017/mem.2023.9

Kilteni, K., Groten, R., & Slater, M. (2012). The sense of embodiment in virtual reality. *Presence: Teleoperators and Virtual Environments, 21*(4), 373–387. https://doi.org/10.1162/PRES_a_00124

Madary, M., & Metzinger, T. K. (2016). Real virtuality: A code of ethical conduct. Recommendations for good scientific practice and the consumers of VR-technology. *Frontiers in Robotics and AI, 3*(3). https://doi.org/10.3389/frobt.2016.00003

Martindale, S., Hook, J., & Carter, R. (2025). A collective interdisciplinary agenda for immersive storytelling: Editorial analysis. *Convergence, 31*(1), 3–17. https://doi.org/10.1177/13548565251321702

Middleton, P., & Spinney, J. (Directors). (2016). *Notes on Blindness* [Film]. Archer's Mark; Creative England; Impact Partners; Arte Cinema; BBC Storyville; Curzon Artificial Eye.

Moscovici, S. (1984). *The phenomenon of social representations.* Cambridge University Press.

Murray, J. H. (1998). *Hamlet on the holodeck: The future of narrative in cyberspace.* MIT Press.

Nichols, B. (2016). *Speaking truths with film: Evidence, ethics, politics in documentary.* University of California Press.

Ryan, M.-L. (2020). *Narrative as virtual reality 2: Revisiting immersion and interactivity in literature and electronic media.* Johns Hopkins University Press.

Schroeder, R. (2021). *Social theory after the Internet: Media, technology, and globalization.* UCL Press.

Slater, M., & Sanchez-Vives, M. V. (2016). Enhancing our lives with immersive virtual reality. *Frontiers in Robotics and AI, 3*(74). https://doi.org/10.3389/frobt.2016.00074

Sora-Domenjó, C. (2022). Disrupting the "empathy machine": The power and perils of virtual reality in addressing social issues. *Frontiers in Psychology, 13.* https://doi.org/10.3389/fpsyg.2022.814565

Tricart, C. (Director & Creator). (2019). *The Key* [Virtual reality experience]. Lucid Dreams Productions; Oculus VR for Good.

Urman, A., Makhortykh, M., & Ulloa, R. (2022). Auditing the representation of migrants in image web search results. *Humanities and Social Sciences Communications, 9*(130), 1–16. https://doi.org/10.1057/s41599-022-01144-1

Warin, C., & Reinhardt, D. (2022). Vision: Usable privacy for XR in the era of the metaverse. In *Proceedings of the 2022 European Symposium on Usable Security (EuroUSEC 2022)* (pp. 111–116). ACM. https://doi.org/10.1145/3549015.3554212

Xynogalas, V., & Leiser, M. R. (2024). The metaverse: Searching for compliance with the general data protection regulation. *International Data Privacy Law, 14*(2), 89–106. https://doi.org/10.1093/idpl/ipac013

CHAPTER 11

Ethical Issues in the Use of VR in the Context of Artificial Intelligence

André Plante

1 INTRODUCTION

The fusion of Virtual Reality (VR) and Artificial Intelligence (AI) has the potential to revolutionize our digital landscape. This will be accomplished by transporting users into interactive 3D worlds that adapt, predict, and personalize user experience in real time. This synergy has profound implications for industries like healthcare, education, entertainment, and workplace applications. But this convergence also raises ethical concerns for users regarding privacy, autonomy, manipulation, and blurred boundaries between real and simulated experiences. For creators, VR-AI poses significant challenges as well, including questions of authorship, ownership, and job displacement. As we navigate this complex landscape, we will focus on the end-user's perspective, as their experience will ultimately determine VR-AI's societal impact.

The lack of unified governance frameworks makes addressing these ethical challenges difficult. According to Kostadimas et al. (2025), VR and AI and other related technologies such as the Internet of Things are advancing independently; their ongoing integration raises questions of feasibility, interoperability, and more notably ethics. Jin and Ryu (2025) also point

DOI: 10.1201/9781003673538-11

out that trust, privacy, and identity threat as well as digital equality play important roles in VR-AI metaverse adoption challenges. These technologies operating without safeguards risk amplifying existing inequalities. On a more positive note, VR-AI can be leveraged to foster inclusion, as Chalkiadakis et al. (2024) demonstrate is possible for students with disabilities. Yet, they also identify threats related to cost, access, and bias. The same two-sided dynamic plays out across various sectors. The current VR-AI convergence, lacking ethical scaffolding, may simply perpetuate existing social problems and introduce new and unforeseen risks.

VR raises pressing ethical concerns as immersive systems collect sensitive forms of user data. Unlike traditional digital media, VR can gather your biometric authentication and feedback data such as eye movements, retina scans, posture, and reaction times, as well as inferred emotional states (EPRS, 2020). A VR head-mounted display also collects information such as your location and time of use, audio, images of your surroundings, and patterns of how you interact with the device, among other data. When analysed with AI, these data allow systems to model and predict user behaviour. This ability opens possibilities for insidious manipulation, exploitation, surveillance, and even psychological harm (Zhuk, 2024). Can we truly afford to ignore the potential risks?

My goal for this chapter is threefold. First, I will contextualize and map the ethical challenges related to the convergence and intersection of VR and AI, focusing on privacy, manipulation, blurred realities, autonomy, and inclusion. This is not an exhaustive survey of all possible challenges but a starting point to underscore their importance. Second, I will examine industry self-regulation, including initiatives such as the OASIS Consortium (n.d.) and policies of platforms like Meta and Roblox. Third, I will consider current and future governance models, including the EU AI Act (European Parliament, 2023), the Council of Europe's Convention on AI and Human Rights (Council of Europe, 2024), and global digital rights debates. This chapter concludes with a call for an "ethics-by-design" (Raja & Al-Baghli, 2025) collaborative approach that embeds human oversight, ethical safeguards throughout the VR-AI development cycle.

2 CONTEXT

VR creates immersive environments that engage our senses, mainly vision and hearing, and occasionally touch through haptic devices such as controllers or gloves with vibration feedback. AI refers to systems capable of tasks requiring human-like intelligence, including pattern recognition, learning, natural language processing, and decision-making. When combined, VR and AI form environments that are both immersive and adaptive: VR provides the setting, while AI is allowed to learn from and respond to users. The virtual experience becomes more tailored to individual needs, predictive, and interactive.

The fusion of VR and AI is not only a technical convergence but also a complex sociotechnical system. Cortese and Outlaw (2021) highlight that social VR intensifies ethical risks, as our embodied presence in virtual worlds makes us more susceptible to manipulative or harmful interactions. AI-driven VR personalization and adaptation create a powerful system which can feel truly authentic and can shape user experiences and decision-making in powerful ways.

3 EVOLUTION

The intellectual roots of a convergence between VR and AI can be traced back to Norbert Wiener's (1948) cybernetic theories, which highlighted the crucial role of feedback loops in human-machine communication. Wiener emphasized that both humans and machines operate using sensors, feedback, and regulation, laying the groundwork for the "Human-in-the-Loop" (HITL) concept. As it became clear that human judgement was indispensable in automated decision-making processes, this principle of human oversight guided aerospace and engineering in the 1960s (Sheridan, 1992).

In the 1990s and early 2000s, VR systems were mainly used in simulation and training applications, such as flight simulators and military use. Facebook's acquisition of Oculus (Albergotti & Sherr, 2014) was a turning point, signalling the entrance of VR into the mainstream consumer market. The next decade saw deep learning gain momentum, enabling AI to enhance non-player character behaviours, generate environments, and offer personalization within VR. Today, AI is being woven into VR through generative models, advanced learning systems, and autonomous virtual agents or companions. Are we on the cusp of a revolution? The integration of these technologies is certainly transforming the digital landscape.

4 CURRENT APPLICATIONS

AI-driven VR is making its mark across education and training, healthcare, social media, and beyond. Commercial tools such as Bodyswaps provide immersive soft skills training (Bodyswaps, n.d.), while Ovation VR helps users overcome public speaking anxiety through simulated audiences and performance feedback (Ovation VR, n.d.). These tools show how adaptive VR-AI systems create controlled learning environments. The workplace is also embracing this tech, offering scalable training programs that focus on communication and leadership skills. Can VR-AI create more effective learning experiences?

Cortese and Outlaw (2021) caution that social VR poses increased risks of harassment, manipulation, and identity-related problems. As AI becomes integrated in multi-user environments as agents or avatars, its physical representation can make harm feel more real and immediate to human users. Beyond shaping user experiences, AI is also being deployed as a moderation tool within these environments. AI integration in social VR in the form of agents or moderation strategy creates a double-edged sword, mitigating some risks while potentially amplifying others.

The healthcare sector shows strong potential for VR and AI integration, such as using Conversational Artificial Intelligence (CAI) agents in mental health therapy. In their scoping review, Rahsepar Meadi et al. (2025) identified many CAI applications, noting both benefits and risks. They outlined ten key ethical themes and warned that reducing human oversight could amplify these issues. This highlights the need to keep human involvement central to ensure responsible use and protect patient well-being.

There have been notable advancements in industrial applications. AI-driven VR is playing an important role in facilitating digital twins and predictive analytics, according to Kostadimas et al. (2025). These systems enhance efficiency but introduce ethical concerns related to surveillance, worker privacy, and job displacement.

Across all these domains, the features that make AI and VR appealing also introduce new vulnerabilities. These concerns are examined in the next section.

5 ETHICAL CHALLENGES

The convergence of VR and AI creates distinctive ethical challenges that are not simply the sum of the issues associated with each technology on its own. In immersive environments, privacy risks arise from the constant and extensive capture of biometric and behavioural data. Manipulation and psychological impact reflect the dangers of persuasive design and emotional influence. Blurred boundaries between reality and simulation complicate consent and authenticity, as experiences increasingly defy a clear distinction between the real and the virtual. Autonomy and digital rights are threatened when AI shapes user preferences, controls avatars,

TABLE 11.1   Mapping VR-AI Ethical Challenges to Floridi & Cowls' AI Principles

VR-AI Ethical Challenge	Floridi and Cowls' Relevant AI Principle(s)	Explanation
Privacy and data collection	Autonomy, justice	Protecting user control over biometric and behavioural data while ensuring fairness in data processing and governance.
Manipulation and psychological impact	Non-maleficence	Avoiding harm by presenting persuasive, addictive, or manipulative immersive design that undermines well-being.
Blurred boundaries of reality and simulation	Explicability, autonomy	Ensuring transparency so users can understand when experiences are simulated and maintaining their ability to give meaningful consent.
Autonomy and digital rights	Autonomy, justice	Safeguarding agency in immersive environments while securing equitable access to rights over avatars, identities, and authorship.
Equity and inclusion	Beneficence, justice	Promoting positive societal outcomes and ensuring that immersive systems reduce rather than reinforce inequalities.

or appropriates identity data. Finally, equity and inclusion concerns high-light the risk of reinforcing societal inequalities and excluding marginalized groups. These five challenges offer a focused sample for evaluating the ethics of VR-AI.

To frame the examination of these ethical challenges, this section adopts Floridi and Cowls' (2019) unified framework of five principles for AI in society: beneficence, non-maleficence, autonomy, justice, and explicability (See Table 11.1). Inspired by principles in bioethics, the framework offers a coherent foundation for assessing how immersive, adaptive technologies affect users. It also bridges abstract theory with the concrete dilemmas raised by AI-driven virtual worlds. Mapping each major challenge onto this framework ensures the study remains systematic and grounded in responsible AI. This approach highlights both the risks of VR-AI convergence and the pathways ethical design can reduce harm and foster fairness.

6 PRIVACY AND DATA COLLECTION

Privacy is one of the most pressing concerns in the convergence of VR and AI. VR systems capture extensive user data to create immersion and presence, including biometric data such as eye movements and even neural signals in emerging brain-computer interfaces. When AI analyses this data, it can model user behaviour with precision. Such models personalize experiences but also introduce risks of surveillance, manipulation, and exploitation.

The European Parliamentary Research Service (EPRS, 2020) warned that immersive environments pose unique data protection challenges due to their ability to collect continuous streams of sensitive biometric data. Unlike web browsing data or application usage logs, VR can generate intimate profiles that reveal emotions, intentions, and vulnerabilities. AI amplifies these risks by predicting choices and potentially nudging behaviour to serve corporate or political interests rather than individuals.

Zhuk (2024) cites metaverse platforms such as Horizon Worlds and Roblox, where AI analyses player behaviour for moderation and engagement. These tools aim to improve safety but also collect vast personal data, raising risks to privacy and trust without strong governance. Chalkiadakis et al. (2024) note similar issues in education, where adaptive VR systems for students with disabilities may not only enhance inclusion but also expose sensitive information if protections fail.

The question of who owns and controls immersive data further complicates matters. Mangina (2021) highlights concerns in education, observing that students often lack meaningful control over the data they generate. These data can be created unknowingly through scanning of the student's physical environment or intentionally created in collaborative platforms.

Stronger ethical frameworks are needed for VR-AI-specific data governance. Existing models like the General Data Protection Regulation (GDPR) (European Union, 2016) offer a starting point but were not designed for immersive, continuous, and biometric data collection.

Within Floridi and Cowls' (2019) unified framework, privacy and data concerns tie directly to autonomy and justice, requiring user control and fair treatment of information.

7 MANIPULATION AND PSYCHOLOGICAL IMPACT

Manipulation and psychological harm represent another central ethical concern. VR systems enhanced by AI are capable of shaping user experiences in highly persuasive ways. AI can adapt environments in real time to trigger emotional reactions, alter decisions, or sustain engagement.

Skulmowski (2023) highlights how immersive experiences can strongly affect attention and motivation. While helpful for learning, these effects also present opportunities for persuasion that are difficult for users to resist. If AI systems optimize engagement for commercial gain, they may encourage addictive behaviours or promote content that maximizes profit rather than well-being.

Anguino (2025), writing for *The Guardian*, described a case in which the release of GPT-5 on 7 August 2025, abruptly ended access to earlier ChatGPT models, leaving users with a system they perceived as less warm and engaging. The sudden change provoked widespread frustration and, for some, even grief, particularly among those who had come to rely on the AI for companionship, emotional support, or therapy. AI systems lack the capacity for genuine empathy, raising questions about whether they can meet the relational needs of vulnerable users.

Manipulation is also a risk in commercial and political settings. AI-driven VR advertising could exploit biometric cues to adapt content in ways that bypass rational decision-making. Disinformation campaigns in immersive environments have the potential to be more persuasive than on traditional platforms because of the embodied user experience. These concerns echo those raised by EPRS (2020), which cautions against behavioural nudging without user awareness.

The literature still lacks empirical studies on long-term psychological effects of AI-driven VR. More research is needed to understand how immersion, persuasion, and manipulation intersect and how ethical guidelines can prevent harm. Risks of manipulation and psychological harm fall under Floridi and Cowls' (2019) principle of non-maleficence, emphasizing the duty to avoid causing harm through persuasive or manipulative immersive design.

8 BLURRED BOUNDARIES

The immersive nature of VR, combined with the adaptive capacities of AI, creates environments where the distinction between reality and simulation is difficult to maintain. This raises ethical concerns related to authenticity, consent, and user well-being.

In their scoping review, Rahsepar Meadi et al. (2025) found that some studies suggested CAI interventions may enhance interactions between humans and machines without necessarily translating into better human-to-human relationships and may even interfere with them. Other studies indicated that users might become adept at using CAI in a superficial way, like playing a video game, without applying these skills in their daily lives. If these findings are extended to VR-AI therapies, it is possible that users may encounter comparable challenges, such as confusing simulated progress for genuine real-world improvements.

EPRS (2020) warns that AI-driven VR systems can shape perceptions of reality in ways that challenge user autonomy. By constructing highly realistic environments, AI systems can encourage users to treat simulations as authentic experiences. This may result in consent fatigue, where users no longer carefully evaluate the risks of immersive engagement.

The risks of blurred realities also extend to cultural and social domains. AI-generated avatars and environments can replicate or distort identities in ways that challenge authenticity. Alkaeed et al. (2023) highlights how generative AI creates conflicts over intellectual property and authorship in creative industries. When these dynamics are combined with VR, questions of ownership and authenticity become even more complex.

Cortese and Outlaw (2021) describe how embodiment in social VR intensifies the perception of reality when it comes to harassment, bullying, or manipulation. If AI systems create or moderate such interactions, the ethical question becomes whether the responsibility lies with developers, platforms, or the algorithms themselves.

Prunkl (2024) argues that blurred realities create new challenges for autonomy, particularly when AI systems shape preferences in subtle ways. If users cannot clearly distinguish between genuine and AI-generated experiences, their ability to make authentic choices is undermined.

Future research should focus on the long-term cognitive and social effects of blurred realities in VR. Under Floridi and Cowls' (2019) unified framework, blurred boundaries between reality and simulation highlight challenges for explicability, as users must be able to understand and evaluate the authenticity of their experiences, as well as for autonomy, since informed consent becomes harder to sustain.

9 AUTONOMY AND DIGITAL RIGHTS

Autonomy is a central concern in debates on AI and VR. Autonomy can be defined both as authenticity or being true to one's values and as agency or the capacity to make meaningful choices (Prunkl, 2024). AI challenges both aspects; manipulative algorithms can influence preferences in ways that undermine authenticity, while opaque decision-making systems can limit agency.

In VR-AI contexts, these challenges are amplified. AI-driven personalization can create experiences so tailored that users lose sight of alternative perspectives. In education, Chalkiadakis et al. (2024) warn that adaptive AI may limit opportunities for students by narrowing learning paths. In social VR, Cortese and Outlaw (2021) raise concerns about identity and agency when avatars are manipulated or taken over by AI systems.

Digital rights are closely linked to autonomy. Mangina (2021) mentions that students and teachers need clear rights over data and identities they generate in immersive contexts. Without such rights, users risk becoming passive subjects of AI-driven environments. Ownership of digital identities remains an unresolved issue. AI systems can replicate voices, faces, and gestures in VR, creating risks of virtual identity theft and unauthorized use. Raja and Al-Baghli (2025) emphasizes that users require clear rights and protections to maintain trust in VR-AI systems. Without enforceable rights, autonomy is eroded.

There is a need for stronger legal and ethical frameworks to protect autonomy and digital rights in immersive media. Current regulations such as the GDPR provide some protection, but they do not address the full complexity of identity, authorship, and agency in VR-AI systems. Questions of autonomy and digital rights map to autonomy and justice in Floridi and Cowls' (2019) unified framework, requiring both personal agency and structural fairness in VR-AI systems.

10 EQUITY AND INCLUSION

Equity and inclusion represent another critical challenge in VR-AI. While these technologies have the potential to expand access and support marginalized groups, they also risk worsening inequalities.

Chalkiadakis et al. (2024) show that VR-AI can provide inclusive learning environments for students with disabilities, offering personalized experiences that are not possible in traditional settings. They also note that high costs, lack of infrastructure, and limited teacher training make these systems inaccessible in many contexts. This creates a digital divide where some learners benefit from immersive innovation while others are left behind.

Zhuk (2024) identifies risks of bias in AI algorithms that moderate VR environments. If these systems reproduce societal stereotypes, they can exclude or misrepresent minority groups. Cortese and Outlaw (2021) describe how harassment in social VR disproportionately affects women and marginalized users, raising concerns about safety and inclusion. AI moderation systems often fail to adequately address these problems.

Rahsepar Meadi et al. (2025) reported that several articles they reviewed highlighted how disparities in factors such as education, language, wealth, internet access, and digital literacy influence who can benefit from advanced AI technologies. Without intentional strategies to improve access, these inequalities risk being deepened, reinforcing the existing digital divide.

Future research must focus on strategies to ensure equitable access and representation in VR-AI. Raja and Al-Baghli (2025) call for co-created ethical codes that include input from diverse stakeholders. Such participatory approaches can help ensure that immersive technologies serve all users rather than reproducing existing inequities.

Equity and inclusion reflect the principle of beneficence, demanding that immersive technologies actively promote well-being while reducing rather than reinforcing existing inequalities. It is my hope that applying Floridi and Cowls' (2019) framework provides a conceptual lens that integrates disparate VR-AI ethical challenges into a coherent structure for further analysis.

11 CURRENT PRACTICES AND INDUSTRY SELF-REGULATION

The rapid convergence of VR and AI has outpaced formal regulatory frameworks, leaving industry players and professional organizations to take the lead in establishing self-regulatory practices. These initiatives vary in scope and effectiveness, ranging from voluntary pledges and ethical codes to technical safeguards built into platforms.

11.1 Voluntary Initiatives

Several multi-stakeholder coalitions have developed voluntary ethical frameworks relevant to VR and AI.

The OASIS Consortium as described by Chow (2022) represents a leading industry-driven effort to promote safety in the metaverse. It unites companies such as Electronic Arts, Roblox, Dentsu, and BBC Studios with safety technology partners to establish standards addressing privacy, inclusion, and the prevention of harassment in immersive environments. Oasis promotes a living standards approach, where guidelines are updated as technologies evolve. Its framework encourages proactive moderation, transparent data practices, and user empowerment. While not legally binding, OASIS provides a shared foundation for ethical design in immersive spaces.

The Partnership on AI (PAI), founded by major technology firms including Amazon, Meta, Microsoft, and Google, focuses more broadly on AI ethics but has relevance for VR contexts (Partnership on AI, n.d.). PAI's initiatives include best practices for AI fairness, explainability, and responsible use in media. Its emphasis on transparency and accountability aligns with the need of VR environments where opaque AI-driven personalization can undermine trust.

The Montréal Declaration for a Responsible Development of AI was launched following an inclusive, multi-stakeholder collaboration, drawing input from citizens, academics, policy makers, industry, and civil society representatives (Université de Montréal & Mila – Québec AI Institute, 2018). It was officially unveiled in 2018 and is non-binding. It is intended to inspire ethical AI development rather than impose legal obligations.

The IEEE Global Initiative on Ethics of Autonomous and Intelligent Systems (IEEE Standards Association, n.d.) has published extensive guidelines that aim to embed ethical considerations into the design and deployment of AI technologies. Although not specific to VR, these guidelines include principles of human rights, accountability, and transparency that apply directly to immersive systems. For example, IEEE recommends that AI systems used in environments with psychological impact, such as VR-AI therapy or education applications, should be subject to heightened oversight.

These voluntary initiatives show an awareness of ethical risks. Their effectiveness depends on adoption by industry stakeholders.

11.2 Platform Self-Regulation

Major VR and metaverse platforms have also adopted their own self-regulatory practices, often in response to public scrutiny.

Meta, through its Horizon Worlds VR platform, has developed internal content and AI risk standards. These standards set boundaries on what AI agents can say or do, and they rely on both automated moderation and human oversight. Investigations by Horwitz (2025) revealed that these rules allowed AI chatbots to engage in inappropriate interactions with minors, raising questions about the adequacy of self-regulation. Meta also emphasizes transparency in data use, but critics argue that its business model, driven by data monetization, creates inherent conflicts of interest.

According to Koneru (2025), Roblox has invested in AI moderation systems to detect harmful behaviours in its social VR environments. These systems rely on machine learning to identify harassment, hate speech, and inappropriate content. As mentioned earlier, Roblox also partners with organizations like the OASIS Consortium to strengthen its safety practices.

Rec Room and other smaller VR platforms have also introduced user safety features such as "safe mode" which allows players to control interactions with others. These features, supported by AI moderation, aim to reduce harassment and psychological harm.

11.3 Strengths and Shortcomings

VR-AI self-regulation has several benefits. By letting companies set their own standards, this approach allows for rapid responses to emerging ethical issues, avoids the delays associated with legislative processes, and encourages innovation. Industry-led initiatives also benefit from technical expertise, enabling guidelines that reflect the practical realities of system design. Can voluntary frameworks foster collaborations across platforms, pave the way for a more cohesive and responsive regulatory landscape?

Self-regulation also has notable drawbacks. First, it lacks enforceability. Voluntary pledges are not legally binding, allowing companies to withdraw or reinterpret their commitment at will. Second, self-regulation is often reactive rather than proactive, implemented in response to scandals or public pressure. Third, conflicts of interest undermine the credibility of the self-regulatory exercise. Can platforms that profit from user engagement and data monetization really be expected to highlight the risks of surveillance or manipulation? Fourth, self-regulation is fragmented. Different platforms adopt different standards, leaving users with a patchwork of protections across similar immersive environments.

This patchwork of self-regulation exemplifies the risk of ethics washing, a practice comparable to greenwashing in environmental policy. Ethics washing occurs when companies selectively promote ethical standards that pose minimal financial impact while avoiding substantial behavioural or structural changes. In the AI domain, this dynamic has been examined under terms such as digital ethics washing or ethics shopping, where organizations publicly endorse ethical AI guidelines but fail to implement supporting mechanisms or accountability. A systematic review by Schultz et al. (2025) reveals how digital ethics washing enables organizations to engage in empty ethical signalling. Can such superficial posturing truly be considered a constructive step? To address this issue, the review outlines frameworks for distinguishing between performative efforts and genuine commitments.

Scholars such as Raja and Al-Baghli (2025) present a persuasive argument for shifting from self-regulation to co-created ethical codes, a collaborative approach that unites industry stakeholders, academics, policymakers, and user communities. Prunkl (2024) stresses that effective governance must address accountability and rights protection, areas where voluntary self-regulation initiatives are weakest.

Although current practices of industry self-regulation demonstrate an awareness of the ethical challenges associated with VR-AI convergence, they cannot adequately protect users.

12 FUTURE DIRECTIONS AND GOVERNANCE

The limitations of industry self-regulation highlight the need for a stronger governance framework to guide the responsible development and deployment of AI-driven VR. Future directions in governance must balance innovation with ethical safeguards, ensuring that immersive technologies enhance human well-being rather than undermine it. This section considers three main directions: the role of HITL oversight, the emergence of policy models such as the European Union's AI Act and the challenges of applying existing frameworks like the GDPR, and finally, the prospect for international coordination through treaties and global principles.

12.1 HITL and Ethical Oversight

The HITL paradigm has long been recognized as an essential principle for ensuring that humans remain central in automated decision-making.

In the context of VR-AI, HITL oversight takes on renewed importance. AI-driven VR systems can collect sensitive data and adapt immersive environments in ways to influence decisions and emotions. Without meaningful human oversight, such systems risk undermining autonomy and trust.

Mosqueira-Rey et al. (2023) argue that HITL systems should represent a genuine collaboration between humans and AI rather than a simple technical extension. They stress the role of explainability, noting that models should be able to clarify why a solution was chosen to support transparency. The authors also propose concepts such as Usable AI and Useful AI, which seek to embed accountability and social value instead of focusing solely on technical performance.

Future governance models for VR-AI should embed HITL at multiple levels. Designers and engineers must be involved in ethical review processes, users must have accessible ways to understand and challenge AI decisions, and oversight bodies must ensure accountability when harm occurs. HITL does not eliminate all ethical risks, but it offers a vital framework to ensure humans remain accountable and at the core of immersive systems.

12.2 Policy Models

Among current policy initiatives, the European Union AI Act (European Parliament, 2023) is the most ambitious attempt to regulate AI. It classifies AI applications according to risk categories. High-risk applications, including those in education, healthcare, and biometric surveillance, must meet strict requirements for transparency, human oversight, and safety. For AI-driven VR, the AI Act offers a structured framework that could ensure ethical safeguards in high-risk contexts. Its success will depend on consistent enforcement across member states and its ability to adapt to rapidly evolving technologies.

The GDPR (European Union, 2016) also could play a central role in governing immersive data. The GDPR emphasizes informed consent, data minimization, and the right to erasure. Yet, scholars such as Rahsepar Meadi et al. (2025) and EPRS (2020) note that traditional consent mechanisms are inadequate for AI, where data collection is constant and deeply embedded in the user experience. Consent fatigue and the complexity of data gathered challenge the effectiveness of GDPR in practice. Future governance will require new models of informed consent tailored to AI and immersive contexts.

In the United States, regulation of AI remains fragmented and largely voluntary. In 2022, the White House Office of Science and Technology Policy released the AI Bill of Rights, which sets out a non-binding framework of five core principles: safety, discrimination protections, data privacy, notice and explanation, and human oversight and responsibility (White House, Office of Science and Technology Policy, 2022). Major technology companies such as Amazon, Google, Meta, Microsoft, and OpenAI have made voluntary pledges to test AI systems for risks, disclose limitations, and watermark AI-generated content. These initiatives demonstrate goodwill, but they lack binding force and often rely on corporate self-enforcement.

Canada's Artificial Intelligence Data Act (AIDA) (Government of Canada, 2023) can be contrasted with the United States' AI Bill of Rights. Both frameworks are non-binding and voluntary at this stage. The AI Bill of Rights outlines broad normative principles, and in contrast, AIDA proposes a more structured, risk-based regulatory model that will be implemented through detailed regulations. AIDA takes a balanced approach, promoting responsible innovation and international market access. It serves both as an ethical governance tool and a pragmatic framework for integrating Canadian AI into global markets.

13 INTERNATIONAL COORDINATION

Because VR-AI convergence is a global phenomenon, effective governance requires international coordination. The Council of Europe's Framework Convention on AI and Human Rights (Council of Europe, 2024), signed in 2024, is the first legally binding treaty on AI. In addition to European countries, the signatories also include Canada, Japan, Israel, and the United States. It establishes obligations to protect human rights, democracy, and the rule of law in AI systems. While not specific to VR, its principles apply directly to immersive technologies, calling for risk assessments, human oversight, and effective mechanisms to address unintended consequences.

Global organizations such as UNESCO (UNESCO, 2021) have also promoted ethical principles for AI, emphasizing transparency, fairness, and inclusivity. These principles can guide national and industry policies for VR-AI. Raja and Al-Baghli (2025) suggest that a co-created code of ethics should complement international frameworks to ensure that governance reflects diverse perspectives.

The challenge lies in aligning different regulatory models across regions. Future governance must therefore combine binding treaties, shared principles, and participatory processes to ensure consistency and legitimacy.

The future governance of VR-AI depends not only on technological progress but also on the commitment of governments, companies, and civil society to work together towards responsible solutions.

14 CONCLUSION

The convergence of VR and AI is reshaping our immersive interactions, but it also creates complex ethical challenges that demand urgent attention. VR-AI systems raise significant concerns about privacy, manipulation, blurred boundaries between reality and simulation, autonomy, digital rights, and inclusion. These concerns are no longer abstract. They are already appearing in education, healthcare, entertainment, and workplaces, wherever immersive systems gather sensitive data, influence user behaviour, and transform social interactions.

Current industry self-regulation efforts demonstrate that technology companies are aware of the risks. These initiatives remain limited in scope, inconsistent across platforms, and often lack enforceability. They provide a necessary starting point but are insufficient on their own.

Future governance must build on strong foundations. This includes embedding HITL oversight, adopting risk-based frameworks, and enhancing international coordination through treaties and shared global principles.

The responsible development of VR-AI depends on an ethics-by-design collaborative approach, where ethical safeguards should be integrated into each phase of the design, development, and implementation process. No matter what your role is, whether you are a policymaker, developer, educator, or user, you can be part of the solution. By engaging actively and demanding accountability, we can ensure that VR-AI systems reach their full potential while protecting human dignity and rights.

REFERENCES

Albergotti, R., & Sherr, I. (2014, March 25). Facebook to buy virtual reality firm Oculus for $2 billion. *The Wall Street Journal*. Retrieved August 12, 2025, from https://www.wsj.com/articles/SB10001424052702303949704579461812019189626

Alkaeed, M., Qayyum, & Qadir, J. (2023). *Privacy preservation in artificial intelligence and extended reality (AI-XR) metaverses: A survey*. ArXiv https://arxiv.org/pdf/2310.10665

Anguino, D. (2025, August 22). AI lovers grieve loss of ChatGPT's old model: 'Like saying goodbye to someone I know'. *The Guardian*. https://www.theguardian.com/technology/2025/aug/22/ai-chatgpt-new-model-grief

Bodyswaps. (n.d.). *Bodyswaps: The VR soft-skills training platform*. Retrieved August 21, 2025, from https://bodyswaps.co

Chalkiadakis, A., Seremetaki, A., Kanellou, A., Kallishi, M., Morfopoulou, A., Moraitaki, M., & Mastrokoukou, S. (2024). Impact of artificial intelligence and virtual reality on educational inclusion: A systematic review of technologies supporting students with disabilities. *Education Sciences*, 14, 1223. https://doi.org/10.3390/educsci14111223

Chow, A. R. (2022, January 6). An industry-backed group thinks the metaverse can avoid the ills of social media. *Here's How Time*. Retrieved July 24, 2025, from https://time.com/6133271/oasis-safety-metaverse/

Cortese, M., & Outlaw, J. (2021). Social multi-user spaces in VR: Trolling, harassment, and online safety [White Paper]. *IEEE Initiative on Ethics of Extended Reality*. Retrieved July 22, 2025, https://standards.ieee.org/wp-content/uploads/import/governance/iccom/social-multi-user-spaces-vr.pdf

Council of Europe. (2024). Framework convention on artificial intelligence and human rights, democracy and the rule of law. *Council of Europe*. Retrieved August 16, 2025, from https://www.coe.int/en/web/artificial-intelligence/the-framework-convention-on-artificial-intelligence

EPRS. (2020). The ethics of artificial intelligence: Issues and initiatives. *European Parliamentary Research Service (STU(2020)634452)*. Retrieved July 26, 2025, from https://www.europarl.europa.eu/RegData/etudes/STUD/2020/634452/EPRS_STU%282020%29634452_EN.pdf

European Parliament. (2023, June 8). EU AI Act: First regulation on artificial intelligence. *European Parliament.* Retrieved July 26, 2025, from https://www.europarl.europa.eu/topics/en/article/20230601STO93804/eu-ai-act-first-regulation-on-artificial-intelligence

European Union. (2016). Regulation (EU) 2016/679 of the European parliament and of the council of 27 April 2016 on the protection of natural persons with regard to the processing of personal data and on the free movement of such data (general data protection regulation). *Official Journal of the European Union*, L119, 1–88. Retrieved July 26, 2025, from https://eur-lex.europa.eu/eli/reg/2016/679/oj

Floridi, L., & Cowls, J. (2019, July 1). A unified framework of five principles for AI in society. *Harvard Data Science Review*, 1(1). https://doi.org/10.1162/99608f92.8cd550d1

Government of Canada. (2023, September 27). *Artificial intelligence and data act (AIDA). Innovation, science and economic development Canada.* Retrieved August 26, 2025, from https://ised-isde.canada.ca/site/innovation-better-canada/en/artificial-intelligence-and-data-act

Horwitz, J. (2025, August 14). Meta's AI rules have let bots hold 'sensual' chats with kids, offer false medical info. *Reuters.* Retrieved from https://www.reuters.com/investigates/special-report/meta-ai-chatbot-guidelines/

IEEE Standards Association. (n.d.). *The IEEE global initiative 2.0 on ethics of autonomous and intelligent systems.* Retrieved July 26, 2025, from https://standards.ieee.org/industry-connections/activities/ieee-global-initiative/

Jin, S. V., & Ryu, E. (2025). Unraveling the dynamics of digital equality and trust in AI-empowered metaverses and AI-VR-convergence. *Technological Forecasting and Social Change*, 210, 123877. https://doi.org/10.1016/j.techfore.2024.123877

Koneru, N. (2025, July 9). How Roblox uses AI to moderate content on a massive scale. *Roblox Corporation.* Retrieved August 9, 2025, from https://corp.roblox.com/newsroom/2025/07/roblox-ai-moderation-massive-scale

Kostadimas, D., Kasapakis, V., & Kotis, K. (2025). A systematic review on the combination of VR, IoT and AI technologies, and their integration in applications. *Future Internet*, 17(4), 163. https://doi.org/10.3390/fi17040163

Mangina, E. (2021). *Extended reality (XR) ethics in education* [White Paper]. *IEEE initiative on ethics of extended reality.* Retrieved August 22, 2025, from https://standards.ieee.org/wp-content/uploads/import/governance/iccom/xr-in-education.pdf

Mosquera-Rey, E., Hernández-Pereira, E., Alonso-Ríos, D., Bobes-Bascarán, J., & Fernández-Leal, Á. (2023). Human-in-the-loop machine learning: A state of the art. *Artificial Intelligence Review*, 56(4), 3005–3054. Retrieved August 15, 2025, from https://link.springer.com/article/10.1007/s10462-022-10246-w

OASIS Consortium. (n.d.). *Advancing digital sustainability through ethical standards and technologies.* Retrieved August 6, 2025, from https://www.oasis-consortium.com/

Ovation, V. R. (n.d.). *Ovation: Virtual reality training for public speaking.* Retrieved August 15, 2025, from https://www.ovationvr.com

Partnership on AI. (n.d.). *Home.* Retrieved August 4, 2025, from https://partnershiponai.org/

Prunkl, C. (2024). Human autonomy at risk? An analysis of the challenges from AI. *Minds and Machines*, 34, Article 26. https://doi.org/10.1007/s11023-024-09665-1

Rahsepar Meadi M., Sillekens, T., Metselaar, S., van Balkom, A., Bernstein, J., & Batelaan, N. (2025). Exploring the ethical challenges of conversational AI in mental health care: Scoping review. *JMIR Mental Health*, 12, e60432. https://doi.org/10.2196/60432

Raja, U. S., & Al-Baghli, R. (2025). Ethical concerns in contemporary virtual reality and frameworks for pursuing responsible use. *Frontiers in Virtual Reality*, 6, 1451273. https://doi.org/10.3389/frvir.2025.1451273

Schultz, M. D., Conti, L. G., & Seele, P. (2025). Digital ethicswashing: A systematic review and a process–perception–outcome framework. *AI and Ethics*, 5(2), 805–818. https://link.springer.com/article/10.1007/s43681-024-00430-9

Sheridan, T. B. (1992). *Telerobotics, automation, and human supervisory control*. MIT Press. https://archive.org/details/teleroboticsauto0000sher

Skulmowski, A. (2023). Ethical issues of educational virtual reality. *Computers & Education: X Reality*, 2, 100023. https://doi.org/10.1016/j.cexr.2023.100023

UNESCO. (2021, November). *Recommendation on the ethics of artificial intelligence*. Retrieved August 30, 2025, from https://www.unesco.org/en/artificial-intelligence/recommendation-ethics

Université de Montréal & Mila – Québec AI Institute. (2018). *The montréal declaration for a responsible development of artificial intelligence*. Retrieved from https://declarationmontreal-iaresponsable.com/la-declaration/

White House, Office of Science and Technology Policy. (2022, October). *Blueprint for an AI bill of rights: Making automated systems work for the American people*. The White House. https://bidenwhitehouse.archives.gov/ostp/ai-bill-of-rights/

Wiener, N. (1948). *Cybernetics; or control and communication in the animal and the machine*. MIT Press. https://archive.org/details/cyberneticsorcon00wien/page/n3/mode/2up

Zhuk, A. (2024). Ethical implications of AI in the metaverse. *AI and Ethics*. https://doi.org/10.1007/s43681-024-00450-5

Challenges and Future Trends in Virtual Content Creation

Victoria Mora de la Torre and
Antonio Díaz-Lucena

1 INTRODUCTION

The rise of immersive technologies and accelerated digitisation has led to a profound transformation in the way virtual content is conceived, produced and consumed. This phenomenon is mainly due to the convergence of several factors, including the potential advancement of computational capacity (Guzmán, 2024), the development of increasingly accessible and sophisticated display devices (Xiong et al., 2021) and the expansion of global connectivity that enables real-time interactive digital experiences (Hazarika & Rahmati, 2023). These scenarios have fostered the emergence of a new paradigm in digital creation, characterised by interactivity, personalisation and deep sensory immersion (Liu et al., 2025).

In this context, technologies such as virtual reality (VR), augmented reality (AR) and mixed reality (MR) have transcended their initial application in the entertainment industry to position themselves as strategic tools in fields as diverse as education (Roncero et al., 2025), medicine (Yeung et al., 2021) and architecture (Wang, 2009). These immersive platforms enable the generation of highly interactive three-dimensional

DOI: 10.1201/9781003673538-12

environments in which users actively participate and which, therefore, are proposed as experiences that facilitate high levels of cognitive and emotional involvement (Lin et al., 2024).

One of the most disruptive trends in this transformation is the use of Generative Artificial Intelligence in content creation. Tools based on generative models such as DALL-E or Stable Diffusion allow the automated production of images, texts, animations and even three-dimensional scenarios, considerably reducing development times and costs (Rahimi, 2025, p. 2). At the same time, these technologies democratise access to digital creation, allowing amateur users to generate high-quality content tailored to their contexts (Zou et al., 2023).

In parallel, the pursuit of realism has become a central objective in the virtual content industry. The implementation of advanced rendering techniques, such as real-time Ray Tracing, global illumination (Papaioannou, 2025, p. 2) and physical simulation algorithms, is making history in visual production. In particular, Ray Tracing allows the behaviour of light to be simulated accurately and is capable of reproducing phenomena such as reflections, refractions and complex shadows. This enhances photorealistic visual aesthetics. When combined with powerful graphics processing units (GPUs), this technique allows for levels of detail comparable to broadcast quality standards (He & Sun, 2024; Zhang, 2024).

In this context, the integration of VR into the metaverse represents another major emerging innovation. The metaverse is configured as a persistent, interconnected and shared virtual space (Ritterbusch & Teichmann, 2023), in which users can interact in real time through digital avatars, participate in economic, social and cultural activities and co-create digital environments. VR amplifies the possibilities of the metaverse by providing total immersion that transcends the conventional two-dimensional experience. Devices such as VR headsets, haptic suits and body tracking systems (Kim et al., 2023) allow users to explore and manipulate digital objects intuitively, as well as reinforce their sense of agency and belonging within these artificial worlds (Evangelou et al., 2023).

Consequently, content creators have become key players within this digital ecosystem, taking on an active role in designing meaningful and socially relevant experiences. However, despite technological and creative advances, substantial challenges remain that limit the scope of these virtual experiences, such as development costs, barriers to access and ethical implications linked to the massive use of data and immersive interfaces. These challenges will be analysed in depth throughout this chapter, with the aim of identifying both their causes and the emerging opportunities to address them.

2 EMERGING CHALLENGES IN THE DIGITAL CONTENT ECOSYSTEM

Despite the remarkable advances in immersive technologies and the growing interest in digital content creation, this field faces a series of structural, technical, economic and ethical challenges that limit its full development. These challenges impact individual creators as well as cultural educational institutions and scientific communities seeking to adopt these tools for educational, expressive or collaborative purposes. The following table shows the main challenges in creating virtual content (Table 12.1).

2.1 Technical and Infrastructure Limitations

One of the main challenges currently facing the creation of virtual content is the existence of significant technical and infrastructure limitations. Although there have been notable advances in computing power and the availability of development tools, the design of high-quality immersive experiences continues to require a complex set of technologies, platforms and technical skills that are not within the reach of all actors in the digital ecosystem (Prabhakaran et al., 2022, p. 8).

To generate virtual environments with a high degree of realism and fluidity, specialised equipment is required, including high-performance GPUs,

TABLE 12.1   Summary of the Main Challenges in Creating Virtual Content

Category	Challenge	Main Implications
Technological	• Hardware and software limitations • Lack of cross-platform standards • Rapid technological obsolescence	• Restrictions on the creation, distribution and maintenance of content
Economical	• High costs • Need for multidisciplinary teams	• Low participation of independent creators
Social	• Digital divide • Accessibility issues • Language and cultural barriers	• Exclusion of users
Ethical	• Algorithmic surveillance • Bias	• Loss of privacy, addiction and discrimination
Environmental	• High energy consumption • Electronic waste	• Negative ecological impact

Source: Own work.

motion sensors, depth cameras, virtual reality headsets (HMDs), workstations optimised for real-time rendering and in some cases, advanced haptic technologies. These technical requirements significantly increase the initial cost of production and constitute a barrier to entry for independent developers, small businesses, educational institutions and non-profit organisations. Devices such as Oculus Quest, HTC Vive and Varjo have improved accessibility in recent years. However, their acquisition, maintenance and updating continue to represent a significant expense (Felnhofer et al., 2025), especially in regions with lower economic capacity or limited technological infrastructure.

The most widely used tools for creating immersive content (such as Unity, Unreal Engine and Blender) offer powerful rendering, physical simulation and artificial intelligence (AI) integration capabilities. However, their effective use requires advanced technical knowledge in programming, three-dimensional design, interaction logic and graphics optimisation (Berrezueta-Guzman et al., 2025). This highly specialised working environment requires creative teams to be composed of multidisciplinary profiles, a fact that complicates autonomous production or experimentation from non-technical educational environments. In addition, the use of emerging technologies such as photogrammetry, volumetric capture or real-time Ray Tracing adds new layers of complexity to the creative process. The absence of simplified or accessible interfaces for non-expert users remains a substantial limitation to the democratisation of virtual content.

Another critical aspect is the network infrastructure required for real-time interactive experiences. Many VR applications require high-speed, low-latency and highly stable data transmission to function properly (Elbamby et al., 2018). The quality of these experiences can be severely affected by bandwidth limitations, connectivity fluctuations or lack of 5G coverage, especially in rural areas or developing countries. The reliance on cloud platforms to process complex data (as is the case with some collaborative virtual environments) also requires robust networks and efficient data centres. Without a solid digital infrastructure, it is difficult to guarantee the quality, stability and security of content distributed in complex virtual spaces such as the metaverse.

Finally, the technological ecosystem for immersive content still lacks universal interoperability standards, which complicates integration between devices, platforms and operating systems (Steed, 2024). This technical fragmentation forces creators to develop different versions of their content for multiple environments, duplicating efforts and resources. In addition, the rapid obsolescence of hardware and software requires constant updating of tools, knowledge and methodologies, which represents an additional burden for production teams.

2.2 High Production Costs

The development of immersive virtual content represents a significant investment in terms of human, technological and financial resources. Although technologies such as VR, AR and AI have advanced rapidly and are becoming increasingly accessible from a technical standpoint, the costs associated with their implementation on a professional scale remain a considerable obstacle to mass adoption, especially among independent creators, small businesses, educational or cultural institutions and non-governmental organisations.

One of the factors that makes virtual content production most expensive is the need for highly skilled multidisciplinary teams. The creation of immersive environments requires the collaboration of professionals specialising in programming (e.g., in C#, C++ or Python), 3D design, modelling, animation, interactive scripting, user experience (UX), spatial sound and, in some cases, AI or physical simulation. These profiles are scarce in the market and hiring them often involves high salaries, as well as ongoing training processes given the constant evolution of the technologies involved (The Royal Society, 2020).

In addition to human talent, the production of virtual content requires the use of specialised software and platforms, many of which involve licence fees, subscriptions or usage fees. While there are open-source tools such as Blender or Godot, the most widely used professional development engines, such as Unity or Unreal Engine, can involve significant costs as the project scales in terms of users or revenue. Developers also often require plugins, asset packs, cloud services and integration solutions that increase operating costs. The use of emerging technologies such as volumetric capture or 3D scanning also requires additional high-end software and hardware.

The acquisition of physical equipment is another cost-increasing factor. To develop and validate an immersive experience, creators must have display devices (HMDs such as Oculus Quest, HTC Vive or HoloLens), motion sensors, depth cameras, workstations with dedicated GPUs and in some cases, haptic technology or body capture suits (WorldViz, 2025). Added to these costs is the need for iterative user testing to ensure that the virtual experience is accessible, functional, immersive and safe. These validation phases involve expenses in logistics, technical personnel, controlled sessions and often content adaptation based on the results obtained.

Virtual environments are dynamic and often require constant maintenance. This includes software updates, bug fixes, compatibility with new versions of operating systems or devices and even partial redesigns to respond to changes in user needs or technological trends. This cyclical nature of updating implies sustained expenditure beyond the initial launch of the product.

Another aspect that drives up costs is the scalability of virtual experiences. As you seek to reach a larger audience or distribute content across multiple platforms (mobile, web, VR headsets, desktop environments), technical adaptations are necessary, increasing development work and budget. In addition, hosting complex virtual experiences (e.g., persistent worlds in the metaverse or collaborative real-time simulations) requires powerful servers and cloud services that incur high operating costs.

2.3 Accessibility and Inclusion Issues

Despite its innovative and transformative nature, the creation and dissemination of virtual content face significant challenges in terms of accessibility and social and technological inclusion. Although these technologies promise to expand the forms of human interaction, learning, work and entertainment, their effective use is still conditioned by various structural, economic, physical and cultural barriers. Thus, these limitations not only restrict the full participation of certain social groups but also compromise the democratising potential of the virtual environment.

Specifically, one of the most obvious obstacles is the persistent digital divide that separates those who have access to immersive technologies from those who do not. This divide manifests itself both in economic terms (ability to purchase devices such as VR headsets, AR mobile phones or specialised workstations) and in terms of technological infrastructure, as many regions still lack high-speed connectivity, stable networks or adequate technical support. The inequality is particularly marked between countries in the North and South but also within developed countries, where rural areas, indigenous communities, older adults and populations with low levels of education tend to have less access to these resources. This imbalance undermines the principle of technological equity and widens the gap in access to information, education and economic opportunities (UNESCO, 2021).

Continuing with this issue, another critical aspect of accessibility is the limited ability of current virtual content to adapt to the needs of people with disabilities. Many virtual and AR environments lack inclusive interfaces (Dombrowski et al., 2019) that take into account conditions such as: visual impairment, for example, lack of audio descriptions or incompatibility with screen readers; hearing impairment, such as lack of subtitles, sign language translation or visual alerts; motor impairment, such as difficulty using controls, sensors or performing the physical movements necessary to navigate the environment; and finally, cognitive impairment or neurodivergence, such as interface complexity, sensory overload or lack of simplification modes.

The lack of universal design in this content directly excludes millions of people who could particularly benefit from these technologies if they were implemented with accessibility criteria from the outset. Most immersive platforms are developed in dominant languages (mainly English) and tend to incorporate imagery, cultural references and forms of interaction centred on Western contexts. This can create an alienating or exclusionary experience for users from other regions, languages or traditions. Furthermore, the lack of localised and culturally relevant content limits the social appropriation of these tools, reducing their usefulness in educational, heritage or community contexts.

Full use of virtual content requires a minimum level of digital literacy, including skills such as navigating three-dimensional environments, using complex interfaces, interpreting multi-channel information and interacting with AI. Many potential users (especially older adults, children and individuals with limited technological training) face these barriers, which prevent them from effectively adopting these technologies. Likewise, in the educational sphere, the introduction of immersive content requires teacher training, curriculum adaptation and the availability of devices to avoid reproducing pre-existing inequalities. In school contexts without access to adequate equipment or connectivity, the use of VR or AR can generate more exclusion than inclusion if accompanying policies and equitable infrastructure are not designed (González & Mora, 2023). Unlike other more established technological media, the development of virtual content still lacks clear and universally applicable accessibility standards. Although initiatives such as the Web Content Accessibility Guidelines and universal design principles exist, they have not yet been fully translated to immersive platforms or consistently implemented in development processes. The absence of specific regulations on accessibility in VR, AR or the metaverse makes it difficult for users, governments or institutions to demand inclusive environments.

2.4 Technical and Infrastructure Limitations

One of the most significant (and least visible) challenges in consolidating virtual content is the fragmentation of the technological ecosystem and the lack of interoperability between platforms, devices and virtual environments. This phenomenon hinders the production, distribution and consumption of immersive experiences, negatively affecting the sustainability, scalability and cohesion of digital proposals. In the context of metaverse development, interoperability becomes a critical condition for ensuring that virtual environments do not function as isolated silos but as part of an interconnected, open and functional system.

Currently, there is a wide variety of proprietary platforms and systems for creating, viewing and interacting with virtual content: From engines such as Unreal Engine, Unity and Amazon Sumerian to metaverse environments such as Horizon Worlds (Meta), Decentraland, Roblox and Spatial. Each of these ecosystems operates under its own formats, protocols, graphic standards and architectures, which prevents digital assets such as 3D models, avatars, scenarios or scripts from being migrated or reused between platforms without costly and complex modifications. This situation creates technological lock-in for creators and users, who must adapt their developments or virtual identities to the rules imposed by each environment. From an innovation perspective, this fragmentation limits the possibility of integrating emerging technologies, such as blockchain or AI, in a cross-cutting and sustainable manner (Li et al., 2023).

In addition to differences between platforms, there are technical incompatibilities between the devices used to access virtual content. For example, an environment developed for a viewer such as Oculus Quest may not be easily compatible with HTC Vive or mobile browsers. Differences in graphics capabilities, sensors, input systems or support software force developers to make specific adaptations for each device, which increases production costs and slows down content expansion. The situation is exacerbated in experiences that require real-time collaboration between users, such as meetings in 3D environments or interactive educational simulations, where synchronisation between heterogeneous devices is essential for a smooth experience.

The lack of interoperability also affects the end user, who must create multiple avatars, accounts, configurations and digital wallets to participate in different environments (Steed, 2024). This fragmentation weakens the continuity of the UX and reduces the perception of cohesion in the virtual space. The inability to transfer a persistent identity between virtual worlds hinders the construction of communities, digital economies and shared narratives, which are key elements for the development of a functional metaverse. Furthermore, digital assets (such as objects, virtual clothing, properties or artistic creations) cannot be easily transferred between platforms, which limits their value, portability and marketability. This represents a significant obstacle to the development of virtual creative economies based on non-fungible tokens, digital licences or decentralised commerce.

Despite some efforts by organisations such as the Metaverse Standards Forum, there are still no widely adopted standards to ensure interoperability between development engines, viewers, servers, data networks and virtual economies. The lack of international consensus on file formats, programming languages, security protocols or avatar representation prevents the construction of a truly interconnected virtual infrastructure. This regulatory vacuum affects not only the technical side but also the social, economic and legal dimensions of the virtual ecosystem: Data ownership, copyright management, digital asset portability and the governance of distributed virtual environments.

2.5 Ethical and Social Risks

The growing use of immersive technologies raises a series of complex ethical and social challenges that must be addressed responsibly and proactively. These risks are not merely collateral but inherent in the way virtual content is designed, implemented and used. In a context where these technologies are becoming part of educational, medical, work and leisure processes, it is essential to reflect on their ethical implications to ensure that their development is not only innovative but also fair, transparent and humanly sustainable.

One of the main ethical risks is related to user privacy and the mass collection of personal data. Immersive platforms often collect extremely sensitive information, including not only browsing and behavioural data but also facial biometrics, body movements, emotional expressions, physiological reactions and social interaction patterns. In many cases, this data is processed using AI to personalise the experience or for commercial purposes, without the user being fully aware of the scope, use or storage of such information. This scenario has been described as an emerging form of algorithmic surveillance (Madary & Metzinger, 2016), where technology companies have access to levels of user knowledge that exceed any previous digital medium. The lack of specific privacy regulations in immersive environments opens the door to potential abuse, especially considering that much of this data could be used for behavioural manipulation, invasive targeted advertising or covert social control.

The design of highly immersive and rewarding virtual environments can lead to forms of psychological dependence or addictive behaviour, especially in children, adolescents and vulnerable individuals (Riva et al., 2019). The possibility of experiencing hyper-realistic, personalised and emotionally stimulating experiences may lead some users to prefer the virtual world to the real world, which is associated with negative effects such as social isolation, anxiety, sleep disturbances and emotional dysregulation. All these conditions should be highlighted because the diagnosis and monitoring of mental health is now much more prevalent and increasingly important (López-de-Ayala & Díaz-Lucena, 2025). In this context, designers and content creators face an ethical responsibility similar to that of other sectors such as video games or social media: To establish healthy limits, design mechanisms for conscious use, and offer alternatives that do not exploit the psychological vulnerabilities of the user.

Another growing risk is the use of virtual environments to distort the perception of reality or manipulate information. Immersive technologies allow the creation of completely simulated scenarios, in which the boundaries between the real and the fictional can easily become blurred. This can be exploited for educational or creative purposes, but also for deceptive, propagandistic or misinformative objectives.

In particular, the use of immersive deepfakes, historical reconstructions without factual basis or manipulated narratives in political or ideological contexts represents a serious ethical challenge, as it can alter the way people interpret events, trust sources or make decisions. In this sense, creators have a responsibility to ensure transparency, traceability and veracity in the content they develop.

Many virtual environments and AI systems used in immersive content are based on algorithms trained with biased data (García-Marín et al., 2025), which can lead to discriminatory practices, both in the representation of avatars and in virtual social interaction or content allocation. For example, facial recognition systems may fail to accurately identify people of certain ethnicities or genders, or recommendation algorithms may render content from cultural minorities invisible. Likewise, the aesthetic or cultural homogenisation of virtual worlds (often designed from a Western, male and technocratic perspective) can reinforce stereotypes or exclude alternative views. In this regard, it is urgent to promote diversity and inclusion from the early stages of content and platform design.

Unlike other more mature technology sectors, the development of virtual content still lacks established ethical and legal frameworks. There are no widely applied international standards to define principles such as informed consent, limits of realism, protection of minors or simulation ethics. This lack of regulation creates a vacuum that leaves users unprotected and creators without clear criteria for professional responsibility. In an environment where technologies advance faster than legislation, it is necessary to promote ethical self-regulation, training in digital ethics for developers and the creation of interdisciplinary observatories to monitor the social impacts of these technologies.

2.6 Towards the Creation of Eco-Sustainable Virtual Content

The development of immersive virtual content, such as VR, AR and MR experiences, requires large volumes of graphics processing, cloud storage and real-time data transmission. As these technologies expand and become integrated into sectors such as education, entertainment, health and remote working, there is growing concern about their environmental impact (Hintemann & Hinterholzer, 2022). Although the digital world has traditionally been considered 'clean', that is, an option that generates less physical waste, as an alternative to resource-intensive physical models, the ecological footprint of virtual content production and consumption cannot be ignored.

Real-time rendering, complex physical simulation, AI model training and the hosting of persistent virtual environments require intensive use of computational infrastructure. This includes servers, data centres, high-performance GPUs and global communication networks, all powered by electricity, often from non-renewable sources.

Recent studies estimate that training large AI models, such as those used in content generation, can emit as much CO_2 as several transatlantic flights. Likewise, platforms such as open metaverses or multiplayer VR games can consume thousands of kilowatt-hours daily, especially if they operate in high definition and with millions of simultaneous users.

The renewal cycle for VR devices, headsets, controllers, sensors and graphics cards is relatively short, leading to a constant accumulation of electronic waste (e-waste). Many of these devices have components that are difficult to recycle and end up in technology landfills, especially in countries without adequate waste treatment policies. This dynamic is exacerbated by market pressure to constantly upgrade hardware and software, driving an unsustainable consumption model (UNITAR, 2024).

Virtual content, especially in three-dimensional, hyper-realistic or AI-generated formats, requires large volumes of cloud storage. The maintenance and cooling of these data centres involve a significant environmental cost. In addition, the global distribution of this content via Content Delivery Networks, streaming platforms or mobile applications intensifies data traffic and, with it, the associated energy consumption. It would also be desirable to encourage the use of renewable energy infrastructures to power data centres and servers used by virtual content creation and distribution platforms.

Beyond the technical dimension, a paradigm shift in digital production culture is required. Sustainability should be considered not as a constraint but as an ethical and innovative criterion that guides the evolution of the immersive ecosystem. This includes everything from the choice of platforms to the training of creative teams in sustainable practices, as well as raising public awareness of the ecological impact of their digital consumption. Specific regulatory frameworks and ecological certifications are also needed for the virtual content sector to help measure and reduce the environmental footprint of each project, similar to green labels in architecture or cinema.

3 TECHNICAL AND INFRASTRUCTURE LIMITATIONS

AI is radically transforming the creation of virtual content, enabling the generation of text, images, 3D environments and animations through simple instructions in natural language. Tools such as ChatGPT, DALL·E, Sora and Stable Diffusion have significantly reduced production costs and times, facilitating access for users without technical training and expanding possibilities for small organisations (Bak et al., 2025). This democratisation has redefined the role of the creator, who has gone from being a technical executor to a curator of algorithmically generated proposals. However, important questions also arise about authorship, algorithmic biases, transparency and aesthetic homogenisation (Al-kfairy et al., 2024). At the same time, advances in graphics engines such as Unreal Engine 5, global illumination and Ray Tracing have increased the visual and auditory realism of immersive experiences. Spatial sound, haptic feedback and advanced physics intensify the sense of presence, generating emotionally meaningful multisensory environments. Virtual content is no longer understood as single-channel media but as integrated experiences where image, sound, interaction, data and emotions converge.

In this context, the metaverse is emerging as a persistent, decentralised and socially interactive environment. Content creation in the metaverse requires dynamic, interoperable and real-time collaboration-oriented approaches, integrating connected worlds, shared narratives and emerging digital economies (Li et al., 2024, p. 8). Platforms such as Virbela and Mozilla Hubs are redefining the logic of creation: From passive consumption to active co-creation. Algorithmic personalisation also drives adaptive experiences that respond in real time to the user's emotional state, rhythm or needs. Technologies such as eye tracking, biometric sensors and behaviour analysis allow the narrative or difficulty of the content to be adjusted, which is key in education, health and therapy. However, it also raises ethical dilemmas about emotional manipulation, privacy and the limits of personalisation. Accessibility and inclusion are becoming fundamental principles. Progress is being made towards content adapted to different cognitive, physical and cultural abilities, with more universal interfaces and narratives that represent social diversity. Design must consider equity from the outset, avoiding the reproduction of technological exclusions or algorithmic biases.

Finally, digital sustainability becomes unavoidable. Real-time rendering, AI models and data centres consume a lot of energy, exacerbated by hardware obsolescence and the generation of electronic waste. In response to this, the eco-design of content, the reuse of digital assets and the use of energy-efficient infrastructures are proposed. Sustainability should be conceived not as a technical limitation but as an ethical and innovative criterion. Thus, the virtual content ecosystem is moving towards more inclusive, critical, collaborative and ecologically responsible creation. The challenge lies in consolidating a horizon where technology and humanity advance in an integrated manner.

REFERENCES

Al-kfairy, M., Mustafa, D., Kshetri, N., Insiew, M., & Alfandi, O. (2024). Ethical challenges and solutions of generative AI: An interdisciplinary perspective. *Informatics*, 11(3), 58. https://doi.org/10.3390/informatics11030058

Bak Herrie, M., Maleve, N. R., & Philipsen, L. (2025). Democratization and generative AI image creation: Aesthetics, citizenship, and practices. *Artificial Intelligence & Society*, 40, 3495–3507. https://doi.org/10.1007/s00146-024-02102-y

Berrezueta-Guzman, S., Koshelev, A., & Wagner, S. (2025). From reality to virtual worlds: The role of photogrammetry in game development. *Computer Science*, 1, https://doi.org/10.48550/arXiv.2505.16951

Dombrowski, M., Smith, P. A., Manero, A., & Sparkman, J. (2019). Designing Inclusive Virtual Reality Experiences. In: Chen, J., & Fragomeni, G. (eds) *Virtual, augmented and mixed reality. Multimodal interaction. HCII 2019. Lecture notes in computer science*, vol 11574. Springer, Cham, pp. 33–43. https://doi.org/10.1007/978-3-030-21607-8_3

Elbamby, M. S., Perfecto, C., Bennis, M., & Doppler, K. (2018). Toward low-latency and ultra-reliable virtual reality. *IEEE Network*, 56(3), 114–120. https://doi.org/10.1109/MNET.2018.1700268

Evangelou, G., Georgiou, O., & Moore, J. (2023). Using virtual objects with hand-tracking: The effects of visual congruence and mir-air haptics on sense of agency. *IEE Transactions on Haptics*, 16(4), 580–585. https://doi.org/10.1109/TOH.2023.3274304

Felnhofer, A., Pfannerstill, F., Gänsler, L., Kothgassner, O. D., Humer, E., Büttner, J., & Probst, T. (2025). Barriers to adopting therapeutic virtual reality: The perspective of clinical psychologists and psychotherapists. *Frontiers in Psychiatry*, 16, 1549090. https://doi.org/10.3389/fpsyt.2025.1549090

García-Marín, D., Roncero Palomar, R., Santín, M., & Mora de la Torre, V. (2025). Perceptions of secondary school students towards virtual reality in STEM subjects. Effect of the gender variable. [El estudiantado de Secundaria ante la RV en materias STEM. Efecto de la variable de género]. *RIED-Revista Iberoamericana de Educación a Distancia*, 28(2), 275–297. https://doi.org/10.5944/ried.28.2.43267

González Caballero, M., & Mora de la Torre, V. (2023). Alfabetización mediática audiovisual en personas con discapacidad visual: El lenguaje y la narrativa audiovisual como herramientas para mejorar la experiencia cinematográfica. *Revista ICONO 14. Revista científica de Comunicación y Tecnologías emergentes*, 21(2). https://doi.org/10.7195/ri14.v21i2.2028

Guzmán, A., (2024). Singularidad de la inteligencia artificial. *ingeniería, innovación, tecnología y ciencia*, 3(1), 8–17. https://revistasuba.com/index.php/InnovaTec/article/view/1132

Hazarika, Á., & Rahmati, M. (2023). Towards an evolved immersive experience: Exploring 5G for real-time AR/VR applications. *Sensors*, 23(7), 3682. https://doi.org/10.3390/s23073682

He, C., & Sun, C. (2024). Research on real-time graphics rendering and interaction optimisation strategies in virtual reality. *Applied Mathematics and Nonlinear Sciences*, 9(1), 2024. https://doi.org/10.2478/amns-2024-3540

Hintemann, R., & Hinterholzer, S. (2022). *Data centers 2021. Cloud computing drives the growth of the data center industry and its energy consumption.* Berlin: Borderstep Institute. https://doi.org/10.13140/RG.2.2.31826.43207

Kim, K, Yang, H., & Lee, W. G. (2023). Metaverse wearables for immersive digital healthcare: A review. *Advanced Science*, 10, 2303234. https://doi.org/10.1002/advs.202303234

Li, K., Lau, B. P. L., Yuan, X., Ni, S.-T., Yuen, C., & Guizani, M. (2023). *Towards Ubiquitous Semantic Metaverse: Challenges, Approaches, and Opportunities.* arXiv. https://doi.org/10.48550/arXiv.2307.06687

Lin, X. P., Li, B. B., Yao, Z. N., Yang, Z., & Zhang, M. (2024). The impact of virtual reality on student engagement in the classroom – a critical review of the literature. *Frontiers in Psychology,* 15, 1360574. https://doi.org/10.3389/fpsyg.2024.1360574

Liu, C., Meng, S., Zheng, W., & Zhou, Z. (2025). Research on the impact of immersive virtual reality classroom on student experience and concentration. *Virtual Reality,* 29, 82. https://doi.org/10.1007/s10055-025-01153-w

López de Ayala, M. C., & Díaz-Lucena, A. (2025). Instagram como Plataforma para la Salud Mental: evolución de las estrategias de publicación y compromiso. *Miguel Hernández Communication Journal,* 16, 467–484. https://doi.org/10.21134/tkb48j06

Madary, M., & Metzinger, T. K. (2016). Real virtuality: A code of ethical conduct. Recommendations for good scientific practice and the consumers of VR-technology. *Frontiers in Robotics and AI,* 3, 3. https://doi.org/10.3389/frobt.2016.00003

Papaioannou, G. (2025). Approximate dynamic global illumination for VR. *Virtual Reality,* 29, 54. https://doi.org/10.1007/s10055-025-01114-3

Prabhakaran, A., Mahamadu, A., & Mahdjoubi, L. (2022). Understanding the challenges of inmersive tecnology use in this architecture and cosntruction industry: A systematic review. *Automation in Construction,* 137, 104228. https://doi.org/10.1016/j.autcon.2022.104228

Rahimi, F., Sadeghi-Niaraki, A., & Choi, M. (2025). Generative AI meets virtual reality: A comprehensive survey on applications, challenges, and future direction. *IEE Access,* 13, 94893–94909. https://doi.org/10.1109/ACCESS.2025.3574779

Ritterbusch, G. D., & Teichmann, M. R. (2023). Defining the metaverse: A systematic literature review. *IEEE Access,* 11, 12368–1237. https://doi.org/10.1109/ACCESS.2023.3241809

Riva, G., Wiederhold, B. K., & Mantovani, F. (2019). Neuroscience of virtual reality: From virtual exposure to embodied medicine. *Cyberpsychology, Behavior, and Social Networking,* 22(1), 82–96. https://doi.org/10.1089/cyber.2017.29099.gri

Roncero, R., Santín Durán, M., Mora de la Torre, V., & García-Marín, D. (2025). *Realidad Expandida. Nuevas perspectivas en Comunicación y educación.* Tiran Humanidades. Editorial Tirant.

Steed, A. (2024). Three technical challenges of scaling from social virtual reality to metaverse(s): Interoperability, awareness and accessibility. *Frontiers in Virtual Reality,* 5, 1432907. https://doi.org/10.3389/frvir.2024.1432907

The Royal Society Report. (2020). Digital technology and the planet: Harnessing computing to achieve net zero. *The Royal Society.* https://royalsociety.org/-/media/policy/projects/digital-technology-and-the-planet/digital-technology-and-the-planet-report.pdf

UNESO (2021). *Reimagining our futures together: A new social contract for educa-tion.* https://doi.org/10.54675/ASRB4722

UNITAR (2024). *The global E-Waste monitor 2024.* https://ewastemonitor.info/the-global-e-waste-monitor-2024/

Wang, X. (2009). Augmented reality in architecture and design: Potentials and challenges for application. *International Journal of Architectural Computing,* 7(2), 309–326. doi:10.1260/147807709788921985

WorldViz (2025). *VR budgeting guidelines for scientific VR labs: Hardware and operational costs.* WorldViz. https://www.worldviz.com/post/worldviz-vr-budgeting-guidelines-for-scientific-vr-labs

Xiong, J., Hsiang, EL., He, Z., & *Zhan,* T. (2021). Augmented reality and vir-tual reality displays: Emerging technologies and future perspectives. *Light: Science & Applications,* 10, 216. https://doi.org/10.1038/s41377-021-00658-8

Yeung, A., Tosevska, A., Klager, E., Eibensteiner, F., Laxar, D., Stoyanov, J., Glisic, M., Zeiner, S., Kulnik, S., Crutzen, R., Kimberger, O., Kletecka-Pulker, M., Atanasov, A., & Willschke, H. (2021). Virtual and augmented reality appli-cations in medicine: Analysis of the scientific literature. *Journal of Medical Internet Research,* 23(2), e25499. https://doi.org/10.2196/25499

Zhang, Q., Shi, R., & Geng, M. (2024). Deep learning-driven optimization of real-time ray tracing for enhanced immersive virtual reality. *Applied and Computational Engineering,* 71, 225–230. https://doi.org/10.54254/2755-2721/71/20241669

Zou, T., Shi, Z., & Wu, Y. (2023). *Welfare implications of democratization in content creation. SSRN.* https://doi.org/10.2139/ssrn.4662282

Glossary

Raquel Victoria Benítez Rojas

A

Action Recognition: The ability of a VR/AR system to recognize and respond to user movements, gestures, or actions.

Adaptive Rendering: A technique used in VR/AR to adjust the quality of rendered graphics based on the system's performance or the user's proximity to objects in the virtual environment, improving performance and maintaining immersion.

Adaptive Resolution: A method used in VR/AR to adjust the resolution of visuals in real-time to optimize performance based on the system's capabilities and the user's position.

Algorithmic Rendering: A type of rendering in VR/AR that relies on algorithms to enhance visual realism.

Analog Input: Input that can vary in value, such as pressure sensitivity in controllers, often used in VR/AR interactions.

Anchor: A fixed point in the real world that AR content is aligned with.

Anaglyph 3D: A technique for displaying 3D content by using two colored lenses (typically red and blue), often used in simple VR or AR systems.

API (Application Programming Interface): A set of protocols and tools for building VR/AR applications.

Artificial Intelligence (AI): The simulation of human intelligence processes by machines, which can be integrated with VR/AR for enhanced interaction.

Artificial Intelligence (AI) in AR/VR: The integration of AI to enhance user experience in immersive environments, enabling features like NPC behavior, content generation, and environment adaptation in real time.

Artificial Presence: The sensation of being in a virtual environment created by sensory stimuli.

Asset: Digital objects, models, or data that are used within virtual or augmented environments.

Asset Pipeline: The series of steps or processes used to create and implement digital assets (models, textures, etc.) in a VR/AR environment.

Asset Pipeline: The series of steps or processes used to create and implement digital assets (models, textures, etc.) in a VR/AR environment.

Augmented Cognitive Reality (ACR): A concept that blends AI and AR to assist users in real-time decision-making, often used in professional or medical applications.

Augmented Navigation: The use of AR to provide real-time guidance for navigation, such as overlaying arrows or points of interest on the user's view of the real world.

Augmented Reality (AR): A technology that overlays digital content on the real world, enhancing the user's perception.

Augmented Reality Interface: The visual interface through which users interact with augmented reality content, such as through graphical overlays, controls, or gesture-based interactions in an AR system.

Augmented Reality Projection: The technique of projecting digital objects onto the physical world in AR, often used for interactive displays or advertisements that appear to coexist with real-world elements.

Augmented Reality SDK: Software Development Kits that help developers create AR experiences. These SDKs provide tools for object recognition, environment mapping, and device integration.

Augmented Reality Cloud: A persistent, shared digital space in AR where virtual content can be stored and accessed by users across various devices, creating a unified, interactive environment in the real world.

Augmented Reality Projection: The technique of projecting digital objects onto the physical world in AR, often used for interactive displays or advertisements that appear to coexist with real-world elements.

Augmented Reality Tracking: The process of detecting and following real-world objects or surfaces in AR environments, essential for placing virtual elements accurately.

Augmented Reality (AR) Cloud: A persistent, shared digital space in AR where virtual content can be stored and accessed by users across various devices, creating a unified, interactive environment in the real world.

Augmented Virtuality (AV): A hybrid between VR and AR, where virtual environments are enhanced by incorporating real-world elements, often used for collaborative applications. Is a technology that overlays digital information or objects onto the real world, typically viewed through a device such as a smartphone or smart glasses, enhancing the user's perception of reality.

Avatar: A digital representation of a user or character in virtual or mixed environments.

Active VR/AR: Experiences in VR/AR where the user actively interacts with the virtual environment or augmented content through gestures, motion, or touch.

Autonomous Virtual Agents: AI-powered digital characters or avatars in VR/AR that can perform tasks and respond to user input autonomously, often used for NPCs in games or virtual assistants.

Audio Spatialization: The process of positioning sound in 3D space to enhance immersion in VR or AR environments.

Axis: A reference line for orientation in 3D space (X, Y, and Z axes).

Alignment: The process of matching virtual objects to the real world in AR.

ARKit: A framework developed by Apple for creating augmented reality applications on iOS devices.

ARCore: Google's platform for building augmented reality experiences for Android devices.

Autostereoscopic Displays: Displays that do not require glasses for 3D viewing.

B

Background Processing: Processes running in the background of VR/AR applications, often used for real-time data rendering and calculations.

Battery Life: The length of time a VR/AR headset can function before requiring a recharge.

Behavior Biometrics: The use of behavior data (such as motion patterns or facial expressions) to identify or verify users in VR/AR systems.

Biometric Authentication: The use of biometric data (such as fingerprint, facial recognition, or retina scanning) for user identification in VR/AR systems.

Biometric Authentication in VR: The use of biometrics, like facial recognition or fingerprint scanning, to authenticate users and provide secure access to VR/AR systems or content.

Biometric Feedback: The collection of physiological data, such as heart rate or skin temperature, that can be used to enhance VR/AR experiences.

Big Data in AR/VR: The integration of large datasets into AR/VR experiences, often used for real-time analytics or creating complex simulations, such as in scientific or industrial applications.

Binaural Audio: Sound recorded or simulated to be heard as if coming from a specific 3D location in a VR/AR environment.

Binaural Beats: Audio designed to create specific brainwave frequencies, sometimes used to enhance immersion.

Binaural Sound: A sound recording or reproduction method that mimics how humans hear sounds in 3D space, creating an immersive auditory experience in VR/AR.

Binaural Sound in VR: Audio technology used to create realistic soundscapes in VR by simulating how sound waves travel to each ear, enhancing the sense of presence.

Blending in AR/VR: The process of seamlessly integrating virtual objects or characters into real-world environments or the virtual world, making the transition between physical and digital spaces feel natural.

Blinks: Small, rapid visual cues used in VR/AR to indicate interactivity or object focus.

Blockchain: A decentralized, distributed ledger technology used to record transactions across multiple computers securely, commonly associated with cryptocurrencies but also used for various other applications such as digital asset ownership.

Blockchain for VR/AR: The use of blockchain technology to provide secure transactions, ownership verification, and data integrity in VR/AR environments, especially for digital assets in virtual worlds.

Body Tracking: Monitoring and replicating the movements of a user's body within VR/AR.

Body-Tracking in VR: The use of sensors or cameras to track the user's body movements, allowing for more natural interactions and a better sense of presence in virtual environments.

Body-Mounted Displays: AR/VR devices worn on the body, such as headsets, haptic suits, or gloves, that provide immersive experiences or track physical motion for user input.

Bounding Box: A rectangular or cuboid frame that defines the boundaries of an object in virtual space.

Bounding Volume Hierarchy (BVH): A method used in 3D computer graphics for efficient collision detection and ray tracing.

Brain-Computer Interface (BCI): A system that allows direct communication between the brain and a VR/AR system, often used for control or immersion.

Brain-Computer Interface (BCI): A system that allows users to control VR/AR environments with brain signals, enabling hands-free interaction or control of virtual environments.

Brainwave Interface in VR/AR: A technology that allows users to control virtual environments through brain activity, offering hands-free interaction for accessibility or advanced control.

Brainwave Monitoring: The use of brain-computer interfaces (BCIs) to track brain activity for enhancing immersion and user control in VR/AR experiences.

Beta Testing: A phase in which new VR/AR software is tested by users before public release.

C

Camera-Based Tracking: The use of external cameras or sensors to track the user's position or movement in an AR/VR environment, often used in AR applications to map the real world and interact with virtual objects.

Camera Tracking: The process of tracking the position and orientation of a camera to render virtual elements in the correct place.

Capture Volume: The physical space used for motion capture in VR/AR applications.

Cave Automatic Virtual Environment (CAVE): A room-sized, immersive VR system using projected images on multiple walls.

Collaborative Mixed Reality: The use of MR to enable multiple users to interact with the same virtual and physical objects in a shared, spatially aware environment, commonly used in enterprise and educational settings.

Collaborative VR: A type of VR where multiple users can interact and collaborate within the same virtual environment, often used for team-based tasks, training, or social experiences.

Collaborative VR/AR: A shared virtual or augmented space where multiple users interact simultaneously.

Collaborative Virtual Reality (CoVR): A shared VR experience where multiple users interact within the same virtual space, often for work, gaming, or educational purposes.

Cloud-Based Rendering: The use of cloud computing resources to render complex VR/AR scenes, reducing the demand on local hardware.

Cloud Computing: The delivery of computing services over the internet, often used in VR/AR for offloading heavy computations.

Cloud Rendering: Rendering of VR/AR content on remote servers to reduce the processing load on local devices and enable high-quality experiences across various devices.

Cloud Rendering in VR: The use of cloud computing to offload the rendering of VR environments, allowing for higher-quality graphics and experiences on devices with less processing power.

Cloud Streaming in VR: The process of streaming VR content from the cloud, allowing users to access high-quality VR experiences without needing high-end hardware to render the experience locally.

Cloud VR/AR: The use of cloud computing to offload VR/AR processing, allowing users to access high-performance VR experiences on lower-end devices through streaming.

Clipping Plane: A virtual plane that determines what is visible in the VR/AR environment.

Collision Detection: The process of determining when two objects in a VR/AR environment come into contact or overlap.

Computer-Generated Imagery (CGI): The creation of still or animated visual content using computer software, essential in VR/AR content development.

Computer Vision: The field of AI that allows machines to interpret and understand visual information, integral to AR.

Computer Vision in AR: The use of cameras and algorithms to enable AR systems to interpret and understand the physical world, helping overlay digital content based on real-time visual inputs.

Convergence of Real and Virtual Worlds: The blending of physical and digital realities in mixed reality, allowing the user to experience both in a cohesive and interactive way.

Contactless Gesture Control: A form of interaction in AR/VR where users control the system by making hand or body gestures, eliminating the need for physical controllers.

Controller: A physical device used to interact with virtual or augmented environments.

Cognitive Augmentation: Enhancing human cognitive abilities through AR/VR by overlaying real-time information or simulations to improve decision-making, learning, or memory.

Cognitive Computing: A form of computing that mimics human thought processes, used in VR/AR to make systems more adaptive and intelligent.

Cognitive Load: The mental effort required to operate or navigate within a VR/AR system.

Cognitive Load in VR: The mental effort required for users to understand and navigate VR/AR environments. Excessive cognitive load can cause fatigue or hinder user performance.

Contextual Awareness: The ability of VR/AR systems to adapt and respond to a user's environment, actions, and inputs based on context, enhancing immersion and utility.

Cross-Reality (XR): An umbrella term encompassing virtual reality (VR), augmented reality (AR), and mixed reality (MR), used to describe experiences that blend the physical and virtual worlds.

Crosstalk: Distortion or interference in VR/AR displays, often occurring when images overlap inappropriately.

Customizable Avatars: Digital representations of users in VR/AR that can be fully customized to reflect appearance, clothing, and movements.

Cybersickness: A term used to describe the symptoms of nausea or discomfort that can result from VR/AR experiences due to mismatches between visual stimuli and physical motion or lack thereof.

Cyberspace: The interconnected virtual environment created by computer networks, often used synonymously with the metaverse or to describe the internet.

D

DAO (Decentralized Autonomous Organization): An organization represented by rules encoded as a computer program that is transparent, controlled by organization members, and not influenced by a central authority or government.

Data Fusion in AR/VR: The integration of multiple data sources, such as sensors, cameras, or user input, to create a more accurate and responsive AR/VR experience, like combining visual data with real-time motion tracking.

Data Streaming: The process of continuously transmitting data, such as high-definition video or interactive elements, into a VR/AR environment.

Data Visualization in AR/VR: The representation of data through 3D objects, graphs, or other visual formats in AR/VR, allowing users to interact with and analyze complex datasets in immersive environments.

Decentralized Identity: A digital identity system where users have control over their personal information and interactions, often built on decentralized technologies like blockchain.

Decentralized VR/AR: A VR/AR system where processing, storage, and control are distributed across multiple nodes rather than relying on centralized servers.

Depth Perception: The ability to perceive the distance and spatial relationship between objects in VR/AR.

Depth Perception in AR/VR: The ability to perceive the relative distance of objects in a virtual or augmented environment, critical for immersion and interaction accuracy.

Depth of Field in VR/AR: The range of distances within a virtual scene where objects appear in focus, with objects outside this range becoming blurred to create a more realistic experience.

Depth Sensing: The ability of AR/VR systems to determine the distance between objects in a scene, crucial for creating accurate spatial awareness and depth perception in immersive environments.

Digital Asset: Any item of economic value that exists in a digital form, such as cryptocurrencies, digital art, or virtual real estate, and can be owned and traded.

Digital Economy: An economy based on digital goods, services, and transactions, encompassing various activities such as e-commerce, online advertising, and virtual currency trading.

Digital Scarcity: The concept of applying scarcity principles to virtual goods, commonly used in VR/AR gaming and virtual economies.

Digital Sovereignty: Control and ownership of digital assets, identity, and data by individuals or entities, emphasizing privacy, autonomy, and protection against external interference.

Digital Twin: A virtual representation of a physical object, system, or environment, used for simulation, analysis, and monitoring purposes.

Digital Twin in AR/VR: A virtual replica of a physical object, system, or process that can be manipulated and analyzed in VR/AR, often used in engineering, design, or predictive analytics.

Digital Wellness: Practices and measures to promote mental and physical well-being in the digital age, addressing issues such as screen time, digital addiction, and online harassment.

Direct Manipulation: Interacting with VR/AR elements through physical gestures or touch.

Device Orientation: The position of a device (headset, controller, etc.) in space, crucial for accurate VR/AR rendering.

Diminished Reality: The removal or suppression of real-world objects in an AR environment.

Directional Sound: Audio technology in VR/AR that allows sound to be positioned and moved in the 3D environment, enhancing immersion by simulating how sound travels in the real world.

Dolly Zoom in VR: A cinematic technique used in VR that distorts perspective by zooming in or out while physically moving the camera, often creating a disorienting or dramatic effect.

Dynamic Lighting: Lighting effects in VR/AR environments that change in real-time based on user actions or environmental factors.

Dynamic Lighting in VR: The process of simulating lighting changes in real time based on user movement, time of day, or environmental conditions, enhancing immersion in virtual spaces.

Dynamic Lighting in VR/AR: The real-time adjustment of lighting conditions in virtual environments based on the user's actions, location, or time of day, enhancing realism.

Dynamic Object Manipulation: The ability to interact with and modify virtual objects in real-time, changing their position, size, rotation, or other properties in VR/AR environments.

Dynamic Object Scaling: A VR/AR technique where the size of virtual objects dynamically changes based on the user's perspective or interaction, improving realism and immersion.

Dynamic Range: The contrast between the lightest and darkest elements in a VR/AR scene.

E

Edge Computing: Processing data closer to the source (e.g., on the device itself) rather than relying on a central server.

Edge Computing in VR/AR: A distributed computing architecture where processing occurs closer to the user's device, reducing latency and improving the responsiveness of VR/AR applications.

Edge Rendering: A technique that optimizes how data is processed for AR experiences by using nearby processing resources instead of relying on centralized servers.

Elastic VR: VR environments that adapt to the user's actions and desires in real-time, dynamically adjusting to provide a personalized experience.

Embodied AI: Artificial intelligence entities or agents within the metaverse that have a virtual body and can interact with users and other entities.

Emotional AI: AI technology integrated into VR/AR systems to recognize and respond to the user's emotional states, often through facial expressions, voice tone, or biometrics.

Emotional Recognition: Technology used to interpret the user's emotional state based on physiological or behavioral data, often for adjusting VR/AR experiences.

Empathetic Virtual Avatars: Avatars in VR/AR that are designed to detect and respond to a user's emotional state, enhancing social interaction through empathy-based responses.

Environmental Effects: Visual or auditory enhancements (like fog, weather, or sound) used to enrich the immersive experience in VR/AR.

Environmental Interaction in AR: When the real-world environment influences or alters virtual content, such as AR systems reacting to physical movements or surface placements.

Environmental Mapping: The process of mapping physical environments into a digital format, crucial for AR.

Environmental Sensing: The use of sensors to capture data about the physical environment (e.g., temperature, humidity, motion) and incorporate it into VR/AR experiences, creating more realistic simulations.

Environmental Sensing in AR: The ability of AR systems to understand and react to the real-world environment, such as detecting surfaces, lighting conditions, and obstacles, to create accurate augmented content.

Environment Mapping in AR: The technique of creating a 3D map of the physical environment in real-time to support AR interactions, enabling digital content to be accurately placed and scaled within the user's surroundings.

Equirectangular Projection: A type of projection used for 360-degree images or videos.

Experience: A specific interactive or immersive event in a VR, AR, or MR environment.

Extended Reality (XR) Cloud: A centralized system in the cloud that stores, manages, and processes XR content, enabling users to access complex immersive environments from any device.

Extended Reality (XR) Ecosystem: The interconnected network of hardware, software, services, and content that facilitates immersive experiences across virtual, augmented, and mixed reality platforms.

Extended Reality (XR) Interface: The user interface designed for XR devices, enabling seamless navigation between virtual, augmented, and mixed realities, with intuitive controls like hand gestures, voice, or gaze.

Extended Sensory Feedback: Technologies that enhance traditional haptic feedback in VR/AR by incorporating additional sensory modalities like smell, taste, or temperature.

Eye Gaze Control: The use of eye tracking to interact with a VR/AR system, allowing users to select options, navigate menus, or control content with their gaze, improving user experience and accessibility.

Eye Tracking: Technology that monitors where a user is looking in a VR/AR environment, used for interaction and focus.

Eye-Tracking Calibration: The process of adjusting an eye-tracking system in VR/AR to ensure accurate tracking of eye movements for improved user interaction, such as foveated rendering or gaze-based control.

Eye-Tracking in VR: The use of sensors to monitor the user's eye movements, allowing for more responsive user interfaces, foveated rendering, and enhanced user interaction.

F

Face Mesh in AR: The detection of facial features in AR, often used for facial animations, filters, or effects, enabling users to interact with their virtual environment via expressions.

Face Recognition in VR/AR: A biometric technology that identifies and tracks a user's face for personalized experiences or interaction, such as custom avatars or security features in VR/AR systems.

Face Tracking: The technology used to capture and interpret facial expressions for use in VR/AR interactions or avatar customization.

Fidelity: The degree of accuracy in replicating real-world environments or interactions in VR/AR.

Finger Tracking: Technology that tracks and responds to finger movements in VR/AR environments.

Field of View (FOV): The extent of the observable environment seen by a user in a VR/AR system.

Flicker-Free Rendering: A technique to eliminate visible flickering in VR/AR displays, improving user comfort and reducing eye strain.

Force Feedback: Haptic feedback that simulates resistance or force felt during interactions in VR/AR, such as when grabbing an object.

Foveated Rendering: A graphics technique used in VR/AR that reduces the computational load by rendering high-resolution details only in the user's direct line of sight (the fovea), while lowering the resolution in peripheral vision areas to optimize performance and save on computational power.

Framerate Capping: A technique used to limit the frame rate of VR/AR systems, reducing the risk of motion sickness and ensuring smoother, more consistent visuals.

Frame Rate: The speed at which frames are rendered in VR/AR; higher rates lead to smoother experiences.

Frictionless Interaction: An interaction design philosophy for VR/AR systems that minimizes barriers between the user and the virtual environment, allowing for smooth, intuitive, and natural interaction.

Full Body Immersion: An immersive VR experience that tracks and replicates the movements of the user's entire body, providing a higher level of interaction and presence.

Full Body Tracking: The use of sensors or devices to track the user's full body movements in VR/AR, often used for motion capture and interaction.

Full-Dome VR: A type of VR experience designed for full-dome environments, such as planetariums or immersive theaters, where users are surrounded by a 360-degree virtual world.

Full-Fidelity VR: A VR system that provides the highest possible quality of visual, auditory, and haptic feedback, often used in professional training simulations and high-end VR experiences.

G

Gamated VR/AR: The incorporation of game mechanics into VR/AR applications to enhance engagement and learning, commonly used in educational or marketing contexts.

Gamification: The application of game-like elements (points, rewards, etc.) to non-game contexts, often in VR/AR.

Gamification in VR/AR: The integration of game-like elements such as rewards, challenges, or levels into non-game VR/AR experiences to increase engagement and motivation.

Geospatial AR: Augmented reality that uses geographic location data (GPS) to place virtual content in the real world based on the user's physical location, commonly used in navigation apps and location-based games.

Geo-Fencing: A virtual boundary used in AR that defines a specific geographic area for interactive content.

Geo-Spatial Awareness: The ability of a VR/AR system to understand the geographical context of the environment and use that data to adjust the experience.

Global Illumination: A lighting technique used to simulate realistic light scattering in VR/AR environments, contributing to visual realism.

Global Positioning System (GPS) for AR: The use of GPS technology to place virtual objects in AR in relation to the user's real-world location, commonly used for location-based AR applications.

Gesture-Based Authentication: A biometric authentication method using hand gestures or movements, integrated into VR/AR devices to verify identity.

Gesture-Based Interface: A control system for VR/AR that allows users to interact by performing gestures, such as swiping or pointing.

Gesture Recognition: The ability of VR/AR systems to detect and interpret physical gestures made by users, often used for input devices like motion controllers or hands-free interactions.

Gesture Recognition in VR/AR: The use of sensors or cameras to interpret hand or body movements as input commands for controlling VR/AR systems, eliminating the need for traditional controllers.

Gesture Recognition Technology: Technology that interprets hand or body movements as inputs in VR/AR environments.

Gesture-based Interaction: A method of interaction in AR/VR that uses hand movements, facial expressions, or other bodily gestures to control or manipulate digital elements.

Glove Interface: Wearable technology that allows users to interact with virtual environments through hand movements.

Glove-based VR Interaction: The use of gloves equipped with haptic feedback and motion tracking to enable tactile interaction with virtual objects in VR, improving realism and immersion.

Gaze Control: A method of interacting with VR/AR systems by using the eyes to control the user interface or select options.

Gaze Interaction: A form of control in VR/AR where users interact with virtual objects by simply looking at them, with actions triggered by prolonged eye contact or blinking.

Generative Design in VR/AR: The use of algorithms to autonomously create complex 3D models or environments based on user-set parameters in VR/AR systems.

H

Hand-Tracking: A technology that detects and interprets hand movements and gestures in VR/AR without the use of physical controllers, enabling more intuitive interaction with virtual objects and environments.

Haptic Feedback: Technology that simulates the sense of touch through vibrations or motions, enhancing immersion and realism in virtual environments.

Haptic Feedback in VR/AR: Tactile sensations provided to the user via controllers, suits, or other wearables, simulating physical interactions like touch, vibration, or pressure in response to actions in the virtual world.

Haptic Feedback Loop: The continuous interaction between user actions and haptic feedback, enhancing the realism and engagement of VR/AR systems.

Haptic Suit: A full-body wearable suit that provides haptic feedback to simulate physical sensations, enhancing immersion in VR/AR.

Head-Mounted Display (HMD): A wearable display device for VR, AR, or MR experiences.

Head Tracking: The process of tracking the position and orientation of the user's head to adjust the virtual environment accordingly.

Head Tracking in VR: The process of monitoring the user's head movement to adjust the VR environment's view, creating a realistic sense of orientation and immersion.

Head-Up Display (HUD): A display system used in AR that overlays key information in the user's field of view, such as speed, direction, or environmental data.

Headset Calibration: The process of adjusting a VR headset to the user's individual preferences, including adjusting the fit, lens distance, and tracking parameters to ensure optimal immersion.

Holodeck: A fictional immersive environment from *Star Trek* used for training, entertainment, and simulations. The term is sometimes used in VR/AR for highly immersive systems.

Holodeck VR: A fully immersive, simulated environment that mimics physical reality, often inspired by the "Holodeck" from *Star Trek*, where users can interact with virtual objects and environments in a lifelike manner.

Holographic AR: The projection of 3D holograms into the real world through AR, allowing users to view and interact with virtual objects as if they were physically present.

Holographic Projection: The display of 3D images that can be viewed from different angles in AR/VR systems without the need for glasses or headsets.

Hololens: Microsoft's augmented reality headset for mixed reality experiences.

Hybrid Reality: A combination of physical reality and digital elements where both interact seamlessly, like mixed reality.

Hybrid VR/AR: A mixed system that uses both VR and AR elements simultaneously, creating a seamless blend of immersive and interactive content.

I

Immersive: The degree to which a user feels part of or surrounded by a virtual environment.

Immersive Analytics: The application of VR/AR to analyze complex datasets in a more interactive and visual way, often used in research or business decision-making.

Immersive Audio: Audio technology designed to create a sense of depth and direction in a VR/AR experience, making the environment feel more realistic by simulating soundscapes based on the user's movement and position.

Immersive Audio Design: The creation of soundscapes in VR/AR that make the user feel fully immersed by simulating 3D sound movement and depth.

Immersive Environment: A virtual or augmented space designed to deeply engage the user through visuals, sound, and interaction, simulating a sense of "presence" as if they are in a real environment.

Immersive Experience: A digital experience that fully engages the senses and creates a feeling of presence, often achieved through technologies like virtual reality (VR) or augmented reality (AR).

Immersive Training: The use of VR/AR to create realistic, interactive simulations for training purposes, allowing users to practice real-world tasks in a safe, virtual environment.

Immersion Level: A measure of how deeply users are absorbed or involved in a VR/AR experience, affected by factors like visual fidelity, interaction quality, and environmental realism.

Illusion of Presence: A psychological concept in VR/AR where users feel that they are truly "present" in a virtual world, which is often the goal of creating highly immersive environments.

In-Game VR/AR Economics: The economic systems embedded within VR/AR worlds, where virtual goods and services can be traded or monetized.

Inertial Measurement Unit (IMU): A sensor system used in VR/AR to detect motion and orientation through accelerometers and gyroscopes, allowing precise tracking of head or hand movements.

Indoor Positioning System (IPS): A system used to track locations within indoor environments for AR applications.

Input Device: A hardware device used to interact with virtual or augmented environments, such as controllers, gloves, or tracking suits.

Interactive Environment: A VR/AR environment where the user can dynamically change elements, affecting the world and its rules in real-time.

Interactive Holograms: 3D virtual objects displayed as holograms that can be interacted with in real-time, often seen in AR and MR applications where users can manipulate the holograms.

Interactive Holography: The use of holographic displays in AR/VR that allow users to interact with 3D objects in real-time.

Interactive Storytelling in VR/AR: A narrative approach where the user plays an active role in shaping the story's outcome, often used in VR/AR to create branching narratives or interactive worlds.

Intelligent Virtual Assistant (IVA): A digital entity in VR/AR that helps the user interact with the environment, perform tasks, or access information using AI-powered voice or text commands.

Interaction Design (IxD): The design of interactions between users and VR/AR systems.

Integration: The process of combining various hardware and software components to create a seamless VR/AR experience.

Interface Lag: The delay in the system's response to user input, a critical factor in maintaining immersion in VR/AR.

Internet of Things (IoT) in VR/AR: The integration of connected devices with VR/AR systems, enabling smart environments where virtual and physical objects can interact based on real-time data.

Intuitive Interaction: Interaction models in VR/AR that are designed to feel natural and easy to use, reducing the learning curve for new users.

J

Jargon in VR/AR: Specialized terminology used within the VR/AR community that may be unfamiliar to newcomers, often tied to development, hardware, or specific use cases of immersive technologies.

Jitter: A visual disturbance or inconsistency in a VR/AR environment, typically caused by latency or tracking errors.

Jitter Compensation: Methods to reduce or eliminate jitter (visual instability) in VR/AR displays.

Jitter in VR: The unintended, rapid, and unpredictable movement of virtual objects or environments caused by poor tracking or low-quality hardware, leading to motion sickness or disorientation.

Joint Angle Detection: Tracking the angles of joints (e.g., elbows, wrists) for motion capture in VR/AR applications.

Joint Collaboration in Mixed Reality: Real-time cooperation between users in a shared MR environment, allowing people from different locations to interact with each other and digital objects seamlessly.

Joint Haptic Feedback: A technique used in VR/AR to provide feedback to users based on the motion or position of their joints (e.g., fingers, wrists, elbows), creating a more immersive and realistic tactile experience.

Joint VR/AR Interaction: The collaborative use of VR/AR technologies by multiple users interacting within the same virtual space in real-time, commonly used for teamwork and virtual meetings.

Joystick: A device used to control movement within VR or AR environments.

Joystick Control in VR: The use of a joystick (often part of a VR controller) to control navigation or interaction within a VR environment, such as moving through the virtual space or manipulating objects.

Jumping VR: A VR experience that simulates the sensation of jumping or falling, typically used in games or experiences where physical movement is incorporated into the virtual world.

Just-in-Time Rendering: A technique that only renders parts of the VR/ AR environment when they are needed, optimizing resource usage and reducing latency.

K

Keyframe: A frame in an animation sequence that defines specific points of change, such as position, scale, or rotation of objects in VR/AR environments, used to create smooth transitions.

Keyframe Animation: In VR/AR, this refers to a technique where key frames (critical positions or states of objects) are used to animate transitions or movements between different points within an environment.

Killer App: A groundbreaking VR/AR application that drives widespread adoption of the technology.

Kinect: A motion-sensing input device developed by Microsoft, used for body tracking in VR/AR.

Kinect-Based Tracking: Using Microsoft's Kinect sensor to track body movements for VR/AR experiences, allowing for motion-based interactions.

Kinematic Feedback: A type of feedback in VR/AR that involves tracking and simulating the user's movements or interactions with virtual objects, providing physical sensations to mimic the interaction with the virtual world.

Kinematic Input: The method of tracking physical movement, such as gestures or body motions, to interact with VR/AR environments. This includes devices like motion controllers, gloves, or full-body tracking systems.

Kinematic Skeleton in VR: A digital representation of the human body used in VR to simulate human movement, where a user's body or avatar is animated based on real-world movement data.

Kinematic Simulation: The process of simulating movements and inter- actions in VR/AR that respond in real-time based on physics and user input.

Kinematic Vibration: Feedback in VR/AR that simulates realistic vibra- tions associated with physical objects or environments.

Kinesthetic Learning in VR/AR: The use of VR/AR for hands-on, active learning experiences where users physically interact with the digi- tal environment to learn new skills.

Knowledge Visualization: The use of VR/AR to represent complex data or information through immersive visualizations, helping users to com- prehend patterns or insights in ways traditional methods cannot.

L

Laser Projection in AR: A technology used in AR to project digital images or holograms into the real world, allowing for more accurate, high-quality visual content that can be viewed from multiple angles.

Latency: The delay between user input and system response in VR/AR, a critical factor for immersion.

Latency Compensation: Techniques used to reduce the delay between a user's action and the system's response in VR/AR.

Latency in VR/AR: The delay between a user's action (e.g., a head movement or controller input) and the system's response, which can significantly affect the realism and comfort of the experience. Minimizing latency is crucial for a smooth experience.

Lifelike Avatars: Highly detailed virtual representations of users or characters in VR/AR, typically featuring realistic facial expressions, body movements, and accurate skin textures.

LiDAR (Light Detection and Ranging): A laser-based scanning technology used in AR for precise depth sensing and environmental scanning to create accurate 3D models.

Light Mapping: A process in VR/AR where lighting information is baked into the texture of an environment, improving performance by reducing the need for real-time lighting calculations.

Lightfield Display: A display technology that uses multiple light sources to create 3D images, providing a more natural and realistic view of 3D objects in VR/AR environments by mimicking how light behaves in the real world.

Lighting Model: A method for simulating the behavior of light in a 3D environment.

Lightfield Technology: A display technology that captures and projects light in multiple directions, creating more realistic and interactive 3D images in VR/AR without glasses.

Liveness in Virtual Environments: Refers to the presence of dynamic, real-time content in a VR/AR experience, such as interactive NPCs, live events, or real-time data feeds.

Location-Based AR: AR applications that use GPS or similar technologies to provide context-specific information based on the user's location.

Location-Based VR: VR experiences that are customized or constrained based on the user's physical location, often used in location-based entertainment and theme park attractions.

Locational Awareness in AR: The capability of AR systems to understand and interact with the real-world location of the user, enabling context-aware digital content placement.

Locomotion in VR: The methods and techniques used to move a user through a virtual environment (e.g., walking, teleporting, or flying).

Low Latency: A key requirement for smooth VR/AR experiences, where there is minimal delay between a user's input (such as a head movement) and the system's response.

M

Machine Learning: A subset of AI that uses data-driven algorithms to improve VR/AR systems.

Machine Learning in AR/VR: The use of machine learning algorithms to enable AR/VR systems to adapt and personalize experiences based on user behavior, environmental changes, or real-time data.

Magnetic Tracking: A tracking technology that uses magnetic fields to detect the position and orientation of objects in VR/AR.

Marker-Based AR: AR that uses visual markers (e.g., QR codes) to trigger the display of digital content in the real world.

Markerless AR: AR that doesn't require physical markers but instead uses environmental data to overlay digital content.

Metaverse: A collective virtual shared space, typically created by the convergence of multiple virtual environments or augmented reality technologies, where users can interact, communicate, and engage in various activities.

Metaverse Analytics: Data collection and analysis within the metaverse to understand user behavior, trends, and preferences, enabling optimization and personalization of experiences.

Metaverse Commerce: The buying and selling of goods and services within the metaverse economy, facilitated by virtual currencies, digital marketplaces, and decentralized platforms.

Metaverse Education: Learning and knowledge-sharing experiences within the metaverse, including virtual classrooms, workshops, and simulations, offering new opportunities for interactive and immersive education.

Metaverse Entertainment: Media and content experiences within the metaverse, such as games, movies, concerts, and immersive storytelling, providing entertainment and cultural enrichment to users.

Metaverse Ethics: Moral principles and guidelines for ethical behavior within the metaverse, addressing issues such as privacy, consent, diversity, and digital rights.

Metaverse Evolution: The ongoing development and transformation of the metaverse over time, driven by technological advancements, user demands, and cultural shifts.

Metaverse Governance: Rules, regulations, and systems for managing interactions and transactions within the metaverse, ensuring fairness, security, and compliance with legal and ethical standards.

Metaverse Infrastructure: The underlying technology and network architecture that supports the operation and growth of the metaverse, including servers, protocols, and communication channels.

Metaverse Interoperability: The ability of different platforms and virtual environments to connect and interact seamlessly within the metaverse, enabling cross-platform communication and content sharing.

Metaverse Platform: Software or infrastructure that enables the creation, management, and interaction within the metaverse, providing tools and services for developers, content creators, and users.

Metaverse Privacy: Measures and protocols to protect users' personal data and information within the metaverse from unauthorized access, misuse, and exploitation.

Metaverse Regulation: Laws, policies, and regulations governing activities within the metaverse, including taxation, intellectual property rights, content moderation, and consumer protection.

Micro-Environment: Small, isolated VR/AR spaces that represent very specific scenarios, such as a virtual room or a single object. They're used for focus-based tasks or simulations.

Micro-Interaction: Small, subtle interactions in VR/AR systems that enhance user experience, such as a sound or animation triggered by a user's action or gesture.

Minimal Angle of Resolution (MAR): Defines the smallest angular separation at which two adjacent pixels on a display can be distinguished as separate by the human eye. Typically measured in arc-seconds, MAR is intrinsically linked to viewing distance: the further the viewer is from the screen, the larger the physical distance must be between pixels for them to appear distinct.

For the average observer, the MAR threshold lies between approximately 30 and 65 arc-seconds—values that form the basis for spatial resolution when contextualized with a specific viewing distance. At 1 meter, pixels spaced less than 0.29 millimeters apart cannot be resolved individually by the human eye. Similarly, at 2 meters, that threshold increases to 0.58 millimeters. In practical terms, this means that beyond these limits, the display will appear visually seamless to the average viewer.

Mixed Reality (MR): A hybrid of VR and AR where real-world and digital content coexist and interact in real time.

Mixed Reality Capture: A technique for recording and broadcasting live mixed-reality content, where both virtual and real-world elements are captured and displayed in real-time, often for gaming or interactive media.

Mixed Reality Interface: The user interface designed for MR systems that blends real and virtual elements for interaction.

Motion Blur in VR: A visual effect used in VR to simulate the blur seen in the real world when an object is moving quickly, adding to the realism and providing a more natural visual experience during high-speed movements.

Motion Parallax: A visual effect in VR where objects move at different speeds depending on their distance from the observer, creating a sense of depth and aiding in spatial awareness.

Motion Sickness: Discomfort or nausea experienced in VR due to mismatched visual and physical motion cues.

Motion Smoothing: A technique to smooth out motion in VR/AR, reducing stuttering and improving visual continuity.

Motion Tracking: The process of capturing movement, typically from users or objects, to animate or control virtual elements.

Multimodal Interaction: The use of multiple input methods (e.g., voice commands, hand gestures, controllers) to interact with VR/AR systems, offering users a flexible and more intuitive way to engage with virtual environments.

Multimodal Interface: An interface in VR/AR that uses multiple forms of input (voice, touch, gesture, etc.) to interact with the system, enabling more natural user experiences.

Multimodal VR/AR: VR/AR systems that integrate multiple types of input (visual, audio, haptic, etc.) and output to create a richer, more immersive experience.

Multi-User VR: VR systems that allow multiple users to interact with each other in the same virtual environment, such as multiplayer gaming or remote collaboration.

Multi-User VR/AR: Environments where multiple users can interact within the same virtual or augmented space.

N

Natural Language Processing (NLP): A branch of artificial intelligence that allows VR/AR systems to interpret and respond to human language, enabling voice commands or interactive dialogue in virtual environments.

Natural User Interface (NUI): An interface that allows users to interact with VR/AR systems in an intuitive, human-like manner, often through gestures, speech, or facial recognition, without the need for a traditional controller.

Navigation: The act of moving through virtual or augmented spaces, often using controllers or hand gestures.

NavMesh (Navigation Mesh): A method in VR/AR used to create a navigable area within the virtual environment, often used in AI pathfinding for virtual characters or objects to move logically and efficiently within the scene.

Near-Eye Display: A display technology used in VR/AR headsets where the screen is placed close to the user's eyes, offering high-quality visuals and minimizing distortion for immersive experiences.

Near Field Communication (NFC) in AR: A wireless communication technology that can be used in AR to trigger specific interactions, such as scanning an NFC tag to display information or launch an experience.

Neural Interface: A system that allows VR/AR applications to interact directly with the brain to control or enhance experiences.

Neural Networks: AI systems that mimic the human brain's structure, used to process data in VR/AR.

Neural Networks in VR/AR: The use of artificial neural networks to improve pattern recognition, object tracking, or user interaction in VR/AR environments, enabling intelligent responses to real-world stimuli.

Neural Rendering: A form of rendering in VR/AR that uses machine learning algorithms to create realistic images or animations by simulating human visual processing and artistic interpretation.

Neuro-Enhanced VR: VR technologies that are combined with brain-computer interface (BCI) systems to enhance immersion or user interaction through neural control.

Neurofeedback in VR: The use of VR alongside brainwave monitoring technology to provide feedback on the user's brain activity. This is often used in therapeutic or performance optimization settings to improve focus or relaxation.

NFT (Non-Fungible Token): A unique digital asset stored on a block-chain, often representing ownership of a digital item or piece of content within the metaverse and used for authentication and provenance tracking.

Non-Linear Interaction: A type of interaction in VR/AR that does not follow a straight path or predictable sequence, allowing users to engage with content in flexible, non-sequential ways. This is often used in storytelling or educational experiences.

Non-Linear Storytelling in VR/AR: A narrative technique in VR/AR experiences where the story is not fixed, and users can influence the course of the plot based on their actions or decisions.

Non-Player Character (NPC): A character in a VR/AR environment that is controlled by the system rather than the user, typically used for storytelling, interaction, or gameplay.

Nose Tracking: A cutting-edge tracking system that uses the nose as a point of reference in VR/AR to improve spatial accuracy and head tracking.

O

Object Occlusion in AR: The technique used to ensure that virtual objects in AR correctly respond to the presence of real-world objects, making it appear as though the virtual object is behind or interacts with the physical environment.

Object Recognition: The ability of a VR/AR system to identify real-world objects and trigger corresponding virtual actions or content.

Object Recognition in AR: The ability of AR systems to detect and identify real-world objects, then place corresponding virtual objects or information on top of them.

Occlusion: The blocking of virtual elements by real-world objects, a key challenge in AR and MR experiences.

Oculus Rift: A VR headset developed by Oculus (now part of Meta) that was one of the pioneers in the consumer VR space, known for its immersive experience.

Omnidirectional Treadmill: A device used in VR that allows users to walk in any direction while staying stationary in the real world, enhancing immersion in virtual environments by enabling physical movement.

Omnidirectional VR: A VR system where users can walk or run in any direction without restrictions, often facilitated by specialized hardware like omnidirectional treadmills.

Omni-Directional VR Treadmill: A piece of hardware that allows users to move freely in any direction in VR without changing their physical location, offering a more natural and immersive walking experience.

Optical Flow: The pattern of apparent motion of objects caused by the relative motion between the observer and the environment. Used in VR/AR to create more realistic movement and interaction.

Optical Flow in AR: A technique for tracking and interpreting the motion of objects in an AR scene by analyzing the apparent movement of pixels in the video feed, improving object interaction and stability.

Optical See-Through AR: A type of AR display technology where digital content is overlaid onto the real world, visible through transparent lenses (e.g., AR smart glasses), providing a seamless blend of virtual and real environments.

Optical Tracking: A tracking system in VR/AR that uses cameras and computer vision to detect the position and movement of objects or users based on visual input.

OpenVR: An open-source platform developed by Valve for supporting various VR hardware devices and applications, often used for creating cross-platform VR experiences.

OpenXR: An open standard for developing and deploying VR and AR applications, providing a unified API across different hardware platforms, allowing for cross-device compatibility in immersive experiences.

Out-of-Body Experience: A sensation sometimes encountered in VR where the user feels as if they are outside their own physical body.

P

Panoramic Video: A 360-degree video format used in VR that captures the entire surrounding area to provide a fully immersive viewing experience, allowing users to explore scenes from every angle.

Perceptual Relevance: In VR/AR, it refers to how well the system adapts virtual content to be meaningful and relevant to the user's current environment or activities.

Peripheral Devices in VR: Devices that enhance VR experiences, such as motion controllers, gloves, treadmills, and haptic feedback suits, offering more immersive and interactive user experiences.

Peripheral Vision in VR: Refers to the visual information processed by the eyes outside the direct focal area (central vision), important in creating natural and immersive experiences in VR.

Persistent Object Interactions: In VR/AR, where virtual objects retain state and behavior across sessions, enabling users to interact with them in a continuous, evolving way.

Persistent Virtual Worlds: Virtual environments that continue to exist and evolve even when users are not actively interacting with them, commonly used in MMORPGs and social VR platforms.

Persistent World: A VR or AR world that continues to exist and evolve even when the user is not interacting with it, often used in gaming or simulation.

Personalized VR/AR: Customized VR/AR experiences tailored to an individual's preferences, behavior, or physical characteristics, such as adjusting difficulty levels or adjusting avatars.

Phantom Limb Sensation: A sensation in VR where users feel the presence of virtual limbs or objects, often used in therapeutic VR applications.

Photogrammetry: A technique for creating 3D models by capturing real-world objects from multiple photographs, often used in AR to generate realistic virtual content.

Photorealism: The level of realism in VR/AR environments that mimics real-world lighting, textures, and objects with a high degree of visual accuracy, creating lifelike scenes and characters.

Photorealism in VR: The practice of designing virtual environments or objects in VR with high levels of detail and accuracy to create visuals that closely resemble real-life counterparts.

Point Cloud: A collection of 3D points representing the surface of a real-world object or environment, often used in AR.

Position Tracking: Monitoring the location of a device or user in space to maintain spatial accuracy in VR/AR.

Positional Tracking: The tracking of a user's position (often through sensors or cameras) in a 3D space, allowing the VR/AR system to adjust the virtual environment based on the user's location within it.

Projection Mapping: A technique used in AR/VR where projectors display digital content onto physical objects or surfaces, transforming static objects into interactive displays or dynamic environments.

Projection-Based AR: A type of AR where digital images are projected onto physical surfaces, often used in interactive installations or public displays where users can interact with projected content.

Pupil Dilation: The measurement of pupil size, sometimes used in VR/AR to track the user's focus and emotional state.

Pupil Tracking: The technology used to track the movement and size of a user's pupils, often used for foveated rendering and eye-based interactions in VR/AR systems.

Position Tracking (duplicate definition removed): The process of determining a user's or object's position in 3D space, typically used in VR/AR systems to track the movement of headsets or controllers for accurate interaction.

Q

Qualitative Immersion: A measurement of immersion in VR/AR that focuses on the emotional and psychological experience of the user, rather than just the physical or technical aspects.

Quality of Experience (QoE): A measurement of how users perceive the quality of their VR/AR experience, factoring in elements such as visual clarity, responsiveness, interactivity, and overall comfort.

Quantum Computing: A future technology that may significantly enhance VR/AR simulations by enabling faster computations.

Quantum Computing in VR: The application of quantum computing technology to VR/AR, potentially offering improvements in real-time simulations, rendering, and processing power for complex virtual environments.

Quantum Computing in VR/AR: The potential use of quantum computers to process complex calculations for VR/AR applications at much faster speeds, enabling more advanced simulations, real-time environments, and AI-driven systems.

Quantum Sensors: Advanced sensors that could significantly improve the tracking and interaction capabilities of VR/AR systems, offering higher precision.

Quantum VR/AR: The integration of quantum computing into VR/AR technologies to improve performance, create complex simulations, and enhance real-time processing of immersive environments.

Quick Access Menu: A user interface design element in VR/AR that allows users to access commonly used settings or tools quickly, enhancing usability by reducing the need for extensive navigation.

Quick Interaction System: A VR/AR interaction system designed for rapid user input, providing immediate feedback and fast response times.

Quick-Response Code (QR Code): A type of barcode used in AR to trigger digital content.

Query Resolution in AR: The ability of an AR system to provide answers or solutions to questions by recognizing objects, locations, or context, delivering real-time data or information.

R

Radial Menu in VR: A user interface design commonly used in VR/AR, where options are arranged in a circular layout around a central point, allowing for intuitive selection with a controller or gesture.

Raycasting: A technique for determining what a user is interacting with in a VR/AR environment, often used for selecting objects or detecting collisions.

Ray Tracing: A rendering technique used to simulate realistic lighting and shadows in VR/AR.

Real-Time 3D Rendering: The ability to generate and display 3D models in real-time, crucial for interactive VR/AR experiences.

Real-Time Collaboration in VR/AR: Multi-user, real-time interaction within a virtual or augmented space, supporting shared tasks, meetings, and communication.

Real-Time Ray Tracing: A rendering technique in VR/AR that simulates the physical behavior of light, creating highly realistic lighting, shadows, and reflections in virtual environments.

Real-Time Rendering: The process of generating and displaying images quickly enough to create a smooth experience in VR/AR systems, often requiring significant computing power for realistic environments.

Real-World Anchoring in AR: The process of fixing virtual content to a specific location in the physical world using GPS, markers, or other location-based technologies, ensuring that virtual objects stay in place relative to real-world surroundings.

Real-World Integration: The seamless blending of real-world elements into VR/AR environments, allowing for better contextualization and interaction.

Real-World Interaction: The ability of VR/AR systems to incorporate real-world objects or environments, allowing users to interact with digital content in realistic ways, such as interacting with physical objects through AR.

Reinforcement Learning in VR: A machine learning approach where an AI agent learns to make decisions by receiving rewards or penalties based on its actions within a VR environment, commonly used in training simulations or gaming.

Reflective VR: A VR system that incorporates real-time reflections and environmental factors into the digital space, enhancing realism.

Remote Collaboration in VR/AR: The ability for users to work together within a shared virtual or augmented environment, often used for team meetings, training, or creative collaboration.

Remote Presence: A VR/AR technology that allows users to feel as though they are present in a remote location, used for teleconferencing, remote assistance, and collaborative work.

Reprojection: The process of adjusting the VR/AR display to match the user's movements to prevent discomfort.

Robot-Assisted VR/AR: A type of VR/AR where robots are controlled remotely via the virtual or augmented environment, enabling tasks such as remote surgery, telepresence, or industrial automation.

Robotic VR/AR: The use of VR and AR to control robotic systems, such as for remote surgeries, dangerous fieldwork, or virtual telepresence.

Room-Scale VR: A VR setup where users can physically move around within a defined area while interacting with the virtual world.

Room-Scale VR (second definition): A VR system where users can move freely within a designated space, with their physical movement being reflected in the virtual environment, often using external tracking systems or cameras.

Reactive Feedback: Real-time feedback given to users based on their actions or interactions in VR/AR, such as visual changes, haptic feedback, or audio cues that respond to user input.

Reactive VR/AR: A form of interactive VR/AR where the system responds dynamically to a user's input, behavior, or environmental changes, creating more personalized experiences.

Reconstruction: The process of reconstructing a real-world object or environment in 3D for use in VR/AR applications.

Retinal Display: A display technology that projects images directly onto the retina for ultra-clear visuals.

S

Scene Graph: A hierarchical structure used in 3D graphics to organize objects and their relationships in a VR/AR environment.

Scene Reconstruction: The process of creating a 3D model of a physical environment or object from images or sensor data, used in AR to place virtual content accurately in the real world.

Sensor-Based Authentication: A method of verifying users in VR/AR by utilizing biometric sensors (fingerprint, retina scan) or behavioral data (gestures, movement patterns).

Sensor Fusion: Combining data from multiple sensors (e.g., accelerometers, gyroscopes) to improve tracking and interaction.

Simultaneous Localization and Mapping (SLAM): A technique used in AR/VR to map the environment and track the device's location in real time, often used in mobile AR apps to place objects on physical surfaces.

Simulated Presence: A technique used to create the feeling of being physically present in a virtual environment, often achieved through VR immersion.

Simulated Reality: A theory or concept where a user experiences a world that is artificially created and indistinguishable from reality, often used as a philosophical or speculative topic in VR contexts.

Six Degrees of Freedom (6DoF): The ability to move freely in 3D space (forward/backward, left/right, up/down, and rotation along all three axes).

Smart AR Glasses: Wearable AR devices in the form of glasses that display augmented reality content while allowing users to maintain awareness of their physical surroundings.

Smart Glasses: Wearable AR devices that overlay digital content onto the user's field of view, often used for hands-free access to information and navigation.

Social VR: A virtual reality environment designed for social interaction, where multiple users can communicate, collaborate, or participate in shared experiences in a virtual space.

Social VR Platform: A VR system that facilitates social interaction between users, allowing them to meet, collaborate, or play in virtual spaces, often featuring avatars and shared environments.

Spatial Audio: Audio technology that simulates the direction and distance of sound sources in 3D space, enhancing immersion in VR/AR by replicating how sound behaves in the real world it simulates direction, distance, and environment-based sounds, increasing immersion and realism.

Spatial Computing: The technology that allows digital content to interact with the physical world in a way that accounts for the spatial positioning of objects and the user, central to both AR and MR.

Spatial Mapping: The process of creating a 3D map of the real world using sensors, enabling AR devices to interact with and overlay digital content onto physical spaces.

Stereoscopic 3D: A technique used in VR/AR that creates the illusion of depth by presenting two offset images to each eye, replicating human binocular vision.

Swarm Intelligence: A collective behavior in VR/AR systems where multiple agents (e.g., AI characters) behave in a way that mimics natural systems.

Synthetic Aperture Radar (SAR): A remote sensing technology used in some AR systems to create detailed 3D environmental models.

T

Tactile Display: A display technology in VR/AR that allows users to "feel" virtual objects through haptic feedback, creating a more immersive interaction with digital content.

Tactile Feedback: Physical feedback in VR/AR that simulates touch or interaction with virtual objects, such as vibrations or forces applied by haptic devices in VR/AR environments.

Tactile Illusion: The creation of the sensation of touch or texture in VR/AR without physical contact, achieved using haptic feedback.

Tactile Interface: An interface in VR/AR that provides physical feedback to users through vibrations, pressure, or other sensations to simulate touch or interaction with virtual objects, often involving haptic feedback devices like gloves or suits.

Tactile VR: The use of haptic feedback systems that provide physical sensations of touch, texture, or resistance when interacting with virtual objects, making the experience feel more realistic.

Teleoperation: Remote control of machines or devices using VR or AR, often in industrial, medical, or space applications.

Telepresence: The perception of being present in a remote location or environment, often facilitated by virtual reality (VR) or augmented reality (AR) technologies, enabling remote communication, collaboration, and exploration.

Telepresence (Additional Definition): A VR/AR system that allows users to feel as if they are physically present in another location, often through robotic avatars or immersive video conferencing systems.

Time-of-Flight (ToF) Sensor: A sensor used in AR/VR systems to measure distances by calculating the time it takes for a light signal to travel to an object and back, aiding in depth sensing and environment mapping.

Time-of-Flight Sensors: Sensors used to measure distances by calculating the time it takes for light to travel to and from an object, often used in AR for depth sensing.

Time Warp in VR: A technique used to compensate for latency in VR by adjusting the position of the virtual environment based on the user's head movements in real-time.

Time Warping: A technique used in VR to adjust frame rates and reduce visual discomfort by aligning movement and viewing perspectives in real-time.

Through-The-Lens (TTL) View: The perspective in a VR system where the user's view is directly influenced by the device's lens or camera system, providing real-time feedback of what they are seeing.

Touchless Interaction: Interaction with VR/AR systems without physical contact, often achieved through gestures or voice commands.

Touchless Interface: An interaction method in VR/AR where users can control the environment or system without physical contact, often relying on gesture or eye tracking.

Tracked Object Interaction: The ability of VR/AR systems to track real-world objects and allow users to interact with them in the virtual environment, such as using physical tools or devices to manipulate virtual elements.

Tracking Area: The physical space in which a user can move freely within VR/AR, tracked by sensors or cameras to ensure smooth interaction with the virtual environment.

Tracking Fidelity: The precision and accuracy with which a VR/AR system tracks the user's movements, impacting immersion and experience quality.

Tracking Marker: A visual marker used in AR to help the system recognize and track the location and orientation of objects in the real world, allowing digital content to be anchored correctly.

Transparency Mapping: A technique used in AR to control the transparency of virtual elements, allowing users to see real-world objects behind digital content.

Tethered VR: A VR system that requires physical cables to connect the headset to a computer or console for processing power.

U

Under-Display Sensors: Sensors embedded beneath the surface of a VR/AR display that track user movements or interactions without visible sensors, enabling a more seamless and aesthetically clean experience.

Undistorted Field of View (FOV): A technique in VR/AR that maintains the user's natural field of view without visual distortion, enhancing comfort and immersion.

Underwater AR: Augmented reality applications designed to work in underwater environments, often used in exploration, research, or recreational diving.

Ubiquitous Computing: The idea of integrating computing devices into everyday life, a concept often associated with AR systems.

Ubiquitous Computing in AR: A concept where computing is integrated into everyday environments, with AR systems enhancing interactions by providing real-time digital information on demand.

Ultra-High Definition (UHD) in VR: A display resolution standard offering extremely high-quality visuals in VR systems, typically at 4K or higher resolutions, to enhance visual realism.

Ultraleft and Ultraright Field of View (FOV): Refers to the extreme left and right boundaries of the visual field in VR/AR systems, important for creating wide and immersive experiences.

Unreal Engine: A widely used game engine for creating VR/AR content, offering robust tools for 3D rendering, physics, and interactivity.

Unrealistic Feedback: A phenomenon in VR/AR where the haptic feedback or visual response from the system feels unnatural, potentially breaking immersion.

Upward Compatibility: The ability of a VR/AR system to support future technologies or content without requiring a full upgrade.

User-Centered Design (UCD): A design approach focused on making VR/AR systems intuitive and easy to use for the end-user.

User-Centric Design: The practice of designing VR/AR experiences around the needs, behaviors, and preferences of users to ensure more intuitive and enjoyable interactions.

User Experience (UX): The overall experience a user has when interacting with a VR/AR system, including ease of use and enjoyment.

User Experience (UX) Design for VR/AR: The practice of creating intuitive, efficient, and enjoyable user interfaces for VR/AR systems that focus on human-centered design principles.

User Experience (UX) in VR/AR: The design and optimization of the overall experience for users interacting with VR/AR environments, focused on usability, comfort, and immersion.

User Experience (UX) in VR/AR: The overall experience a user has when interacting with a VR/AR system, focusing on comfort, ease of use, and the effectiveness of the interaction.

User Interface (UI): The visual elements that users interact with in a VR/AR application.

User Interface (UI) in VR/AR: The system of visual elements, controls, and interactions that allow users to engage with and navigate through virtual or augmented environments.

Universal Input System: A system that can accept a wide range of inputs, such as hand gestures, eye-tracking, voice, and physical controllers, in a VR/AR environment.

V

Vaporwave AR: A visual style in AR characterized by retro-futuristic aesthetics, such as neon colors and glitch effects, often used in artistic or experiential projects.

Varying Degrees of Freedom (VDoF): A term used to describe systems where the user experiences different levels of motion freedom within a VR or AR system, such as 3DoF vs. 6DoF.

Vibration Feedback: Feedback sent through vibration to simulate sensations of touch or impact within VR/AR experiences.

Virtual Agent: A digital character or assistant in VR/AR environments, often powered by AI, capable of interacting with users.

Virtual Assistant in VR/AR: An AI-powered tool within a VR/AR system that provides guidance, assistance, or control, responding to voice commands or user interactions.

Virtual Collaboration: Working together in a digital environment, often using tools and platforms within the metaverse, to facilitate communication, collaboration, and productivity across distances.

Virtual Currency: Digital currency used within virtual environments for transactions and purchases, often tied to specific platforms or economies within the metaverse.

Virtual Economies: The simulated economic systems that exist within virtual worlds or VR games, where users can trade, earn, or spend virtual currencies and assets.

Virtual Event: An event or gathering that takes place entirely within the metaverse, often attended by avatars representing real-world participants, offering opportunities for networking, entertainment, and education.

Virtual Fashion in VR/AR: The creation of digital clothing or accessories for avatars in VR/AR environments, allowing users to customize their virtual appearance.

Virtual Goods: Digital items or assets that have value within the metaverse, such as virtual clothing, accessories, or virtual pets, and can be bought, sold, or traded for real or virtual currency.

Virtual Human: A 3D human model used in VR/AR applications, typically for training, simulations, or gaming experiences.

Virtual Identity Theft: Unauthorized access or manipulation of digital identities within the metaverse for fraudulent purposes, such as impersonation, data breaches, or identity fraud.

Virtual Item Economy: A digital economy within VR/AR worlds where virtual items or currencies have real-world value, often seen in gaming or virtual marketplaces.

Virtual Land: Digital space within the metaverse that can be owned, developed, and monetized, like real-world land, offering opportunities for investment, creativity, and entrepreneurship.

Virtual Object: Any object created digitally within a VR/AR/MR environment.

Virtual Object Manipulation: The ability to interact with and modify virtual objects in VR/AR, including rotating, scaling, or moving them as if they were physical objects.

Virtual Object Occlusion: The process in VR/AR that makes virtual objects realistically appear behind or in front of physical objects, mimicking real-world interaction.

Virtual Object Recognition: The ability of a VR/AR system to identify and track virtual objects within a 3D environment, allowing users to interact with them or manipulate them within the virtual world.

Virtual Ownership: The concept of owning digital assets, rights, or property within the metaverse, often facilitated by blockchain technology.

Virtual Reality (VR): A fully immersive digital environment that replaces the real world, often experienced through a headset.

Virtual Reality SDK (Software Development Kit): A collection of software tools and resources that enable developers to create VR applications and content.

Virtual Reality Sandbox: A VR environment that allows users to experiment with digital content in a dynamic, freeform manner.

Virtual Set: A digitally created background or environment for use in VR or AR productions.

Virtual World: A simulated environment created in VR where users can interact and navigate digitally represented spaces.

Voice Recognition: Technology used to recognize and process spoken commands in VR/AR systems.

Volumetric Capture: The process of capturing 3D data from real-life objects or people for use in VR/AR environments.

Volumetric Capture: A technique used to record 3D data of physical spaces or people, which can be used to create lifelike models for VR/AR applications.

Volumetric Video: A 3D video format that captures real-world scenes from multiple angles.

Volumetric Video: A video technique where a scene or object is captured in 3D, allowing for free movement around it in VR/AR.

Voxel: A pixel with volume, used in 3D modeling in VR/AR for representing physical objects.

Voxel-based Rendering: A 3D rendering technique used in VR/AR that creates environments and objects from small cubic units (voxels) instead of polygons, often used for more realistic modeling of complex environments.

VR Headset: A device worn on the head to provide immersive visual and auditory experiences in VR environments.

VR Locomotion: The method or technique used to allow users to move within a virtual environment. This can include teleportation, walking in place, or using controllers for movement.

VR Mapped Area: The virtual space where the user can move around in a VR environment, often defined by room-scale limits.

W

Walkthrough VR: A VR experience designed for users to explore and navigate through virtual environments by physically walking, often used in architectural visualization and gaming.

Wall-Walking: A VR experience that allows users to interact with virtual environments by walking along walls or surfaces that defy gravity.

Wearable AR: AR technologies integrated into wearable devices like smart glasses, headsets, or clothing, allowing users to experience augmented reality content without holding or manipulating a device.

Wearable Computing in AR: The integration of computing systems into wearables (such as smart glasses or VR/AR headsets) to provide immersive AR experiences with mobility.

Wearables: Devices worn on the body, such as VR/AR headsets or haptic gloves, that enable interaction with virtual environments.

Warping: A visual technique used to adjust distorted or off-angle images in VR to match the user's perspective.

Wavefront Propagation: A method of simulating how light waves travel and interact with objects, often applied in VR/AR for realistic lighting, shadow effects, and depth rendering.

Waveguide Display: A type of optical display used in AR glasses that uses light guides to project images directly into the user's eyes, often offering a compact form factor with minimal visual distortion, allowing virtual images to be projected onto the user's view of the real world.

WebXR: A standard for building XR (VR/AR) applications that run directly in web browsers.

Wide-Field of View (FOV): The extent of the observable area in a VR headset, with a larger FOV providing a more immersive and expansive experience by covering a wider portion of the user's vision.

Wide Field of View (FOV): The extent of the observable world seen at any given moment in a VR/AR headset, usually measured in degrees.

Wireless VR: A type of VR headset that does not require cables to connect to a computer or console, providing greater freedom of movement and eliminating the risk of tripping over wires.

Wireless VR: A VR system that does not require any cables or physical connection to a computer or console, offering greater mobility and freedom.

Wired VR: A type of VR that relies on wired connections for power and data transfer between the headset and computer, offering stable performance but less mobility compared to wireless systems.

World Anchors: A reference point in AR or virtual markers in AR used to hold virtual objects in place within the real world, typically anchored to specific physical locations or surfaces.

World Anchors in AR: Digital points that are fixed in the physical world and used to position virtual objects, ensuring consistency in placement as the user moves or changes perspective.

World Coordinate System: A 3D coordinate system used in VR/AR to define the positions of objects within a spatial environment.

World Interaction: The process in VR/AR where users can interact with objects or the environment around them, including manipulating virtual or physical elements to achieve tasks.

World Reconstruction: The process of building a digital model of a real-world environment using sensors, cameras, or other data sources, typically used in AR for mapping.

World-Scale VR: A type of VR system that allows users to move freely within a large physical space, typically using multiple sensors or external tracking systems to map out the environment in real-time.

Wrist-Based Interaction: Interaction in VR/AR using devices or sensors worn on the wrist, such as smartwatches or haptic devices.

Wrist Tracking: The use of sensors or devices to track hand and wrist movements for interaction in VR/AR.

X

X-Axis: One of the three axes in 3D space, representing horizontal movement (left to right) in VR/AR environments.

X-Plane: A flight simulation VR system that provides immersive flight experiences with realistic physics and environmental models.

XR (Extended Reality): An umbrella term encompassing VR, AR, and MR, which all immerse users in digitally enhanced experiences.

XR Cloud: A cloud-based service designed for storing, processing, and rendering VR/AR content, enabling efficient multi-user experiences.

XR Ecosystem: The interconnected network of hardware, software, platforms, and services that support immersive experiences across virtual, augmented, and mixed realities.

XR Spatial Computing: A term that refers to the interaction between physical and digital spaces in immersive environments like VR/AR, where digital content is anchored to the physical world in a meaningful way.

XR Toolkit: A set of development tools and libraries designed for creating cross-platform immersive experiences, enabling developers to create VR, AR, and MR applications with shared components.

X-Reality: Another term for extended reality, emphasizing immersive digital environments.

X-Reality: An umbrella term that encompasses all forms of immersive technologies, including VR, AR, and MR, and sometimes other digital environments such as 360-degree video.

X-Reality Cloud: A cloud-based system that stores, processes, and delivers XR (Extended Reality) experiences, allowing users to access shared content and environments from multiple devices.

X-Reality Interface: A unified platform that integrates VR, AR, and MR experiences, allowing seamless transitions between the different types of immersive technology.

Y

Y-Axis: The vertical axis in a 3D coordinate system, used to define upward and downward movement.

Y-Axis Gimbal: A gimbal system used in VR/AR headsets to stabilize the head tracking on the vertical axis, ensuring smoother movements and preventing nausea.

Y-Axis Rotation: The rotation around the vertical axis in VR, often responsible for turning or rotating the user's viewpoint to the left or right.

Yarn (in VR/AR): A scripting language used in VR/AR development for creating interactive narratives, dialogue systems, or branching storylines.

Yaw: The rotational movement of the user's head or an object along the vertical axis in a 3D space. It controls the turning of the head or viewpoint in VR/AR environments.

Yellow Box in AR: A visual tool or marker used in AR development that shows the boundaries or limits of a virtual object or AR interaction, helping users or developers gauge the space within which AR content appears.

Yellow Brick Road (YBR) AR: A navigation feature in AR where digital paths are superimposed on the real world to guide users to specific locations or destinations, commonly used in museum tours or retail experiences.

Yield Management in VR/AR: The process of optimizing resource allocation (such as GPU or CPU power) in real-time to ensure smooth performance in VR/AR applications.

Yielding in AR: The ability of an AR system to adjust and adapt in response to environmental changes, like modifying virtual content to suit different lighting conditions or user behaviors.

Z

Z-Axis: The axis in a 3D coordinate system that defines depth (forward and backward) in space.

Z-Axis Alignment: In VR/AR, the proper positioning and orientation of objects or elements in relation to the user's depth perception (the Z-axis), which is essential for realism in spatial interaction.

Z-Axis Movement: Movement along the depth axis in VR, allowing users to move forward or backward in a virtual environment, which adds to the feeling of immersion.

Z-Axis Translation: The movement along the depth axis in a 3D space (forward and backward). In VR/AR, it is used to adjust the position of objects or users in the virtual world.

Z-Buffer: A buffer used in 3D graphics to store depth information, ensuring objects closer to the user are rendered in front of distant ones in VR/AR.

Z-Buffering: A rendering technique used in VR/AR to manage depth information, ensuring that objects are drawn in the correct order based on their distance from the viewer, preventing objects from appearing incorrectly layered.

Z-buffering in VR: A method used in 3D rendering to handle depth information, ensuring that objects closer to the viewer appear in front of those farther away, enhancing the realism of virtual environments.

Z-Coordinate: The third dimension in a 3D coordinate system used in VR/AR to define depth, moving away from or toward the user.

Zero-Delay Input: A technology designed to reduce the delay between the user's input (e.g., controller action or gesture) and the system's response, critical for maintaining immersion in VR/AR experiences.

Zero Gravity VR: A VR experience that simulates a zero-gravity environment, allowing users to float and move freely in space without the limitations of Earth's gravity.

Zero Interaction VR: A VR experience designed for users who are not physically interacting with the environment, but rather experiencing it passively, such as in cinematic VR.

Zero-Latency VR: A VR system that operates with no detectable delay between the user's actions and the system's response, vital for avoiding discomfort or disorientation during immersive experiences.

Zenith Angle: The angle measured from the top of the user's head, often used in tracking and controlling view orientation in VR/AR.

Zoom: The act of magnifying or reducing the view of an area or object within a VR/AR environment.

Zoomable AR: An augmented reality feature that allows users to zoom in and out on virtual objects, providing greater detail or an expanded view of the augmented content.

Additional Resources

References for Future Readings

Allison, C., Miller, A., Oliver, I., Michaelson, R., & Tiropanis, T. (2012). The Web in education. *Computer Networks*, 56(18), 3811–3824.

Bainbridge, W. S. (2007). The scientific research potential of virtual worlds. *Science*, 317(5837), 472–476.

Bartle, R. (2004). *Designing virtual worlds*. Indianapolis, IN: New Riders Publishing.

Bell, M. W. (2008). Towards a definition of "virtual worlds". *Journal of Virtual Worlds Research*, 1(1).

Bolter, J. D., & Grusin, R. (1999). *Remediation: Understanding new media*. MIT Press.

Boughzala, I., De Vreede, G. J., & Limayem, M. (2012). Team collaboration in virtual worlds: Editorial to the special issue. *Journal of the Association for Information Systems*, 13(10), 714–734.

Brown, E., & Cairns, P. (2004). A grounded investigation of game immersion. In *Proceedings of the Conference on Human Factors in Computing Systems (CHI 2004)* (pp. 1279–1300). New York: ACM Press.

Castronova, E. (2005). *Synthetic worlds*. Chicago, IL: The University of Chicago Press.

Dionisio, J. D. N., Burns, W. G., & Gilbert, R. (2013). 3D virtual worlds and the metaverse: Current status and future possibilities. *ACM Computing Surveys (CSUR)*, 45(3), 34.

Duncan, I., Miller, A., & Jiang, S. (2012). A taxonomy of virtual worlds usage in education. *British Journal of Educational Technology*, 43(6), 949–964.

Emotions and cognitive marvels: Methodology, tools and applications. Germany: Springer Nature Switzerland.

Fares, O. H., Aversa, J., Lee, S. H., & Jacobson, J. (2024). Virtual reality: A review and a new framework for integrated adoption. *International Journal of Consumer Studies*, 48(2), e13040.

Fisher, E. (2010). Contemporary technology discourse and the legitimation of capitalism. *European Journal of Social Theory*, 13(2), 229–252.

Gee, J. P. (2003). *What video games have to teach us about learning literacy*. New York: Palgrave Macmillan.

Ghanbarzadeh, R., Ghapanchi, A. H., Blumenstein, M., & Talaei-Khoei, A. (2014). A decade of research on the use of three-dimensional virtual worlds in health care: A systematic literature review. *Journal of Medical Internet Research*, 16(2), e47.

Grassian, E., & Trueman, R. B. (2007). Stumbling, bumbling, teleporting and flying… librarian avatars in second life. *Reference Services Review*, 35(1), 84–89.

Grenfell, J., & Warren, I. (2010). Virtual worlds to enhance student engagement. *The International Journal of Technology, Knowledge and Society*, 6(1), 25–40.

Hillis, C., Bhattacharjee, M., AlMousawi, B., Eltanahy, T., Ono, S., Hui, M., Ba' Pham, Swab, M., Cormack, G. V., Grossman, M. R., & Bagheri, E. (2025). Teaching postsecondary students about the ethics of artificial intelligence: A scoping review protocol. *PLoS One*, 20(7), 12. https://doi.org/10.1371/journal.pone.0329020

Honey, M., Connor, K., Veltman, M., Bodily, D., & Diener, S. (2012). Teaching with second life: Hemorrhage management as an example of a process for developing simulations for multiuser virtual environments. *Clinical Simulation in Nursing*, 8(3), 79–85.

Jarmon, L., & Sanchez, J. (2008). The educators coop: A virtual world model for real world collaboration. *Proceedings of the American Society for Information Science and Technology*, 45, 1–10.

Johnson, L., & Levine, A. H. (2008). Virtual worlds: Inherently immersive, highly social learning spaces. *Theory into Practice*, 47(2), 161–170.

Kemp, J. W., Livingstone, D., & Bloomfield, P. R. (2009). SLOODLE: Connecting VLE tools with emergent teaching practice in Second Life. *British Journal of Educational Technology*, 40(3), 551–555.

LaValle, S. M. (2023). *Virtual reality*. Cambridge: Cambridge University Press.

Manovich, L. (2001). *The language of new media*. MIT Press.

Marchioro, D. M., Fonseca, A. A., Benatti, F., Zuin, M. (2024). *Virtual reality: Unlocking*.

Marks, S., Estevez, J. E., & Connor, A. M. (2014). *Towards the Holodeck: Fully immersive virtual reality visualisation of scientific and engineering data*. In *Proceedings of the 29th International Conference on Image and Vision Computing New Zealand* (pp. 42–47). https://doi.org/10.1145/2683405.2683424

Marougkas, A., Troussas, C., Krouska, A., & Sgouropoulou, C. (2024). How personalized and effective is immersive virtual reality in education? A systematic literature review for the last decade. *Multimedia Tools and Applications*, 83(6), 18185–18233.

McArdle, G., & Bertolotto, M. (2012). Assessing the application of three-dimensional collaborative technologies within an e-learning environment. *Interactive Learning Environments*, 20(1), 57–75.

Minocha, S., Tran, M., & Reeves, A. (2010). Conducting empirical research in virtual worlds: Experiences from two projects in second life. *Journal of Virtual Worlds Research*, 3(1), 3–21.

Ng, P. (2024). Challenges and opportunities of using metaverse tools for participatory architectural design processes. *Virtual Worlds*, 3(3), 283–302. https://doi.org/10.3390/virtualworlds3030015

Paul, J., Ueno, A., Dennis, C., Alamanos, E., Curtis, L., Foroudi, P., ... & Wirtz, J. (2024). Digital transformation: A multidisciplinary perspective and future research agenda. *International Journal of Consumer Studies*, 48(2), e13015.

Ryan, M.-L. (2015). *Narrative as virtual reality 2: Revisiting immersion and interactivity in literature and electronic media.* Baltimore, MD: Johns Hopkins University Press.

Salen, K., & Zimmerman, E. (2004). *Rules of play—Game design fundamentals.* Cambridge: The MIT Press.

Schroeder, R. (2008). Defining virtual worlds and virtual environments. *Journal of Virtual Worlds Rresearch*, 1(1).

Sclater, M., & Lally, V. (2013). Virtual voices: Exploring creative practices to support life skills development among young people working in a virtual world community. *International Journal of Art and Design Education*, 32(3), 331–344.

Singh, N., & Lee, M. J. (2009). Exploring perceptions toward education in 3-D virtual environments: An introduction to "second life". *Journal of Teaching in Travel & Tourism*, 8(4), 315–327.

Soliman, M. Mona, Ahmed, E., Darwish, A., & Ella Hassanien, A. (2024). Artificial intelligence powered metaverse: Analysis, challenges and future perspectives. *The Artificial Intelligence Review*, 57(2), 36. https://doi.org/10.1007/s10462-023-10641-x

Stone, J. (2013). Immersive virtual reality, presence and engagement: What is the pedagogic value of immersive virtual worlds?. In *EC-TEL Doctoral Consortium* (pp. 115–122). Paphos, Cyprus.

Tang, Y., Wang, D., Ma, Y., & Li, H. (2024). Advancing haptic interfaces for immersive experiences in the metaverse. *Discover Internet of Things*, 4(1), 19. https://www.sciencedirect.com/science/article/pii/S2666998624001728

Todino, M. D., Eliza, P., Argyro, F., Antonia, M., Lucia, C., Francesca, P., Stefano, D. T., & Maurizio, S. (2025). Bridging tradition and innovation: Transformative educational practices in museums with AI and VR. *Computers*, 14(7), 257. https://doi.org/10.3390/computers14070257.

Truong, V. T., Le, L. B., & Niyato, D. (2023). Blockchain meets metaverse and digital asset management: A comprehensive survey. *IEEE Access*, 11, 26258–26288. https://ieeexplore.ieee.org/document/10068493

Webber, S. (2013). Blended information behaviour in Second Life. *Journal of Information Science*, 39(1), 85–100.

Yee, N., Bailenson, J. N., Urbanek, M., Chang, F., & Merget, D. (2007). The unbearable likeness of being digital: The persistence of nonverbal social norms in online virtual environments. *CyberPsychology & Behavior*, 10(1), 115–121.

Index

For Product Safety Concerns and Information please contact our EU
representative GPSR@taylorandfrancis.com
Taylor & Francis Verlag GmbH, Kaufingerstraße 24, 80331 München, Germany